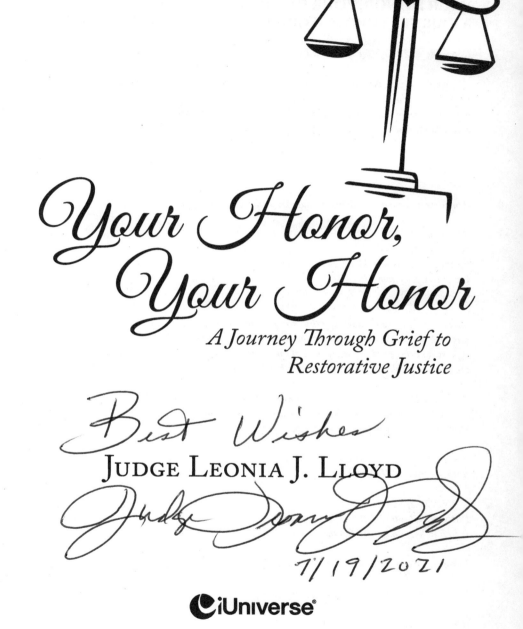

Your Honor, Your Honor

A Journey Through Grief to Restorative Justice

Best Wishes

Judge Leonia J. Lloyd

7/19/2021

YOUR HONOR, YOUR HONOR
A JOURNEY THROUGH GRIEF TO RESTORATIVE JUSTICE

Copyright © 2020 Judge Leonia J. Lloyd.

All rights reserved. No part of this book may be used or reproduced by any means, graphic, electronic, or mechanical, including photocopying, recording, taping or by any information storage retrieval system without the written permission of the author except in the case of brief quotations embodied in critical articles and reviews.

iUniverse books may be ordered through booksellers or by contacting:

iUniverse
1663 Liberty Drive
Bloomington, IN 47403
www.iuniverse.com
844-349-9409

Because of the dynamic nature of the Internet, any web addresses or links contained in this book may have changed since publication and may no longer be valid. The views expressed in this work are solely those of the author and do not necessarily reflect the views of the publisher, and the publisher hereby disclaims any responsibility for them.

Any people depicted in stock imagery provided by Getty Images are models, and such images are being used for illustrative purposes only.
Certain stock imagery © Getty Images.

Front cover photo by Victor A. Toliva
Author Photo by Al Cooper

ISBN: 978-1-6632-0182-9 (sc)
ISBN: 978-1-6632-0184-3 (hc)
ISBN: 978-1-6632-0183-6 (e)

Library of Congress Control Number: 2020913005

Print information available on the last page.

iUniverse rev. date: 10/06/2020

Dedication

In loving memory of my parents, Leon T. Lloyd Jr. and Mattie N. Lloyd. Thank you for your continuous love and support and for teaching us the values of courage, strength, love, and compassion. You showed us how to brightly shine our lights to touch humanity.

In loving memory of my twin sister, Judge Leona L. Lloyd, who I know is watching. Thank you for always believing, encouraging, and supporting me in all my endeavors, no matter how crazy they were. Between us, life and love are eternal. I wrote this book to fulfill a dream of ours and a loving promise to you.

Contents

Dedication v

Author's Note ix

First Foreword xi

Second Foreword xiii

Introduction xvii

PART 1: 1945–1967

Chapter 1: Back to Where It Began 1

Chapter 2: Our Parents 15

Chapter 3: Motown Sounds and The Detroit Riot 25

PART 2: 1967–1979

Chapter 4: The Challenges of College 53

Chapter 5: Teaching Young Minds to Be Strong 69

Chapter 6: Law School 91

Chapter 7: Our Father's Struggle 103

Chapter 8: The Abandonment and Rebounding of Mattie Lloyd 111

PART 3: 1979–2001

    Chapter 9: Here We Come 119

    Chapter 10: Practice of Law versus Sexism 129

    Chapter 11: My Election for Judge 155

    Chapter 12: Leona's Election For Judge 169

PART 4: 2001–2009

    Chapter 13: A Day That Changed My Life Forever 179

    Chapter 14: The Funeral—for Whom? 193

    Chapter 15: Returning to the Courtroom 201

    Chapter 16: A Story from a Drug Court Graduate 211

    Chapter 17: Project Fresh Start: A Way Out of the
                  World of Prostitution 219

    Chapter 18: A Story from a Graduate of PFS 233

    Chapter 19: Paying It Forward 255

    Chapter 20: Amazing Grace: A Bond That Death
                  Could Not Break 261

PART 5: 2009– TO PRESENT

    Chapter 21: Veterans' Court 271

    Chapter 22: You Have Only One Life to Live 283

    Chapter 23: From Where I Sat 289

Appendix 295

Acknowledgments 297

Photo Album 303

About the Author 321

Author's Note

This book is a memoir. It reflects the accurate portrayal of my journey in life. I have changed some names, characteristics, identifying details, and events to conceal and protect the identities of those involved. This book is not meant to give any professional, medical, or legal advice. I hope you enjoy the story of my life.

First Foreword

The word *forward*, by definition, denotes motion and progress.

In this foreword, I'm writing about the word *forward* and its application to this book you're holding and perhaps contemplating buying. It's a book I read multiple times as I participated in the author's creation of this manuscript.

As a child of the '60s, I cannot read or hear these stories without also feeling the soundtrack of our lives and of the times. Fortunately, our author has provided her personal playlist to enhance your score to this memoir. As children of '60s Detroit, Leona and Leonia Lloyd marinated daily in the rarified Motown air. They naturally inhaled its sounds. The music influenced every aspect of their lives, motivating them spiritually, culturally, and physically, and it always moved them *forward*.

This book, *Your Honor, Your Honor*, is a compilation of thousands of words, yet the essence of Judge Lloyd's life story, its many lessons, and its applications upon those who crossed paths with her can be broken down into one word: *forward*. It's a directive, as in "Keep moving forward."

As children of the civil rights generation, we were constantly instructed to move forward. We were forced to learn of our history wherever we could because it wasn't being taught to us in school. In order for us to move ahead in our education and within our society, we had to move beyond our segregated communities and schools. We had to move forward in our preparation for participation in this society.

The Lloyd sisters were always moving forward and improving the quality of their lives. That upward mobility and forward progress they were raised in and instructed upon followed them throughout the course of their professional careers.

As educators, they were about moving students forward, not just passing them along. *Forward*, in this case, means more than movement. It takes on the gravitas of knowledge and of responsibility.

Forward indicates enhanced placement and earned location.

As entertainment lawyers, they moved those who were talented but undiscovered forward. They enhanced the existing careers of known artists. Whether that progress was measured in record units sold, including Gold and Platinum, or measured on accounting ledgers, it was all about one word: *forward*.

When they moved onward to the judiciary, they brought the defendants who came before them forward. They knew their responsibility was far greater than mere sentencing; they had the duty of restorative justice, of moving these people and their families forward and, consequently, moving society forward.

Now, as Leonia publishes her memoir and shares her lessons learned with her readers, this book is a continuation of her commitment to moving others forward.

Judge Lloyd overcame the challenges she experienced in her personal and professional life by moving forward. Recovery from loss of life is not in mourning the life or grieving the loss but in moving forward in a way representative of that life and how that life was lived.

Most important to me as I write this foreword is that those of you who buy and read this book will gain the same valuable lesson Judge Lloyd has gained and is sharing with us all: to move *Forward*.

Reginald Turner

Managing Partner at Momentum Management,
Founder and Executive Director of the Tulsa Project, and
Executive Producer and Director at Mportant Films

Second Foreword

Your Honor, Your Honor is the true story of identical twin sisters Leona and Leonia Lloyd. They were a dynamic duo whose professional careers led them to become models, schoolteachers, and entertainment lawyers, and eventually, with their unique moniker, Twins for Justice, they became the first identical-twin district court judges to sit on the same bench at the same time in the country. Their careers were on a meteoric rise until the unexpected and sudden death of Judge Leona Lloyd, who died in the presence of her sister, put an abrupt halt to their successful lives together.

The death of Leona changed the trajectory of Leonia's life in ways she never could have imagined and led her into a deep and abysmal hole of depression and fear that caused her to be uncertain about her own health and doubt her future without her sister.

The story of how Judge Leonia Lloyd was able to find her way back from depression and regain a life of purpose and meaning is an inspirational testimony and an instructional lesson of survival and triumph. As she pulled back the layers of her life, the lessons Leonia learned at an early age from her parents about strength and endurance surfaced and carried her through some of her darkest days.

The journey Leonia traveled returned her back in time to her somewhat dysfunctional early home life with a mentally ill mother and an alcoholic father. Her mother's misunderstood mental illness drove her father to drink excessively and, eventually, to leave the family. The soul-searching and courage of the twins, who had to learn to lean on each other, ultimately led Leonia to stand in her own truth and rely on those early lessons from the past when, for the first time in her life, she was left to stand alone. In helping others suffering through addiction, codependence, and abusive relationships, Leonia found herself uniquely prepared for the challenge.

I met and became friends with Leona and Leonia early in my own career as an attorney. For a few years, in the mid-1980s, when the twins were successful entertainment lawyers, our law offices were in the same building, on the same floor, in the Detroit Renaissance Center. Because the Lloyd twins had become lawyers before I had and had more legal experience than I did, I often sought their sage wisdom and consulted them for legal advice. I also admired their stunning good looks and the fact that they seemed inseparable. I seldom saw them apart. They were a little mesmerizing in that way. In conversation, they often finished each other's thoughts and sentences. Their closeness was uncanny.

One campaign year, when Judge Leonia Lloyd was running for reelection, one of the Detroit police department precincts invited Judges Leona and Leonia to speak at a regularly scheduled monthly community meeting at the precinct. The meeting was open to the public, but it was particularly intended for the residents living in the police precinct. These meetings were intended to promote better relationships between law enforcement and the citizens. Judges Leona and Leonia Lloyd were special guests invited to speak about law enforcement from a judicial perspective and to discuss the operation and the jurisdiction of the Thirty-Sixth District Court.

I was curious since, at that time, I had not participated in one of these programs, so I talked my husband into going with me to hear the judges speak. I will never forget the big smile on his face as he turned his head repeatedly from one side to the other, looking first at Leona and then at Leonia as they spoke. The two beautiful identical twin sisters were impeccably dressed, articulate, energetic, and knowledgeable, and they were sitting judges. Their speech was almost synchronized, although neither one of them ever referred to any notes while speaking. They were natural and fluid, as if they were having a conversation with the audience. My husband was so fascinated by them he seemed to be almost hypnotized. I had to shake his arm to break the spell. I still tease my husband about that evening and how captivated he was by the judges' presentation.

Soon after Leona and Leonia became judges, I too became a judge on the same district court bench. As judges, we saw each other nearly every day. They had the same closeness as judges that they'd had as lawyers.

When Leona passed away, I had my doubts and concerns as to whether Leonia would ever recover from the overwhelming sadness and loneliness of the loss of her sister and best friend. I was amazed and surprised by her strength and resilience. After reading *Your Honor, Your Honor*, I now understand how Leonia was able to come safely through the devastating pain of her loss and thrive. Leonia's story is a lesson in courage and survival. It is also an inspiration to anyone experiencing his or her own overwhelming grief.

HONORABLE MIRIAM MARTIN CLARK

Introduction

I am a retired judge who had a long, interesting legal career, but that is not why I wrote this book. I wrote this book because I am keeping a promise, I made to my identical twin sister, Leona Lloyd. We had side-by-side careers as models, teachers, lawyers, and judges.

After our varied life experiences, we had a story to tell the world. We agreed we would write a book together for people who were going through difficult times and who did not feel they were good enough, smart enough, or strong enough. We wanted to tell them not to give up on themselves and to hold on to their dreams no matter what. We wanted readers to understand that no matter how many failures they experienced, they had to own them but remember their true potential. Understanding that, they could not let failures stop them. Instead, they needed to learn that failures could teach them life lessons.

Our lives took many different twists and turns due to all the unexpected challenges life hurled at us. We dealt with issues that caused excruciating pain: discrimination, depression, family tragedies, and an array of both physical and mental health issues. With all our hearts and souls, we used the failures, obstacles, and pain cast upon us to become strong and resilient. The many horrible things that entered our lives and were meant to hurt or stop us became the wind beneath our wings that made us soar. We would wipe away our tears and say to each other, "We are enough, and we can do this. We will do this."

One of our mantras, taken from an old African American spiritual, and often used in the Civil Rights demonstrations was,

"Ain't Gonna Let Nobody Turn Me 'Round." This motivating force was so deeply rooted in us that we felt required to pass it on to those who entered our lives. Both the classroom and the courtroom were empowerment zones to us. It was our opportunity to give advice and motivation to uplift a downtrodden person.

When my sister passed, I made a promise to her that I would continue what we started and write this book. This is not an autobiography but a memoir that highlights pivotal moments in our lives that helped shape us into the women we became together and individually.

The subtitles of the book chapters are the names of Motown songs and popular songs of that time in our lives. Each song carries the theme for the section that follows it. I included the song titles because music was the backdrop of our lives. My sister and I were born and raised in the city of Detroit, known as the Motor City to some and Motown to others. Music was in our bones, and it was an integral part of our lives. As young girls, we had transistor radios glued to our ears, and there was not an R & B song or popular pop song we did not know. It was no coincidence that music played a large role in our teaching careers as well as our careers as entertainment lawyers. Music was no stranger to my courtroom, as the many people who walked through my courtroom doors discovered. Until my sister joined me on the bench, I was the only judge in the courthouse with gold records adorning the walls of my judicial chambers. My nickname became the Rock 'n' Roll Judge.

Leona's patio, where we relaxed and cooked on the grill

I hope the journey with my sister, as well as the path I traveled alone after she passed, will motivate anyone out there to set a goal and devise a plan to accomplish that goal. When my sister died, I knew that our steps had been ordered by God and that I had steps yet to take. However, in order to do that, I had to break the paralyzing grip that tragedy had over me. That was the only way I could go forward with my life. I had to listen to my inner voice, which screamed, *You, can break these chains of bondage and live and accomplish your goals, no matter what!*

Let me tell you our story.

Part ONE

1945–1967

CHAPTER 1

Back to Where It Began

INSEPARABLE

It seemed to be a typical morning in my courtroom, until I heard voices screaming through the walls of the criminal exam courtroom next door. Next, I heard sounds of large objects crashing. Not only was this highly unusual, but it was my sister's courtroom. I began to panic.

I rose from my seat on the bench and focused on my court officer, screaming, "Go next door, and help my sister!" My officer immediately ran out the door. The people seated in my courtroom were in a frozen state of disbelief as they looked at a panicking judge. However, I could not focus on them; I was worried about my sister, Leona. What was going on in her courtroom?

Was it a brawl? Was she all right? For a few seconds, a scary thought flew through my brain about an incident that had happened a few months earlier in my own courtroom: a violent physical altercation had nearly broken out following a murder examination hearing. I'd had to hit the panic button on the bench, which immediately summoned ten extra police officers to my courtroom.

Was something like that happening next door? Often, tempers flare in criminal courtrooms because of the nature of the cases heard in them. I could not hide my concern from the people in my courtroom. I stood up and told the people in my courtroom that my sister was next door and that I had to go check on her and would be right back. I thought; *I cannot, let anything happen to her.*

Heads in my courtroom nodded in agreement, and one voice yelled, "Go ahead, Judge!"

At that moment, my court officer reentered the courtroom and yelled out, "Judge Lloyd!"

I turned around, stepped back toward my seat on the bench, and said in a nervous and strained voice, "Yes?"

He said, "Everything is all right. There are about ten officers in there now. Your sister is fine."

I stopped trembling, and my racing heart calmed down as I slowly sat down in my chair. Even the audience in my courtroom looked relieved.

My reaction to that event was second nature to me. From the crib to the courtroom, my sister and I were extremely close and protective of each other. Wearing a black robe was not going to change that.

◆ One Heartbeat

Leona and I were the best-kept secret in the world. We were inside our mother's womb, as close as two peas in a pod, except Leona was lying upside down. But no one knew we existed as a duo.

Our mother, who was a petite lady, only five feet three inches tall and barely a size 7, had no idea she was expecting twins, because her doctor had heard only one heartbeat. This was in the days before the use of ultrasound.

Our tiny mother grew as large as a house during her pregnancy. Our father, Leon, along with everybody else, was certain the baby was going to be a boy. The boy was to be named Leon. The baby shower was planned for a boy, as well as the nursery decor. But as fate would have it, a boy was not born.

On August 6, 1949, in the delivery room, the startled doctor pulled Leona out feet first and exclaimed, "Wait—oh my God, there's another one!" Within three minutes, I was taken out headfirst. This was a surprise to the doctor, who revealed to our father, "All through her prenatal care, I only heard one heartbeat."

Even though the two little bundles of joy were a shock to our father, the news was an even bigger shock to our mother when she woke up in her room and was told by our father that she had two girls instead of one baby boy. Dumbfounded, our mother said, "What did you say? Two girls? Oh my, guess I've got to think up two names."

But with this twist of fate, he quickly announced to her that he had already named us. My mother looked at him, a little thrown off, and asked, "What did you name them?"

"Leonia and Leona," he proudly answered. This surprised but tickled our mother because he had named us after himself.

Our mom settled into being a registered nurse, her trained profession; a wife; and a mother after our birth. She thought she could juggle three balls in the air. She balanced a career and marriage

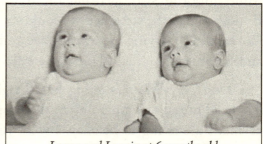

Leona and Leonia at 6 months old

while taking care of two babies who babbled in a language only, we understood. Our father and mother worked out the shifts to take care of us, but it was too much of a strain on her. She broke out in a stress-related rash over her entire body. Her doctor recommended she stop working, stay home, and take care of her two newborns. Even though she was opposed to the idea of quitting her job, our mother agreed it was the only way to stop her nervous condition, so she gave in and did not go back to work as a nurse. To her it was a temporary setback.

Little did our father know, life was going to throw him a curveball and cause that temporary change to become permanent.

For the next five years, we grew up under the watchful eyes of our parents.

In the fall of 1954, at age five, we attended Courville Elementary School for kindergarten. Every morning, after dressing us, our mother walked us to school, and she returned for us when it was time to come home.

However, one day we were shaken out of our normal routine. Suddenly, we were taken out of our kindergarten class early and brought home; we did not know why.

Our Mother with us in 1954 at 5 years old

Upon arriving at our house, we saw an ambulance with flashing red lights waiting near our open front door. Strange men dressed in white uniforms swooshed out the front door, pushing a stretcher. Running up to the stretcher, we could see our mother lying on it. She looked afraid. Crying hysterically, we grabbed her outstretched hand and screamed, "Mama! Mama, where are you going? What's wrong?"

"Don't cry. Mama's going be all right, but I do not feel well. My head hurts, so I am going to the hospital for a little while. Stop crying. I am going to be okay. I want you to mind your father and your auntie, okay?" Tears washed over her face. We watched, as the men placed her in the big red ambulance.

As Leona and I looked up, our eyes met the haunting gazes of our father and aunt. Our aunt was trying to get us to stop crying, but we could not stop. Those men had just taken our mother away. We wanted our mother to stay and could not understand what was happening or why. Our father came over to us to say he was going to the hospital with our mother, and we were to stay with our aunt. We promised to be good girls while he was gone, but there was a quiet panic in our father's eyes as tears cascaded over his cheeks. He kissed us and left.

Our mother remained in the hospital for three months, through the Christmas holidays. We were too little to visit her, but we were determined to communicate with her, so every day we colored pictures for her and insisted that our father take them to her. Every night, when our father returned home, he smiled at us and said, "Yes, I gave your mother your pictures." Even at the age of five, we were determined to stay connected to her. A trait of strong determination was forming at an early age within us. When our father reported to us how our mother was doing every day, we were okay.

As we got older, we learned that our mother had suffered a subarachnoid hemorrhage of the brain, a serious condition that cause a lot of people to die. She said back then that the usual treatment was to bore holes in the skull and insert a tube to drain excess fluid from the brain. This was done to limit the amount of possible damage to the brain as well as to prevent death. However, our mother made our father promise he would not let them surgically enter her head. She said, "If you do, I won't be the same."

I can only imagine the pressure our father was under, but he felt compelled to honor our mother's wishes. After all, she was a registered nurse and knew a whole lot more about the body than our father did, but that did not make it any easier.

Our mother's health took a turn for the worse, and the doctors tried to convince our father that surgery was the only option besides death for her, but our father said no. No matter what they said to scare him, they could not, get our father to break the promise he made to our mother. He prayed in the hospital chapel that night about his decision.

Our father visited her every night. She was hospitalized for a long time. Sitting by her bed, he was not sure if she could hear him as he talked to her; she just lay there, motionless. Many days passed, but one miraculous day, when he walked in, she was awake. Our father was ecstatic. However, he quickly discovered she did not know who he was, and she did not know she had twin girls. Our mother remembered nothing about her past life. It was obvious to him that her brain had been affected.

Following the doctors' suggestions, our father brought in pictures of us, as well as our drawings, to try to bring back her memory. During his daily visits, our father would tell her stories of her life to help her remember. This continued during the time she was hospitalized, as well as, after her day of her release. The doctor advised my father not to return to the previous place she had lived before her hospital stay, because something from her past caused her to worry. He did not want her to remember whatever caused that fear and worry.

Therefore, while our mother was still hospitalized, our father arranged to buy a newly built house in southwest Detroit and move everything from the old home to the new home, and that was where she was taken as soon as she was released from the hospital.

How our father juggled all those balls in the air was a question we often thought about when we got older. It was our father who combed and braided our hair, dressed us for school every day, and made sure we had our daily meals. It was our father who reassured us every evening and said nightly prayers with us as he put us to bed upon his return from the hospital. On top of all that, he moved us all into our new home, where my sister and I grew up. That is how we spelled l-o-v-e. The depth of our father's love was a lesson to us that with love, you can climb mountains that you previously thought were impossible to climb.

Our new Childhood Home that our father moved us to after our mother got out of the hospital

We were overwhelmed with joy when Daddy finally brought our mother home, which was around February 1955. We were just glad she was back. Everything was normal to Leona and me. We had no idea that this was like a new beginning for our mother. As little girls, we were oblivious to the depth of her brain injury. In fact, our parents worked together to make sure our lives fell into comfortable daily routines. They shielded us from the harsh realities they were handling.

As two skinny little tomboys growing up, we went fishing and skating with our father, but with our mother, we were always studying or learning how to cook something in the kitchen. Those cooking lessons paid off when we grew up and started living on our own.

Our parents never missed seeing us in school performances. From the stage, we always searched for their smiling faces in the audience.

We dressed alike until we finished high school, but that was our choice. Even though we dressed alike, my mother instilled in us that we were two distinct individuals.

"Don't select or not select something because the other one has chosen the same outfit. You pick what you like. If your clothes are different, that is fine, and if they are alike, that is fine too because you're picking what you like," she said. She drilled independent thinking into us, which prepared us for other criticisms later in life that had to do with any decisions we made independently or jointly.

◆ Learning the Bond of Unification

Our mother taught us to always have each other's back. Once, in the fifth grade, a girl on the school bus tried to pick a fight with Leona.

As soon as we came home and reported what had happened on the bus, our mother asked, "Did you stand up there and protect each other?"

We said yes.

"Good. If not, I would whip your behinds," she replied.

Our mother's lesson on the bond of unity was one we used all our lives. We stood up for each other against anyone who dared to try to bring harm against the other—and I mean anyone. Remember the courtroom scene in the beginning of the book?

◆ The Meaning of Sisterhood

Even though we had a united front outside the house, it was a different story inside the house. As twins, we argued over stupid stuff, just as all sisters and brothers do. If I felt strongly about an object belonging to me, the argument would often result in a tug-of-war and then a hitting match. Whenever any hitting started, our mother would break up the fight and tell us to stop it before we both got a whipping from her.

We were about eight or nine years old when Leona and I got into a particularly loud, heated argument—over what I could not tell you, but at the time, it was important to us. When the verbal arguing changed into a hitting match, our mother decided to end the fight in a different way. That day, our mother decided to teach us a valuable life lesson about the importance of being sisters and the bond we shared. Instead of coming into the room and breaking up the fight, as she usually did, she decided to use reverse psychology. Our mother walked into the room and stood there with her arms folded as we passed licks back and forth.

She said in a loud, booming voice, "That's right—hit each other! Go on and kill each other."

After hearing that, we immediately stopped hitting each other. That did not sound like the mother we knew, but we were still primed to continue the fight.

Leona and I stared at each other, still mad, but something clicked inside us. I no longer wanted to hit her, and she no longer tried to strike me. Our mother had used the word *kill*, and that word had never crossed our minds. We stopped, went to our individual twin beds, sat down, and said nothing. But our mother did not stop; she wanted to drive her point home. She stood between our twin beds with folded arms and teary eyes as she stared at us.

"One day your father and I will die, and all you will have is each other, but if you kill each other now, you will have no one." With those words, she turned and walked out of the room.

We sat on our beds quietly. All I could think about was that I did not want to kill my sister.

After about five minutes, I said, "I don't want to kill you."

"I don't want to kill you either," Leona said, and she came over to my bed and hugged me. "I'm sorry."

"Me too," I responded.

From that day forward, arguments still happened from time to time, because sisters are not going to agree on everything, but one thing that did change after that day was the hitting. Never again did we raise our hands against each other. After all, Leona was not just my twin sister; she was my best friend. We shared a bond that time revealed could not be broken.

❖ Hard Lessons of Life

Summertime is a period of playful, lazy days for a lot of kids, but it was not in our household. Every year, when school was out for summer vacation, our mother had other vacation plans for us: she would go through a ritualized cleaning frenzy that she pulled Leona and me into like a tsunami. This occurred from the third grade through high school. We were forced to scrub and wipe down windowsills and blinds as well as the walls and the floors. This process was extra hard because our parents smoked a lot of cigarettes, and our mother wanted to be sure we got rid of any evidence of smoke or nicotine residue in the house when we cleaned. The result of the work had to be a spotless room; anything less would have to be recleaned. Lastly, we had to help our father repaint the rooms in the house right before the fall school semester began. Yes, these were the same walls we had previously washed and scrubbed at the beginning of summer vacation. Can you spell *child abuse*?

In our minds, this felt like child slavery because while we were working our bodies to the bone, all our friends were outside playing. But we were obligated to do the work, or we would have hell to pay. We realized later in life that our mother was teaching us the lessons of hard work and discipline. Demonstrating to us, that this type of manual labor could be our future, if we did not continue our education. With an education, we would have more choices in life.

She showed us we had a choice: we had to either do the hard work and obtain a college education after high school graduation or be prepared to immediately get a manual-labor job.

Leona and I never shied away from any type of hard work, because our mother had made us tough. We felt there was nothing wrong with manual labor, if that was what you wanted to do. However, we wanted more choices for employment, and if manual labor was the only type of work we would be qualified to do after finishing high school, then we were definitely going to college because we wanted to broaden our choices for employment.

My mother's lesson to us about hard work, education, and choices was one we both passed on as teachers and judges. We wanted young people to have more choices in life when they finished high school. We also wanted defendants who appeared in front of us and were on probation to know there were more opportunities for them out there as well. Whether they selected job training for certification for employment opportunities, apprenticeship programs that created a pathway to skilled jobs, or college, we wanted them to keep growing and exploring what was out there for them. But we told both groups they would have to work hard to attain those goals, because nothing was going to be handed to them.

◆ Never Giving Up (Quitting Is Not an Option)

Even though Leona and I had our share of arguments with each other, there were times when we had to team up with each other against our parents, especially in the case of something we really wanted.

One of those times occurred at the ripe age of ten. Leona and I wanted to play instruments in school, but my parents did not want us lugging some beat-up old instruments home. We decided to ask our parents to get us a piano, and we begged and pleaded.

Our mother made her case that pianos were expensive, and they did not have that kind of money. She said, "Besides that, you two will be interested in it for a year, and then I won't be able to drag you to the piano to practice, and guess what? Your father and I will still have to make payments on a piano that will be sitting with cobwebs on it. So, the answer is no!"

That was when Leona and I discovered, if you really want something, you do not take the first *no* as a final answer. We had to fight for what we felt was right, even though it was against our parents. We had to use our brains and the power of persuasion.

Leona had a rebuttal. "What if we could find a used piano that didn't cost much? Then would you get us the piano?"

"And where are you going to find a used piano?"

"The want ads," Leona answered.

Our mother rolled her eyes at Leona. We knew what that meant, so we continued pleading since we had countered her argument.

"Find it first, and show it to me, and then we'll decide," our mother said.

Leona and I combed the Wednesday and Sunday want ads every week for a few months, and then bingo—we hit the jackpot! We found a used piano for twenty-five dollars. We ran to our mother with the ad.

"You found a piano for twenty-five dollars? It must be a piece of junk," she retorted.

"Well, can we go look at it?"

Our parents had a discussion and then placed a call and made an appointment for the next day to see the piano. Leona and I had won round one.

The next day, we went to view the condition of the piano. It was an old antique piano that had been painted a drab gray. The lady who owned it reassured us it was playable but said it needed tuning.

Glaring at us with a smirk on her face, our mother said, "You don't want this piano, do you?"

"Yes!" was our resounding answer.

She looked at us and said firmly, "If we get this piano, you have to take piano lessons and practice on it every day. I mean it. I'd better hear those keys singing, or you will forfeit your weekly allowance for every week that you miss a day playing during that week."

We jumped up and down with excitement and said, "We won't miss a day."

After the piano arrived, it was tuned, and we started our weekly piano lessons. We did not know our piano lessons would be a little over a mile away in a city named River Rouge, and we had to walk there and back every week. On a good day, it was at least a brisk thirty-minute walk, but the lessons started at specific times. Rain, sleet, or snow, there would be no excuses or missed lessons. We bundled up, put our boots on, and walked.

One day there was a snow blizzard so thick we could not see a foot in front of us. There were already six to seven inches of heavy snow on the ground, and it was colder than the North Pole, but our mother would not listen to any excuses or make any exceptions to her iron-clad rule. Even the TV weatherman said, "If you don't have to go out, don't."

Our mother looked at us, handed us extra scarves, and said, "Put these around your necks for extra warmth, but you are going."

Leona and I could not believe she was sending us out into the cold, snowy beyond-belief blizzard, but she was. Once we arrived, we had to thaw out our hands first before we could touch the piano keys. I shiver to this day when I think about how cold we were, but we pushed through.

Leona and I kept each other company as we walked. This went on for five years, until we completed the last John Thompson piano lesson book. What a feeling of accomplishment. Our teacher, Mrs. Royal, congratulated us and told us, "Most kids don't stick with it long enough to get this far."

At fifteen, we stopped taking lessons because we had finished what we had started. Those five years indirectly taught us the meaning of fighting for what you want and believe in and the importance of having the commitment, strength, and endurance to see it through. We learned that your word means everything, and you do not give up just because a task becomes hard and obstacles are put in your way. You push on through. These lessons served us well as we grew up and fought for other meaningful things that were worth fighting for. *Quitting* was not in our vocabulary.

With timing being everything, we had now picked up a new interest: listening and dancing to Motown music.

CHAPTER 2

Our Parents

AIN'T NO MOUNTAIN HIGH ENOUGH

When you examine the strength and determination of our parents and see the challenges life put them through, you will understand how Leona and I became who we were.

Our mother, Mattie Naomi Chisolm, was born in Rock Hill, South Carolina, on September 6, 1922, to Fannie Louise Irvin Chisolm and Anderson Chisolm Sr. She was the tenth of eleven children. Growing up in a household in which education was stressed, she and all her siblings completed college, except for two brothers, who received training and became certified licensed morticians. My uncle, Napoleon Chisolm, a self-made man, went to Boston, Massachusetts, after he finished his military service in the army during World War II. He arrived in Boston on a bus with two quarters in his pocket. He went on to build two of the largest funeral homes in Massachusetts; one was in Boston, and one was in Springfield.

Our grandmother, Fannie L. Chisolm, who was born on May 21, 1886, owned two houses located across the street from one another in Rock Hill, South Carolina. She also owned a gas station that had a store—no small feat for a black woman back in those days. Being a black businesswoman in the South must have been scary back then. According to our mother, our grandmother told her to hide under her bed when the Ku Klux Klan raged through town one evening and placed burning crosses in the front yards of her homes. Our grandmother was no stranger to the acts of hangings and house burnings by the Klan. They burned down one of the two houses our grandmother owned and an elementary school her son, my uncle William Chisolm, a Yale graduate had built for the black children in Rock Hill. The combination of ignorance and racial hatred was the match that lit the fire that burned down the school for young, innocent children. Determined that the children would continue their education, my uncle bought a bus that transported the children daily to their new school that was a greater distance away.

Our mother told us that her mother was a female entrepreneur and a businesswoman with a good heart. She would give food and goods to neighborhood people who had no money during the Great Depression. With eleven children to raise, our grandmother was a strong, no-nonsense, spunky lady, just like our mother and just like Leona and me. I guess the apple does not fall far from the tree, because Leona and I became business owners when we started our law firm.

Our grandmother died on May 25, 1949, a few months before we were born in August. Our mother said she took her mother's passing hard because in a discussion they had, her mother expressed joy and excitement, as she anticipated the birth of her first grandchild. Boy, the two of us would have been a big surprise for her.

When I visited my grandmother's tombstone, I felt a real connection to her. On her tombstone are two tributes etched in granite, which describe her perfectly and speak volumes about her:

A pioneer devoted to building character, educationally, morally, and religiously. Seeking her own in another's good.

A civic leader devoted to the betterment of mankind, a friend to all.

I never met her, but I believe she, Leona, and I are kindred spirits. Like our grandmother, Leona and I have spent our lives dedicated to improving and uplifting the lives of others, as teachers, lawyers, and judges.

Our mother did exceptionally well in school, despite the racial turmoil in Rock Hill. She was valedictorian of her high school class at Emmett Scott High School. I know the climate of violent and brutal racial tension had a long-term effect on my mother, because she never wanted to go back to visit. No matter how much we begged her to show us where she grew up, she never wanted to go back there. More than half of her brothers and sisters had moved away from Rock Hill when they became of age, and with her mother and father no longer alive, she felt she had no reason to go back.

Education, as a necessity for a good life was a major belief of our grandmother and our mother, which is why our mother felt it necessary to give us grueling work tasks every summer when school was on recess. Even though her sisters all became teachers, she wanted to become a nurse to give medical assistance to people. Our grandmother thought all the hard work would be too demanding and stressful and cause her daughter, an early death. Nevertheless, our mother's mind was made up: she was going to be a nurse. My twin and I were the same way. Every occupation we selected was to help people. Just like our mother and father, Leona and I had a stubborn streak. When we made up our minds to do something, we did it. Our mother's early lessons about not quitting what we started stayed with us our entire lives.

Mattie, our mother, keeping that learning curve high, was the valedictorian of her graduating class in nursing school. She delivered the valedictory commencement speech, just as she had done in high school. After graduating from nursing school, she moved to Florida to take her first nursing job as a registered nurse. Our grandmother was not thrilled about her daughter moving to Florida, but she gave Mattie her blessing.

A popular lady, our mother loved to dance. She was a petite woman with a smooth caramel-colored complexion that turned a warm shade of crimson if she stayed in the sun for a long period of time. Not one to be bothered with long hair, she kept her curly black hair in a stylish bob. One could find her at the United Service Organizations (USO) clubs on the weekends, dancing the night away with the black soldiers. That was where she met our father, Leon T. Lloyd, Jr.

Even though USO policy expressly forbade discrimination on the basis of race or creed, it was not uncommon for separate USO centers to spring up in the same town, either because of local regulations or by request of African Americans who deplored the tensions that arose when they entered the USO center.

Our father was born in Memphis, Tennessee, on October 22, 1918, to Leon Thomas Lloyd, Sr., and Juliece Alma Lloyd. Leon was the oldest child of seven children born to the couple. He learned responsibility at an early age. Because he was the oldest of the children, the younger ones had to follow his orders when he took care of them.

Father was handsome, charming, confident and fashionable. When he was growing up with his brothers, they would stride down the streets of their Memphis neighborhood dressed to the max in suits, which earned them the title of the Lloyd Boys. He was five foot nine, with a strong, muscular build on a medium frame. His hair was medium to dark brown, which accentuated his light complexion. When he was younger, the hot Memphis sun would turn his hair a reddish color.

He attended the Memphis public school system and graduated from Booker T. Washington High School. Later, he attended Henderson Business College, where he received his associate degree in business. He was enlisted in the US Army from 1941 to November 1945. While serving in the army, he rose through the ranks. He entered as a private and remained a private for one month; then he advanced to sergeant, a position in which he served for nine months. Then he was promoted to first sergeant and served in that capacity for thirty-three months. While serving as a first sergeant, he was commanding a detachment of four hundred soldiers overseas in England, France, and Germany. As a first sergeant quartermaster, he commanded a company of 212 men. While serving as a quartermaster officer, he studied company administration, transportation, military law, and supply administration.

As you can see, we had an intelligent father, and he was not afraid to tackle challenges that led to self-improvement.

Furthermore, our father passed a test to become a first lieutenant, but he turned down the position because back then, an officer could only sit and eat with other officers. The problem was that the other officers were all white, and my father, being "colored," could not sit with the white officers, so he would have been sitting by himself in isolation, and that he would not do. Isolation can be a tool of destruction and control. It is used in prisons as a method of behavior control and punishment. However, my father was not a prisoner; in fact, he passed a test that a lot of Caucasian soldiers could not pass. Rewarding him by separating him from others because of his race was not only a method of discrimination but also a form of punishment. As an officer, his living quarters would have been isolated as well, which, in my opinion, was degrading, cruel and heartless. It makes me angry that my father had no choice but to turn down the higher ranking as an officer, which he had earned, or choose segregation, that would result in forced separation and isolation in a restricted area. This type of quarantine, under these terrible conditions, represents the inhumane treatment of a human being, more specifically black men. Unless, a black man wanted to subject himself to that type of cruelty, he had no chance of elevating to the ranks of an officer. What kind of choice is that?

Our father, Leon T. Lloyd Jr., First Sergeant, US Army

As I mentioned earlier, the racial divide in the military service left scars on our father that we could not imagine. Later in life, we tried to give my father a green suit as a Father's Day gift, but he said to take it back and get it in another color. Our mother said, "Never buy him any clothes that are green, because that color reminds him of the military, and he will never wear it." Our father would never talk to us about his time in the service, but our mother helped us understand why it was a subject that was off limits. Even though my father had many lifetime friends he met in the military, the military experience, seasoned with racism, was something he preferred to forget.

Leon was deployed often while in the service, but he always came back, looking for Mattie, his true love. While Leon was still in the service, he and Mattie decided to get married. They were married on April 7, 1944, but not without hitting a few obstacles. According to the law in Florida, Mattie was too young to get married without first obtaining parental consent from at least one parent, so she nervously called her mother to get her permission. She told Leona and me that she dreaded making that call.

When Mattie's mother found out she wanted to marry Leon, a young man she had yet to meet, she asked her if she knew what she was doing. Mattie said she did.

Due to Mattie's youthfulness, her mother interrogated her further. "Are you sure you want to get married?"

"Yes," she replied.

Reluctantly, Mattie's mother granted her permission to marry.

Shortly after Mattie and Leon got married, Leon was deployed to Germany. Not long after he arrived in Germany, the war ended. Leon boarded a ship, that was deployed back to the United States. Upon returning, he quickly proceeded to join Mattie in Florida. In 1945, Leon had finished his time in the army.

After his return, he took Mattie to Memphis so his family could meet his new bride. He was proud of her. Then they returned to Florida, where they began their new life together. Leon had to get a job, and everyone knew about the booming auto industry in Detroit. Black folks could get a job that paid five dollars a day, which was good money back then. So off to Detroit they went. They lived in a segregated area of the city, known as Black Bottom. It used to be a German ghetto and was named Black Bottom because of its rich black soil.

The black population of Detroit exploded in the 1900s, growing from 5,701 to more than 120,000 by 1930. It became a commercially sound area and a melting pot. The entertainment area was called Paradise Valley. There were black businesses, social institutions, and nightclubs. Major blues singers, big bands, and jazz artists performed, such as Duke Ellington, Billy Eckstine, Pearl Bailey, Ella Fitzgerald, and Count Basie. The area had been thriving for some time before Leon and Mattie moved there, but by 1946, people, including my parents, were moving to the northern and western areas of Detroit. During the 1950s, because so many people had moved out, it became a blighted eyesore. Our parent's new residence was located on the northeast side of Detroit.

Leon initially found a job at the Ford Motor Company plant, but he did not find the work challenging. He had a creative, artistic spirit. He wanted to become an auto body mechanic, so he and Mattie agreed he would return to trade school. He finished training and received his certification. But life was rough for a black man in those days. He would go for interviews after being told on the phone there was a job opening, but when he got there, mysteriously, the job had just been filled, the white employer would tell him. Even though this happened time after time for the same apparent reason, Leon was determined to get a job that he was fully trained in.

As luck would have it, a good buddy of his, who was also a good friend of the family, Mr. Dick Sears, helped him get hired at an auto repair shop as a body mechanic. Mr. Sears was a fair-skinned black man with straight black hair, who was also a body mechanic. Mr. Sears spoke up for my father, and that was how my father was hired. His employers quickly saw that everything Mr. Sears had said about my father was true. My father proved to be an asset to the company.

We learned the character traits of strength, belief in oneself, and knowing one's own self-worth from our father. He knew who he was and would not let anyone else define him or tell him what he could or could not do.

A proud, take-no-mess kind of man, Leon would not back down from a confrontation. And guess what? Leona and I were the same way. He was a man of few words. When the situation called for it, he went into action. I still remember one incident like it was yesterday. It was a sunny day, and our father was sitting in the La-Z-Boy reclining chair in the front yard with a cast on his left leg from a previous fall. We had bought our father that chair to relax in after his fall. A car cruised by with some young men inside who challenged him saying, "Old man you better not to be in front of this house when we come back again or else." This threat made our father angry. Our father, immediately hobbled into the house, retrieved his shotgun, and proceeded to return outdoors and sit there well into the night. Knowing our father's stubborn streak, this made our mother extremely nervous.

I went outdoors and walked over to my father to get a better understanding of why he took that stance, my father looked into my eyes and said, "No one tells me what to do on my property." The conviction in his eyes and in his voice was unflinching. This was his house, a place he called his home, a place where he should be able to come rest after a day's work. It was not a place where he should run to hide from any man. This was his home and his castle, and he was not going to cower in fear or isolation.

His explanation said it all. His human rights were being threatened and he just could not look the other way. I fully understood why my father stood his ground. I quietly returned into the house. As a black man who faced discrimination all his life, he was not going to let anybody, black or white, tell him what he could do on his property. I told my mother I understood why my father took that stance and said I would have done the same thing. My mother heard the explanation but felt he still might get hurt. She knew, as well as I, my father would rather face the possibility of harm or death, than live as a caged scared animal in his house, fearing to come out. That would have destroyed the quality of my fathers' life.

I stayed late into the night to make sure my father was not alone; plus, it made my mother feel better. Nothing happened that night or any of the following nights my father sat on his lawn.

My sister and I displayed that same trait of speaking out against injustice and what we felt was wrong. I have spoken out for those who had no voice, and I was warned against it. As with my father, threats did not scare me, because I knew in my heart and soul that what I was doing was right, and I could not operate out of fear.

A great example of Leon's protective fatherly love was shown on one hot summer evening. Leona and I were downstairs in our basement, watching television. We had claimed the basement as our teenage cave. That evening, it was dark outside, and our dog kept barking at the basement window. We told him to be quiet and sit down, but he kept barking. Leona got up and peered out the window, but she could not see anything because it was dark, so she grabbed our dog and put him in her lap. But his persistent barking continued. This went on for more than ten minutes, and finally, he quieted down. Shortly after that, our father came down the stairs into the basement and asked us if we had heard anything outside. We told him, "No, but the dog kept barking and looking up at the basement window."

"There was a young man peeping in the basement window, looking at the two of you," our father said. "The man stared for about five minutes and then went to the guest bedroom window and started unscrewing the screen." Our eyes grew as big as saucers as we listened. By the time the man got to the third screw, our father had popped open his switchblade knife and rushed through the bushes toward the man.

"He saw me coming through those bushes and took off. I chased him for a block and a half before I stopped. He probably thought you two were home alone," he said. Our father was not going to let anything happen to his girls. That man had picked the wrong house. He never returned to try it again.

The surprising thing about the event was that my father made the whole neighborhood block feel safer. One neighbor, an older man, said, "Mr. Lloyd, when I see or hear anything, I am going to call for you." Did my father take the law into his own hands? Yes, to protect our lives. I was proud of my father, and a feeling of safety surrounded my sister and me like a blanket because he was there. Our father demonstrated that type of strength and love for his family his whole life.

The examples my father showed us did not go unnoticed. We were not physically as strong as my father, who could protect others, but he gave us the gift of wanting to help protect those who could not protect themselves. We chose to wield the law as an instrument as strong as any sword to help people who could not help themselves. We used restorative justice to uplift the downtrodden. Our father watched us in our law practice and as judges, and he not only approved of our actions, he was proud of us.

CHAPTER 3

Motown Sounds and The Detroit Riot

Heaven Help Us All

In our early teenage years, from thirteen to sixteen, Leona and I saw ourselves as any other teenagers who loved dance music, especially Motown music. This became the soundtrack of our lives. We knew the names of all the Motown artists, as well as the lyrics to all their songs. We had eight-by-ten pictures of Motown artists on our walls in our bedroom, including the Miracles, Marvin Gaye, Little Stevie Wonder, the Temptations, the Supremes, the Marvelettes, and Martha Reeves and the Vandellas, to name a few. The Motown sound not only was big in Detroit but also was catching on throughout the world.

As young teenagers, we were lucky to have the opportunity to see the entire roster of Motown artists perform live in the Motown Revue at the beautiful Fox Theater in Detroit, Michigan. The shows took place in the winter, but wind, snow, and freezing temperatures did not stop us from standing in line for hours to be rewarded with front-row seats, which we barely used because we could not sit down.

Even though Leona and I were good students, our parents could not understand how we could do our homework with the radio blasting. However, we felt the music helped us study. The music made us feel great; it was mood-changing and stimulated our motivation. The Motown sound was imbedded in us. The lyrics and the fast-paced music had us on our feet, jumping in our bedroom.

We danced along while watching a local television dance show called Robin Seymour's *Swingin' Time*. The show was recorded in Canada but televised in Canada as well as in Michigan. My sister and I became courageous enough to go appear on the show. All the teens in Detroit were tuned into that show, along with my high school teachers, who said, "I saw you on television yesterday." The show was Detroit and Canada's version of *American Bandstand*. Because we danced regularly on the show, we were often recognized while out in public. Our junior and senior years in high school were positively impacted by this show. This foreshadowed our relationship with the media when we later became lawyers and judges.

Our early teenage years were filled with a lot of fun but also unexpected pain and anger and had an impact on our future career choices as well as the narrative we chose for our lives.

◆ You May Discriminate Against Me, But You Will Not Stop Me

We arrived at Mumford High School in 1965, and at that time, the school had a predominantly Jewish school body. Black students made up only about 20 percent of the student body population. We were entering tenth grade.

Leona and I were excited about starting at the new school and sat anxiously in our new counselor's office as she prepared our class schedule. On the third morning, she handed us separate cards with our class schedules. Leona and I split up and went to the classes listed on our cards. Classes had been in session for about three days, so we had not missed much. The class I was going to was geometry, and Leona was headed off to the advanced algebra class.

Up until that day, Leona and I had never experienced discrimination or racism firsthand. We knew the history of the civil rights movement and watched the marches for civil rights on television with our parents. I saw people being sprayed down with water hoses. Some were viciously attacked by dogs, and some were beaten and dragged for sitting at a lunch counter. I knew they were fighting for the right of black people to be treated as humans and given the same rights as those of the white race. I saw the unflappable human spirit in people who sang "We Shall Overcome" as they were beaten. When I was a young girl, tears would well up in my eyes because I knew they were fighting for me.

I had never dealt with racism but, everything was about to change for me the moment I entered that geometry class. What happened to me in that class would affect me and every major decision I made for the rest of my life.

I headed to my first class, geometry, and looking through the window of the door to the classroom, I saw that class was already in session, so I walked in quietly and tried to hand the teacher my enrollment card, but she didn't take it. Instead, she looked me up and down and said, "Can I help you?"

I smiled and said, "Yes, I'm a new student, and here is my enrollment card."

She still would not take the card. Instead, she said, "Are you sure you are in the right class? This is an honors geometry class."

"Yes, this is the classroom I am to report to. See? It says it on the enrollment schedule."

She abruptly snatched the card, glanced at it, and gruffly said, "Take a seat in the back of the room."

As I walked back there, I noticed there were only three other black students in the class, and they were in the back of the classroom as well. I had never felt so unwelcome in my entire life. I wanted to run out of that classroom to my counselor and ask her to place me in a different class, but instead, I quietly took my seat in the back.

After a few days in her class, I was playing catch-up. I noticed she had the habit of asking if anyone had any questions before she moved on to what was next on her agenda. So, the next day I had a question I needed answered, so I could comprehend what was happening in the class. I raised my hand when she asked for questions. She looked directly at me and continued to scan the classroom. No hands were up except mine. She said, "Since there are no questions, we will move on."

The next day, the same scenario happened. I raised my hand because now I had a compounded question and desperately needed clarification regarding the problems we were working on and again, she rolled her eyes and turned her back to me and said, "Since there are no questions, we will move on." She was intentionally not answering my questions, so for me, there was no moving forward. It was as though she did not want me to comprehend what was going on, as if to prove her belief that I did not belong in her honors class.

This continued the next week, until I just stopped raising my hand. After all, by looking at me with my hand raised, she was making a point that she was not going to entertain any questions from me. For the first time in my life, I was doubting my ability. I began to question *if I was suitable for that class.*

By the third week, I came home and burst into tears as I told my mother what was happening in the classroom. I told her we were going to have a test the next day, and I knew I would not pass it, because I did not understand geometry, and my teacher wouldn't help clarify anything by answering my questions. I was usually an

A student in math, so I did not understand why I could not ask questions in that class. If the teacher did not want to answer any questions, why did she ask the students if they had any questions? My mother listened but, at that moment did not have an answer for me.

The next day, I took the test, and as I had predicted I, along with the other black students, failed the exam. On the next test, I received the same result. The situation was driving me crazy. I came home crying hysterically to my mother about the class and how the teacher smiled as she handed me my failing test score. My mother saw how upset and angry I was because I felt the class could affect my ability to get into college. I felt this woman wanted me to feel I was less than, was not smart enough, and did not belong with the other nonblack children in the class. She was trying to break my spirit and make me quit trying to learn. She wanted me to accept failure.

However, there was a problem with her equation she did not see: my parents always declared to my sister and me that we were smart. They taught us that when we hit a wall, we should back up and figure out another way to get over it and not quit. My mother told us one day when she looked at our report cards, which contained straight *A's*, "Your daddy is smart, and so am I, so you two have no excuse for not being smart."

All those thoughts were running through my brain when my mother, who now had been thinking about my dilemma for a few days said, "Baby, I can't help you because I never had geometry, and your father never had geometry, so you are going to have to teach yourself. Start from page one in the book and read and follow all the directions. Answer all the work questions, and then review the past exams you had, and answer those questions."

I thought my mother had lost her mind at first, but I stopped my crying, wiped my swollen eyes, and quietly said okay. Then I went back to my bedroom, opened my book, and started reading page one.

Every day I just sat in class, not really listening to the teacher anymore, because she had mentally excluded all the black students from her class. I worked diligently at home, as my mother had told me to. After a few weeks, I had caught on to geometry. I ran and told my mother, "Mama, I understand geometry now! I understand."

My mother smiled and said, "I knew you would figure it out; you are smart."

In another week, I had caught up with the class, just in time for a test the next day. This time, I welcomed the test. After I finished the test, I told my girlfriend in the class, "I know geometry, and I know I passed that test."

The following day, the teacher walked down the aisle, passing back our exams, and when she handed me my exam, I saw a big *B* at the top of the page. I wanted to jump up and scream, "I know geometry!" but I had to maintain my cool.

She handed me my paper and said with sarcasm in her voice, "This was an easy exam."

I thought to myself; *Well, the boy in front of me received a D, as he has on all his exams, so if the test was so easy, why doesn't he have a B on his paper like me?* I did not care what she said, she was not going to steal my joy. On every test, thereafter, including the midterm and final exams, I received only grades of *B's and B+'s*. I no longer questioned my ability nor my sense of belonging in that class.

Based on the average of all my scores, combining the first card marking grade with the totality of my test grades in my final semester, I should have received nothing lower than a *C-* for a final grade. However, my racist teacher had the audacity to give me a failing final grade. When she handed me my report card, she made sure she scratched out the *H* for *honors* and replaced it with an *R* for *regular.* That was her way of saying, "I don't care how many exams you passed in my class; I am still going to fail you and put an *R* by the grade to remind you that you, little black girl, shouldn't have been here in the first place."

When the other black students saw my grade, they were angry because they knew my grades, and they felt at least one of us had passed with a great grade. One black male student wanted to go cuss her out, but I stopped him. The only thing that stopped my tears from flowing was the fact that at least he wanted to stand up for me.

He said, "I am not scared of her, because she can't do nothing to me." I was scared for him, as I did not want him expelled, so I told him my mother would handle things.

Our mother called the counselor and explained the problem, so the counselor set up a meeting in her office with the teacher and my mother. The problem was the date of the meeting coincided with classes being officially over. We were there for the meeting, but the teacher called in and left a message that she could not attend because she was out of town on vacation. The counselor claimed the grade could not be changed without the teacher's sign-off on it. I cried my eyes out because I had never experienced an injustice like that before. There I sat with a folder filled with graded exams. It was not fair! I did not understand how a teacher could do that, feel no remorse, and not experience any consequences for her wrongful actions. I felt as if no one cared to make the teacher accountable for her actions regarding the final grade she gave me or for intentionally missing the meeting. My mother and I were made to feel powerless against a system that had no remedy for a prejudiced teacher. The system did not have a fair way of correcting the havoc she had caused in my life nor the damage that could possibly ensue to hurt my future admittance into college.

Sometimes adversity can cripple a person, but for Leona and me, it caused us to work that much harder and be more determined to make it. Our parents had instilled in us that no one could stop you but you, and damn it, that teacher was not about to stop me.

I took the class over again because I was not going to let a failing grade remain on my transcript, but this time, I had a new teacher. Every time I took an exam or quiz, I finished it in a matter of minutes. I would hand in the tests, and the teacher would review and grade them before the others in the class had finished and turned in their exams. I received an *A* on every exam or quiz. At the end of the semester, I went up to receive my report card. The teacher looked at me and said, "I don't know why you were put in this class. It has been obvious all semester that you knew geometry." I responded, "I was not supposed to know geometry!" She shook her head as she handed me the final grade of *A* on my report card. I was determined that the racist teacher I previously had was not going to win, nor was her grade going to remain on my transcript.

The lesson I learned from that experience was to speak up to a teacher I felt was wrong or prejudiced. I was no longer going to bite my tongue. Even if that teacher did not change, I would receive satisfaction that this young black student was never again going to sit silently in the face of injustice. I would call teachers out on it to their faces. That would replace tears with the satisfaction of knowing the teachers were not going to get away with behavior that was unfair and unjust. There would be no more tears for me.

That was the beginning of my standing up for what was right and fair and against injustice—period. I carried that value into the courtroom. The importance of fairness for every person who came into my courtroom and appeared in front of me was what I ruled by.

Even though that incident was a horrible one to go through as a teenager, Leona and I had other experiences that were spirit- and morale-boosting and made high school a joy for us.

◆ Our First Election Experience

The next year, Leona and I decided to run for student council. At the time, there were only one or two black students on the council. We felt that all students should have an equal say in what happened at their school, thus the need for more people of color on the council to make representation equal in the school. The race was on.

It was our first campaign, so we learned as we went. We saw signs go up for those running, so up went ours. We did not have the money our opponents had that made it possible for them to plaster the school walls with campaign paraphernalia, but we did the best we could. A lack of money was not going to stop us.

Three days before the election, that morning, we were feeling a little down because we couldn't advertise like we wanted to, when all of a sudden, as we walked through the front doors of the school, we saw large, colorful campaign posters with pictures painted of Leona and me. They were three times the size of our homemade signs, and they were plastered everywhere. They were on every floor, in front of every set of stairs, and lined up on all the hallway walls. We had an anonymous guardian angel helping us.

Faith carried us through, and we won the council election two years in a row. Little did we know that our courage to run in a high school council race that no one thought we could win was setting us up for unforeseen future judicial elections that people thought we didn't have a chance in hell of winning.

◆ From Cool Jerk to Class Treasurer

During our senior year in high school, I ran for class treasurer, and Leona ran for class secretary. Leona did not make the primary, but I did. Of course, even though she was sad about her loss, Leona threw her support behind me.

All the candidates were supposed to give a campaign speech in the school auditorium a day before the election. I did not want to get up there and give a dry "Vote for me" speech. I wanted to be different and do something outside the box, something my classmates would remember. I decided to pantomime a popular record out at the time, "Cool Jerk by the Capitols."

The song focused on a theme of coolness that this guy possessed. I figured if I turned it around and mouthed the same words but dressed up as a trashy-looking derelict, I would have their attention. I was not trying to be cute, as my opponent was, just cool. My sister and our girlfriend Gretchen Sears were my backup singers. We dressed up in our fathers' oversized old clothes: hats, shoes, and suits. All were at least three sizes too big. We used an eyebrow pencil to draw mustaches and stubble over our faces. We were the bomb—we looked great! We looked as if we had rolled off a park bench.

As soon as the music started, we pranced out in step as we pantomimed the song, never missing a beat or a word. The rhythm to the song was jumping; as the lyrics stated, "I was the King of the Cool Jerk." After we finished, I stepped to the microphone and yelled, "Vote for me, Leonia Lloyd, for treasurer!" Then we took a bow. As I looked up, my eyes met the audience, and I could see them on their feet, cheering.

I won the election hands down. My classmates supported me 100 percent.

The lesson I learned from that campaign was to do something that was not predictable. Do not follow the pack and stick with the traditional. Sometimes, it is necessary to draw outside the lines. Do the unexpected. Not only will it get you noticed, but you will be remembered. That rule was good in my high school campaign and good when I campaigned many years later for judge. In my judicial campaign, I used strategies the other candidates did not use; that way, I stood out from the pack. I was not afraid of being different. Being different helped me win.

♦ Turning the Negative into a Positive Force

When Leona and I decided to become teachers, we wanted to be a positive force in the lives of the children we taught in high school.

This idea of positive empowerment was implanted in our brain by our speech teacher, Mrs. Zimmerman.

In 1967, we were high school seniors who had completed two years as school councilwomen, and I had just won an election as senior class treasurer. We were doing well in our classes and had our minds on college selection. We both were A students in Mrs. Zimmerman's speech class and enjoyed the class. She believed in the talent and abilities Leona and I had and encouraged us to go to modeling school. Her belief gave us the courage to step out on faith and enroll in, and later graduate from, the John Robert Powers Modeling, Acting and Finishing School, which led to several professional modeling jobs after we graduated high school.

The second display of confidence she had in us was when she selected us to be the first black graduation commencement speakers at Mumford High School for the morning graduation. Even though she knew the administration would challenge her for choosing black speakers, she said, "I selected you because you are the best speakers in my class, and I stand by my choice."

It meant a lot to us that she had faith in us. We said to ourselves; *If she thinks we can do it, then maybe we really can.* Being speakers for the graduation would also allow us to continue the legacy our mother had started as a past commencement speaker for her high school class.

Were we really that good? Well, that question was answered the morning of the graduation commencement. When we finished our speeches and looked out into the packed auditorium, we saw the audience giving us a standing ovation that lasted for several minutes.

Mrs. Zimmerman planted a seed of positivity in us that never disappeared. Years later, as judges, Leona and I spoke, jointly and separately, in many graduation commencements—in fact, too many to count. Each time we gave speeches, they were always to uplift and empower the graduates. Without question, each time we ended our speeches, we gazed with pride at audiences that gave us standing ovations. Mission accomplished. As teachers and judges, we were aware that words were power. That is why, year after year, in the classroom and the courtroom, we continued to pass on the words of positivity Mrs. Zimmerman had so graciously showered on us.

◆ The First Nervous Breakdown

Our mother's helpful and guiding hand was the reason our graduation commencement speeches were received so well. She helped us day and night.

Unfortunately, a few weeks before we were to give the speeches, my mother had her first nervous breakdown. The subtle signs pointing to a nervous breakdown were there, but at the time, as teenagers, we had no way of knowing what we were witnessing. For example, we once were watching TV with our mother, laughing at something funny, then suddenly, our mother asked, "Do you see Jesus on the TV screen?"

We laughed, saying, "What? Where? Jesus isn't on TV."

"Yes, he is. He's right there," she responded with a serious tone.

Joking, we asked, "Where? Do you see him?"

My mother responded in a serious tone, "Yes."

Our laughter stopped when we realized our mother was dead serious. We became silent and just stared at her and then asked again if she still saw Jesus. Our mother quickly returned our stare, and she must have sensed something was wrong with her response, because she said, "No, I don't see Jesus." We did not know she was hallucinating. She saw things that were not there several other times, but she sounded sincere.

Then there were the sleepless nights. Our mother would wander around in the middle of the night, not able to sleep, or stare at a blank

TV screen. That was just the beginning of her strange behavior. Eventually, her behavior turned violent, and she began hitting our father with her fists or any object close by. He called her doctor for help and followed the doctor's suggestion to drive her to the hospital and admit her through the emergency room. How he managed to get her there we did not know because we were at school.

After the doctors examined her and indicated that she had suffered a nervous breakdown, they placed her in the psychiatric wing of the hospital for treatment.

When Leona and I arrived at the hospital, we waited with our father for the doctor to come tell us what was happening with our mother and why she was in that ward at the hospital. At the time, we did not know what had caused her nervous breakdown. We did know, however, that it was serious enough for her to be hospitalized for thirty days, which seemed like an eternity to Leona and me.

Finally, the doctor came out to talk to us. He explained that our mother suffered from depression, which had led to her nervous breakdown. We were confused because our mother did not walk around acting or looking depressed. The doctor explained that depression can manifest in forms you do not see right away. We asked, "What could she be depressed about?"

He said, "She could be upset about something in her past that she is unhappy about or about unfulfilled expectations for her life that never came to fruition. A person with depression cannot simply just snap out of it. It is a medical condition that affects the quality of her life. The person must receive treatment. Normally, we give shock treatment to patients to help them forget what may be bothering them so they can be themselves again; however, because your mother has had a subarachnoid hemorrhage of the brain, we cannot take a risk in giving her that, so we are going to treat her with medication and hope that within thirty days it works.

"But I must warn you that this medication she must take is relatively new and still deemed experimental, so, Mr. Lloyd, you will have to sign for permission for us to give her the medication. We have had success with this medication in the past, but I cannot predict the outcome for your wife's case because of her past subarachnoid hemorrhage. I pray it does go well, and if so, she will have to continue therapy sessions with a psychiatrist as part of her outpatient treatment plan."

Leona and I just sat and looked at each other. Our heads were spinning. We were not prepared for the dilemma our mother was in. We felt helpless. My father reviewed and signed the papers and returned to sit with us. When they finally let us see our mother, she became enraged at our father and told him to get out. To calm her down, he left and remained in the hallway. He knew that person was not our mother. She began to calm down when just Leona and I remained in the room, but she was disoriented. She did not know she was in the hospital.

Later that night, when we went home, our father sat quietly at the kitchen table with a drink of alcohol. That was unusual because our father never drank on weekdays. Even on a rough day, our father never sat at the table silently by himself and drank.

Every day we went to see our mother, praying for a change, but to no avail. There was no change, and every night, our father would sit quietly with a drink. It became a pattern for our father. We knew the situation was breaking his heart.

With each day that passed, our mother became a little calmer, and then, on day twelve, she looked at us when we entered the room and was happy to see us and asked for our father. We told her she had said she did not want him in the room. She responded, "No, I want your father here. Please ask him to come in."

We got our father, who waited patiently outside. He had come every day, hoping for a change or a breakthrough. Finally, a breakthrough had happened, but she could not remember anything that had caused her to be there. With tears in her eyes, she apologized to our father for anything she had done to hurt him. He gave her a big hug and a kiss. We asked our mother what she was depressed about, and she said she was not depressed. That response never changed her entire life. It finally was a good day, but the drinking at night for our father never stopped.

As time moved on, Leona and I kept wondering what could have made our mother depressed. We wondered if the depression was because of the lasting effects from the subarachnoid hemorrhage, such as not being able to go back to work as a nurse, a job she had loved with all her heart. Was it because of our graduating from high school and closing that chapter of our lives? Did she have empty-nest syndrome? Or was it because of problems associated with our father; rarely socializing with their friends or going out for an evening. We knew that whatever it was, my mother was holding it close to her chest, and we knew only a skilled doctor might be able to penetrate her protective shell.

When I became a drug treatment court judge and a veterans' treatment court judge, I came across many things that affected the minds of the people in my programs. Some I realized right away had issues that led them to try to find solace in drugs or alcohol. Substance abuse was not their answer. I learned from my mother's case that the brain is a delicate instrument, and the slightest thing can affect it. My experience with my mother gave me a unique benefit and advantage that I used as a tool to help the defendants in front of me get the help they needed. Whether they suffered from PTSD, addiction to substances, or other outside issues, I knew that the sooner they got treatment the better off they would be.

Given her timeline of residency in the hospital, our mother was going to miss our graduation, including the speeches she had helped create for us to give. Even though our mother would be coming out of the hospital five days after our graduation, the doctor would not allow her to conditionally leave on our graduation day to see us speak and then return. That put a damper on our enthusiasm, even though our mother encouraged us to go do a great job. It was not going to be the same with her absence. We knew we had to give the commencement speech without her present, but we were just two sixteen-year-old girls. We cried our eyes out at night in our room, wondering how we were going to do it without her. Through all our tears, we said to each other, "We have to do it. Mama wants us to do it and do it the same way we practiced it in front of her." We knew our father and his sister, our aunt Kathryn from Chicago, would be there for us. We had to pull ourselves together.

Miraculously, the morning of the graduation, we fought back the tears and persevered. In our speeches, we talked about what the future could hold for the graduates, and we ended the speech with a poem called "Don't Quit." Fittingly, we could not quit that day—or any other day—when life threw us curveballs. "Don't quit" would become the mantra for our lives, a theme that would echo time and time again as I spoke to the students I taught in high school, as well as, to the defendants in my drug court many years later. Quitting was not an option!

Thirty- five years later, that same poem was printed on bookmarks that I and Judge Jefferson, gave out on the date of graduation to the graduates of drug court. I instructed my graduates, to read the poem every day so they would remember that when things got hard for them, they could not quit.

That "Don't quit" attitude got us through situations that dealt with discrimination in school as well as in the workplace. During our mother's multiple nervous breakdowns and our father's drinking problems, we had to remain strong. That poem rang in our heads and propelled Leona and me forward. Quitting was not an option. Dogged determination and a "Don't quit" attitude helped us make it through.

Don't Quit
John Greenleaf Whittier

When things go wrong, as they sometimes will,

When the road you're trudging seems all up hill,

When the funds are low and the debts are high

And you want to smile, but you have to sigh,

When care is pressing you down a bit,

Rest if you must, but don't you quit.

Life is strange with its twists and turns

As every one of us sometimes learns

And many a failure comes about

When he might have won had he stuck it out;

Don't give up though the pace seems slow—

You may succeed with another blow.

Success is failure turned inside out—

The silver tint of the clouds of doubt,

And you never can tell just how close you are,

It may be near when it seems so far;

So stick to the fight when you're hardest hit—

It's when things seem worst that you must not quit.

Right after our graduation from high school, our mother came home, and everything seemed great, so after she settled in, we decided to seek work as models. We called the agency we had been given; a contact by the modeling school we had graduated from. We called numerous times, but no one answered. Undisturbed by that, Leona and I decided to make an unannounced trip to the agency.

We drove downtown to the talent agency building, took the elevator to the office, walked in, and sat down on a couch. On the walls were pictures of beautiful models and actors we gawked at. As we sat there, we could not help but overhear a loud conversation going on in the other office. A lady with a gruff voice was talking to a man, and we heard her say, "Okay, I have your pictures and your information, and if I get something for you, I'll call you. In the meantime, don't quit your day job." There was a moment of silence, and then a handsome Brad Pitt type of guy walked out.

Leona and I exchanged glances. She read my mind and said, "Leonia, let's go, and we can come back when we have our photos."

We got up to leave, when a plump, short middle-aged white lady with spiked hair, wearing bifocals, came to the door of the inner office and asked, "Who are you two?"

We froze like statues for a minute but turned toward her. I am sure our eyes showed the fear of possible rejection. We told her our names.

"Are you twins?"

"Yes," we replied.

"Where were you two weeks ago when I needed you?"

"Graduating from high school."

"Come in. My name is Louise. What are your names?"

Right away, we felt she was interested in us, so we calmed down and answered the questions she fired at us. She asked us if we had any pictures?

Sheepishly, we said, "We only have our high school pictures."

"Fine. If that is all you have, give me that."

We opened our wallets, pulled out our pictures, and gave them to her.

Sizing us up, she said, "You two are cute. I want to send you for an interview for the Detroit Auto Show. That is the biggest modeling job in Detroit. They have two shows: the executive show in July and the regular auto show in November. Since we are in the month of June, it is probably too late for the July show, but I will get you an interview for the November show. The interviews are in September, so you'll have your photo composites by then, right?"

We nodded.

"Great. I'll be calling you later in August for the interview in September, but I need pictures ASAP so I can get you other jobs before then, okay?"

"Yes, we'll get them to you soon," I said.

We returned the completed employee information contact form to her, and then we left. We were excited at the prospect of our first modeling job. Heck, it was our first job, period. Leona and I chatted in the car all the way home. We felt modeling school was going to start paying off.

When we returned home, we told our mother, who seemed as excited as we were about what had transpired. A few days later, around nine o'clock in the morning, Louise called. She had scheduled an interview for us at 1:00 p.m. that day at the main headquarters of the Ford Motor Company. They wanted to interview us for the auto show. Louise asked us to wear the cute outfits we had worn to her office. While I talked to Louise, Leona sat on the edge of her bed, trying to understand what was happening. When I got off the phone, I filled Leona in on what was happening and told her to get dressed.

We arrived in a timely manner at the office for the interview and sat in the waiting room with the other models. The other models appeared to be professional and had larger-than-life picture portfolios, and there we were with just our high school graduation pictures.

It was not long before we heard our names called. We walked into the interviewing room, and the lady at the desk said, "Stop, and turn around." We did as she asked. She peered over her reading glasses at us and asked for our pictures. We handed her our high school pictures, which she glanced at.

"This is all you have?"

I explained to her that we had just graduated from high school and had not gotten our composites back yet. Looking at the papers on her desk while talking to us without eye contact, she said, "Well, we have your information. It's too late for the executive show, but if you get selected for the November show, we'll call you in September." Then her eyes met ours as she asked, "By the way, what do you girls do? What job are you working now?"

Leona proudly and unapologetically said that we had just graduated from high school and were not employed but would be attending Wayne State University in the fall. At that point, the lady put her pen down and took her glasses off. She focused directly on us and responded, "My son attends Wayne State University. It is a very nice school. Nice meeting both of you." We smiled, thanked her, and left.

While driving home, Leona said, "That lady barely looked at us throughout the whole interview until I said we would be attending Wayne State in the fall. Then her voice and whole demeanor changed, and she really looked at us." Leona and I figured they probably would not call, but we thought it was a good learning experience.

Bright and early the next day, Louise called. I answered, and she sounded excited when she said, "Girls, you got the executive show at the Detroit Auto Show! I do not know what you said in the interview, but you impressed them. You are in both shows, and you have a clothes fitting, today at two o'clock, so write this information down."

I immediately woke Leona up and told her what was happening. We started screaming and jumping up and down. We told our mother, who beamed. I said, "Mama, we are going to be in the Detroit Auto Show. This is the biggest modeling gig in the city of Detroit, and we got it right out of high school with no portfolio!"

When something like that happens in your life and you have no justification for it; it has to be God showing off one of his miracles.

We were fitted for mini dresses with long patent-leather boots. The outfits were cute. Generous donors, who were exquisitely dressed, attended the executive show. As models, Leona and I posed by two trucks. One featured Twin I-Beam lights, and the other was a futuristic truck that cost $300,000. The truck looked like a car, with hydraulic doors that lifted like wings, like the DeLorean, which made a debut about twenty years later.

With the executive show completed, we were ready for the regular auto show, which was going to be in November of 1967. Louise kept her word and kept us busy with a few modeling jobs throughout the summer.

◆ The Detroit Riot of 1967

As our excitement was calming down from the executive auto show held in the beginning of July, something else began to heat up. Out of the clear blue, we started to see announcements on television about a riot that had broken out in Detroit. The riot started on July 23 and lasted five days. It was sparked by a Detroit police raid at a black bar that operated after hours. Governor Romney deployed nine thousand Michigan Army National Guard to help restore order, and then, upon his request, on the second day, President Lyndon B. Johnson authorized five thousand federal troops to be sent in from the US Army's Eighty-Second and 101st Airborne Divisions. As mentioned in the Kerner Commission Report, the cause of the riots in Detroit, as in other inner cities, was that many Detroit residents were infuriated over poor economic conditions, racial injustice, and long-simmering tensions between black residents and Detroit's majority-white police force. A total of forty-three individuals were killed in the riots, and thirty-three were African American. More than 7,200 people were arrested, and as for property damage, around 1,400 buildings in Detroit were heavily damaged or demolished.

Beginning in April and continuing throughout the rest of the year, 159 race riots erupted in the United States. The most devastating ones were in Newark, New Jersey, and Detroit. The music at that time reflected what was happening all over the United States. It voiced the sentiments of the black race. For example, Marvin Gaye's 1971 album, which some call a protest album, asked questions in its songs, such as "Inner City Blues" and "What's Going On?" His lyrics were an outcry about the riots, the Vietnam War, the unrest in America, and police brutality.

There were songs of encouragement meant to uplift the spirit, such as the Impressions' 1965 songs "We're a Winner" and "People Get Ready." Both had an impact on the civil rights movement. The 1969 song "Choice of Colors" and the 1970 song, "If There's a Hell Below We're All Gonna Go" by the Impressions and Curtis Mayfield sent a message to serve as a warning regarding the state of race relations and the tempers raging in the inner cities. All these songs were politically conscious music. James Brown's 1968 song "Say It Loud: I'm Black and I'm Proud" and Nina Simone's 1970 song "To Be Young, Gifted, and Black" became anthems of the black power movement.

The riots were not physically near our house where we lived, but we were glued to the TV, watching the black clouds of billowing smoke and the multitudes of armed guards. Our mother gave us strict warnings that we could not drive anywhere in the area of the riots.

One day Leona and I went outside to go to the store, and we heard a loud, unfamiliar noise coming from the street. We stepped onto the porch, and before we knew it, a huge US Army tank was easing down our street. Leona and I had never seen a tank in person. The colossal size of the armed tank scared us to death. One blast from the gun on the front of that monster could have taken out our house. Why it rolled down our street we did not know, but we were glad when it was gone. Our neighborhood was nowhere near the riots, so why were soldiers charging through a quiet residential street? We became suspicious and untrusting of their motives.

That summer, the messages in the music we sang and danced to, left their subliminal impact on us.

◆ The November Auto Show

It was fall, and the riot had been over for a while. We were attending our college classes, but we knew the auto show dates were right around the corner.

Finally, it was November 26, 1967, and the 51st annual Detroit Auto Show had arrived. Attendance rose that year to more than 250,000 people. Our parents came to see us on the first day of our ten-day modeling stint, and we were excited when our aunt Kathryn from Chicago came to see us on the fifth day of the show.

When we took our lunch break, we spent it talking to our aunt. We told her they were going to talk to us about being in the Chicago Auto Show.

"It'll be right there where you live!" we excitedly blurted out.

But to our surprise, she said, "I won't come out the door to see you in Chicago."

"Huh?" we said. We were not prepared for that response.

Aunt Kathryn thought we would get distracted while traveling with the auto show and pull away from school, and she could not support that.

"I want you in school. I've come all the way here because you're still in school, but I won't support something that will take you away from school." Life had taught our aunt some wise lessons. She was a former beauty queen and had lived a glamorous life. She felt that sometimes the glitter and bright lights could steer people off, even determined persons, and sometimes they never found their way back. No matter how much we said that would never happen to us, she was not hearing it. Our aunt left a few days later because she had come to Detroit only to see us.

It was December 2nd, and the auto show would be finished in a few days, when an older model named Marie, who was also an announcer, came over to speak to us. She said she had been watching us and knew we were new models for the show. She told us a little bit about herself and how long she had been with the auto show. We realized she had been with them for a long time and traveled with all the auto shows. We in turn told her our brief modeling history and said we were students at Wayne State University. When she asked if we wanted to see her pictures from previous shows, we said yes enthusiastically, so later, when we finished our shift at the end of the show, we went to her trailer. She showed us a huge photo book. Marie was still pretty, but twenty years ago, she had been a knockout.

When we got to the end of the photo book, she blurted out, "That's it. There is not anything more to show you. That is my life. Do not let this be you. I have a few more years left, and then modeling's over for me. I do not know what I will do then. So, stay in college, and finish. Don't be like me."

We responded, "Okay." Feeling deflated, we thanked her and told her she had given us a lot to think about.

The ride home was quiet until Leona asked me if I was thinking about what Marie had said.

"Yes, because it was kind of sad. I do not want to end up like that, where all I have is a bunch of pictures in a scrapbook. I want my life to really mean something. I want to finish college and teach."

Leona said, "So do I. Now I understand why Aunt Kathryn was so dead set against us coming to Chicago for the auto show. With the demands of the show and our absences from class, it would have distracted us from our main goal, which is finishing college. The Chicago show can be done by other models, and we should just focus on school, like Aunt Kathryn said."

"I was thinking the same thing," I said. Feeling better about our decision, we laughed and sang with the car radio blasting all the way home.

That show taught us a valuable lesson: all that glitters is not gold. With our paychecks, we treated ourselves to fox-trimmed coats and some clothes for school and our mother to outfits of her choice. We continued to do sporadic modeling assignments and photo shoots while in college, but the glitter the modeling world once had held for us lost its sparkle after the auto show. Modeling was not an easy job, but it was glamorous enough to lure a person away from the not-so-glamorous world of studying. The decision we made that night on the drive home was one of the most important ones we had made in our lives. Our aunt Kathryn and Marie had a profound effect on our decision.

Part TWO

1967–1979

CHAPTER 4

The Challenges of College

A Change Is Gonna Come

In the fall of 1967, with all the changes in the household concerning the health of our mother, my sister and I entered Wayne State University in September. It soon became obvious our father would not be able to help us financially, as he was behind on a few payments to the school, so we knew we had to work our way through college. We found jobs on campus and adjusted our class schedules so we could do both school and work. With only one car to use, we had to coordinate our study, job, and class schedules to make them work before we drove home. We also obtained scholarships and loans because our part-time jobs were not going to cover the costs of tuition, books, food for lunch, parking, and gas to get to school. We cut corners as much as we could. Buying used books for classes and reselling them back helped a lot. We were going to school from home, but our mother made living at home almost impossible.

The aftermath of our mother's first nervous breakdown resulted in her behavior becoming increasingly bizarre. She cooked meals that she should have known we never liked. One night, when we were studying, she zipped into our room and clicked the lights off, stating that she and our father needed to save on the electricity bill. We pleaded that we needed to study, but she was not having it. That was unlike the sweet, caring mother who had raised us. She never would have done anything to stop or interfere with our studying. With tears in our eyes, we wondered when our real mother would return.

Her wave of meanness had a negative impact on our father, whose drinking increased more and more. We began to worry about him. He seemed to block out her tirades with his use of alcohol.

We tried talking to our mother, but this person was not her. Classes had started in September, and by November, matters did not improve. In fact, they got worse. We had tackled the tuition problem so we could enroll in January for the next quarter, but our mother's behavior was something we could not control. To drive from home to our classes, we used the family car; however, gas and parking for school were our responsibility, as our father did not give us an allowance anymore. Our mother constantly hinted at taking the car away from us. The threat was based not on need but on meanness. Many nights, my sister and I cried over the way she treated us. Often, she would threaten to take away all the comforts of home from us for no reason. This continued for the entire school year.

Even though we did not want to, we felt we had no choice but to move if we wanted to stay in school. We were eighteen years old, and it was our first major move, leaving the only home we knew. It was stressful for us, but we felt we could not stay. The money we had saved from our jobs, would enable us to move into a dormitory on campus. We selected January 1969 as the month to move; it was the beginning of the new quarter of school. We were determined to continue in college; after all, our mother had preached the importance of college to us since we were young. Nothing could change our minds now, not even her.

As I was packing and wiping away tears, a book caught my attention as I was about to place it in a box: *The Autobiography of Malcolm X*. As I held it in my hand, I fondly remembered the reading game Leona and I inadvertently had gotten into with our father. We were required to read the book for a sociology class at Wayne State University. When we were busy with other schoolwork, if we left our copies of the book lying on a table, our father would grab one to read. One day we saw him reading it, so we started discussing the book with him. To our surprise, he told us that he had met Malcolm X when he was in Detroit and that his nickname was Detroit Red because of the color of his hair. Fascinated by the stories our father told us about that time in Detroit, my sister and I listened, spellbound. He finished the book before the two of us did, which reminded me that our father was not only an avid reader but also one of the smartest men we had ever known.

That memory ripped at my heart because I knew how much we were going to miss our father, but when it came to our mother, he was helpless and caught in the middle. We did not want to move, but we could not stay in constant conflict with our mother. Wiping the tears from my eyes, I placed the book in the box and continued to pack. We loved our mother with all our heart, but we could not continue to live with the abusive side of her personality.

Our move was fast because there was not much to pack. Our boyfriends loaded their cars with our boxes, but right before we pulled off, our father came home. He asked my mother what was going on, and she told him the girls were moving. That came as a shock to him, as we had not announced our moving to either one of them. If we had told our father ahead of time, we felt it would have been more agonizing for him.

He wanted to know the location we were moving to, so we told him we were moving onto campus and gave him the address. Our father was not prepared for this, and he stood there quietly with tears welling in his eyes, looking at the address on the paper I had given him. Emotional, I turned away. I had seen my father cry only once before, at his mother's funeral. We knew he did not want us to leave, but he understood why we could not stay. Our father knew our mother was taking out her misplaced anger and aggression on us, and no matter what he said to try to intervene, she did not listen to him. "Too many women in the house," she would say. My father stood on the porch and, with unblinking eyes, watched as the cars holding our belongings pulled away.

Once we arrived at the dorm, we unpacked and stacked a bunch of canned goods in the two drawers of the desk. Suddenly, we heard a knock on our dorm room door. Having no idea who it was, Leona opened the door, and there was our father; he wanted to see where we were staying. We showed him our small room, which consisted of two beds, a long study desk for two, and our bathroom, which we shared with the girls next door. Showing him the drawers stacked full of canned goods, fighting back tears, we assured him that it was peaceful and that we would be all right. In our hearts, we hoped we would be all right.

Once again, we saw sadness and water flood our father's eyes. Immediately, he pulled out his wallet and gave us fifty dollars each, saying in a trembling voice, "Look, you let me know if you need anything. Do you understand me? I mean anything!" We agreed. We knew it was not a lot of money, but it was what my father had after paying all the bills of the household. After long hugs, he left.

I could smell the alcohol on my father. I knew he had been drinking. I did not want his sadness to cause him to increase his drinking. I mentioned my concern about his drinking to Leona as we sat on our beds quietly crying because our father, who had had our hearts since the day we were born, had just walked out the door. Our father believed in family and was protective of all of us. His presence always made Leona and me feel, that no harm would ever come to us. There to help us when we needed anything, he was a man of his word. That man was our hero. When he went out that door, we looked at each other and, without speaking, realized we were alone.

But we did not want our leaving to increase his drinking. Our aunt Kathryn told us several years later that our moving broke his heart, but he knew and understood why we had to leave.

I lived in the dorm from January 1969 until graduation in 1971, and Leona lived there for a little over a year. She wanted more room, so she decided to move to a two-bedroom apartment close to campus with one of our girlfriends who had lived in the dorm. She wanted me to move in with her, but I felt safer in the dorm, so I stayed.

Once our father knew Leona had moved, I knew he would pay her a visit. When our father paid her a surprise visit and went over there to check out the place, he saw that Leona and her roommate did not have beds. Leona was sleeping on a stack of comforters and her roommate slept on a mattress. That upset our father, who said, "No child of mine sleeps on the floor. You go down to the furniture store tomorrow and get yourself a bed. Charge it to my account and get that other girl one too." My sister bought two twin beds the next day, one for each room. After that, our father was satisfied. Even though we were no longer living at home, our father was always going to be protective of us, no matter what.

While in college and living on campus, I was the slightly more politically involved twin. I became active in the Black Student Union (BSU) and the causes it supported. I attended the evening meetings, which were close by. The organization was active on campus in pushing for more support for minorities on campus through financial grants, scholarships, additional black studies programs, classes and minority counselors. Everything was within walking distance for me, but it was quite a distance for Leona since she no longer lived on campus. Unfortunately, because of the physical distance, there were several activities she could not participate in.

It was the height of the civil rights movement. The Black Panthers, Angela Davis, and Stokely Carmichael were in the news all the time. Black students protested, demanding more justice and presence in colleges.

My sister was not surprised when I participated in a protest with the Black Student Union (BSU) to help a woman who had worked in the kitchen on campus. The lady, who was a mother to several children, came to the BSU for help. After looking into her case, we felt she had been unjustly fired a few days before her ninety-day probationary period was completed, after which she would have become a permanent employee. The BSU, led by officers; Jihad Hud, PhD; Derrick Humphries; Paul Taylor; David Booker; and Adam Shakoor, decided we were going to try to help get her job back.

When the administration failed to honor our request for a meeting, we took action that we knew they would understand, interfering with their money stream. The BSU decided to form a line at the cafeteria where the fired employee had worked. Lunchtime was their busiest part of the day, so we decided to protest then. We lined up around eleven o'clock and started yelling about why people should not buy food from the cafeteria. We described the injustice being done to this poor single mother trying to earn a living for her children. If a person picked up a tray, we went up to him or her and started talking. The folks I approached would look at me and listen and then put the trays back down and leave. The protest was working. After an hour, there were no people lined up to purchase lunches.

With no customers it had become quiet, but not for long. Suddenly, we saw armed tactical military units storming down the hall. They were dressed for combat, from their helmets down to their combat boots, with rifles, handguns, and shields. They were heading our way. They lined up in a single file formation, facing us. I was scared as all heck, but I kept thinking; *If, we do not speak up for her, who will?* The answer to that question was *No one*. She had no one else—that was why she had come to us. So, the members of the Black Student Union and I stood our ground. If the soldiers were meant to scare us away, it did not work. Their presence only scared away the people who might have wanted to eat. As I stood there, I began talking to the armed guard in front of me, explaining how the firing of this poor woman had been wrong.

He was silent as he looked straight ahead, trying not to make eye contact with me. That did not stop me, because I knew he could hear me, and I felt that if he had one drop of compassion in him, it would strike a silent chord. While watching me, he said, "Ma'am, we aren't allowed to talk to you."

"That's okay; you don't have to talk. I will do all the talking," I said, and I continued to speak nonstop. Standing there, he had no choice but to listen. I wanted him to know the real reason we were there. I wanted him to see us as human beings helping another human being. We were unarmed students, and we had not displayed any violence. The customers were gone, so they could not say we had done anything harmful to them.

After thirty to forty-five minutes, the military men were told to leave, and they did so, as the cafeteria was closing. The protest was over for that day. Our plan was to come back to continue the protest the next day, but the administration had a change of heart and agreed to meet with the president of our organization. The meeting happened the next day between the officers of our organization and the administration. The administration listened to our representatives explain how the woman had been unfairly treated and intentionally fired based on false information a few days before her ninety-day probationary period ended, which resulted in no employment benefits. They said they would follow up on the allegations.

They kept their word. The lady was reinstated and made a permanent employee. The supervisor who had fired her was terminated. That was the first time I had ever participated in a protest of any kind, and it showed me the power of organizing and fighting for something when you know it is the right thing to do. We were a voice for a woman who had no voice. We stood up for what was just. We had no idea they were going to call in armed guards on us, but we were not backing down. At that moment, I thought about what Martin Luther King Jr. and his followers must have felt when they peacefully marched only to be met with guns, vicious dogs, and water hoses and get beaten and dragged.

When I say my sister and I showed our political consciousness differently, that type of involvement was what I meant. She might not have physically marched with me in that protest, but if I needed her to be there with me for anything, all I had to do was ask her, and she would be there in a heartbeat. Later, in law school, she would demonstrate her political consciousness in another protest.

When the lady from the cafeteria was reinstated, we considered the matter resolved. The BSU recognized that their success was a result of the legal guidance we received, as well as, the evidence that was presented to the administration, that supported our fight for her. The incident showed me early on that in order to help and protect people, I had to know the law. I never forgot that, and it became one of the factors in my decision later to become a lawyer and then a judge, because then I could really help people from a position of knowledge and strength. It did not surprise me when two of the officers of the Black Student Union also went into the field of law. Derrick Humphries became a lawyer, and Adam Shakoor became a lawyer, a judge and Deputy Mayor for the City Detroit.

As students, we both had double majors in English and Speech because public speaking came naturally to both of us. In my Persuasive Speech class, I tried to educate those who did not understand the Black Power movement at that time. I gave a powerful, persuasive speech on Black Power to a shocked and amazed class, proudly wearing a miniskirt, boots, and a huge Afro and raising my fist while shouting, "Black Power! Black Power!" That was my attention-getting move.

At first, the almost totally white class looked petrified. The only other black person in the class was a much older black male, who thought I was crazy to do that speech. The class didn't get it at first, but by the end of my speech, I think all of them understood that the Black Power movement emphasized racial pride, economic empowerment, and the creation of political and cultural institutions for black people in the United States. Their new awareness was reflected by how the students rated me on the required grade slips they turned in at the end of class. Each of the thirty students gave me a grade of A, including my instructor, who was a young white male from the South.

Public speaking was a subject we taught as high school speech teachers. In law school, a required part of the writing class in the first year was Moot Court, wherein students showed their research and advocacy skills. Leona and I teamed up in Moot Court, and not only did we win against our opponents, but we shined. As lawyers, we found that possessing the knowledge of the law and great advocacy skills were a winning combination. This was particularly true when we were in contract negotiations and the stakes were high or when Leona was arguing in front of the Michigan Court of Appeals or the Michigan Supreme Court, for the City of Detroit.

From 1967 through 1971, while I was a student at Wayne State University, there was tremendous unrest around the country. Students were protesting everywhere. In 1970, Kent State University's unarmed students had a massive protest, against the bombing of Cambodia by the United States military forces, and they clashed with Ohio National Guardsmen on the campus. Four students were shot and killed. This showed how deeply divided the nation was about the Vietnam War.

Race problems were also at an all-time high. Angela Davis, Stokely Carmichael, H. Rap Brown, Bobby Seal, Malcom X, and Kathleen Cleaver, to name a few, were political activists who sought equal access, privileges, and rights for all citizens of the United States. The Black Power movement grew out of the civil rights movement. Young people wanted to be more effective in changing race relations. These were the new social leaders whom people of my generation listened to and admired.

If young black adults saw an injustice, they were not afraid to speak up. Injustice anywhere would not be tolerated. Things in society had to change.

During that time period, I worked as a student assistant in the Wayne State Art department, a job on campus that allowed me to work no more than twenty hours a week at $1.50 per hour. Such work-study funds earned were to assist students in paying for books, food, and lodging. In the art department, I did clerical work: I typed, answered the phones, filed documents, and did other miscellaneous jobs.

When I first started working there, I dressed like an average student and wore my hair in straight, loose curls. My boss was a middle-aged white woman in her fifties. The other two younger secretaries who worked under her were also white. After completing my work assignments, I would go directly to my classes. Everyone there was nice to me—until they were not.

After about four months of working there, I changed my hairstyle to an Afro. The Afro was symbolic of the appreciation of black pride and black beauty. When I first came to work with that hairstyle, no one said a word to me about my change in hairdo. In fact, it was unusually quiet—that was, until the head of the art department breezed in and stared at me. When he reached the doorway of his office, he stopped, turned around, and asked, "New hairstyle?"

My eyes met his as I said, "Yes."

Smiling, he said, "I like it."

Returning his smile, I thanked him.

I wore that hairstyle for about a month to work and had received no additional comments, until one day, out of the blue my boss walked up to my desk, where I was typing and said with a smile on her face, "Excuse me, Leonia. I know you were busy, but I wanted to let you know that I liked your hairstyle better the way you wore it before." She was trying to be pleasant, and I noticed that the other two secretaries suddenly stopped typing and chimed in with her in agreement regarding which style they liked.

I thought to myself; *This was planned because they agreed in unison.* Glaring at them and smiling, I wondered; *Are you trying to tell me in a nice way to go back to my old hairstyle while I am working here? Well, if I do not tell you how to style your hair, then you are not about to start telling me how to style mine.*

I reared back in my chair and said, "Really. Well, I like my hair this way, and I plan to wear it like this for a long time. In fact, who knows? I might wear it like this forever." When I said that, their fake smiles disappeared from their faces, and my boss's face turned crimson as she politely went back to take her seat. For the rest of that afternoon, the icy silence in the office was so intense that anyone walking in could have felt the chill.

What bothers me is that we are still having a discussion today about the issue of how black people should wear their hair. A black high school wrestler had to forfeit his hairstyle of locks or not compete with his team for the championship. Under duress, he chose to compete, and they cut his hair right on the gym floor in front of the crowd. The referee was later fired for that call. Even today, black actresses are ostracized if their hairdos are considered "too black." My hairstyle, then as well as today, is an expression of me as a person, and only I can make that decision.

Mirror photo of me (front) and Leona with our new hairstyles as we modeled at the Autorama

With all the similarities and differences between my coworkers and me, I had worked a little more than a year there, new hairstyle and all, so I thought it was time to request a raise. My boss promptly replied with a smile on her face that there was a freeze on hiring and giving raises to employees, but as soon as it was lifted, she would let me know because I was a good worker and deserved a raise. I said fine and went back to my desk. Was she telling the truth? There was no proof that she was not.

Well, as fate would have it, one day the entire office was planning to have a holiday lunch, and she asked me to watch the office and sit at the main secretary's desk so I could answer the phone. I said, "Sure, no problem."

After they left, in between answering incoming phone calls, I began to read the school newspaper lying on the desk. An article with a headline in bold letters showing that the freeze had been lifted in hiring and giving raises to employees, grabbed my attention. My eyes skipped down to the chart for raises for student assistants. Now, the raise I was entitled to was only an additional ten cents per hour, raising my salary from $1.50 to $1.60 an hour, but it wasn't the amount that was important; it was the principle of their not giving me what I deserved and lying to me. I reviewed the paper with a fine-toothed comb and noticed the date on the paper. It was a month old, which meant the week before, when I had asked my boss about the raise, she had known or should have known the freeze had been lifted. My boss methodically read every school newspaper, from page to page, that came in a timely fashion to our office, so there was no way she had not seen that large article.

I was angry because when I had asked her for the raise, she could have applied for it then, since she valued me as a great worker. Instead, she had looked me right in my face with a fake grin and lied to me. The issue was about being fair and honest, and she lost on both counts.

When they returned from lunch and were seated, I waited for about ten minutes and then marched over to her desk with the paper down at my side in my hand and made the request for a raise again. She had the nerve to appear disturbed that I would ask her about the topic again so soon. She coldly but politely told me she would let me know when the hiring freeze was off.

I blurted out, "The freeze is off. It says so right here in the paper. It's been off for a month." She looked at the paper I handed to her. Her make-believe smile was no longer there. In fact, her face turned bright red. Yes, I had caught her in a lie and confronted her. I had no problem questioning people in authority, because I had learned long ago as a young high school student that those in authority are not always right and often lie. Without facing me, she coldly said she would check into it and get back to me.

"Fine," I responded. I did not care that she felt uncomfortable that I had exposed her lie. I had my own mind-set and was not afraid to speak my mind or defend myself. I was not afraid to stand up to any group of people, nor was I worried about their retaliation.

The next day, while I was filing a lot of documents, my boss came up to me and said she had put in for my raise, which would date back to the beginning of that month. She did not explain why she did not know about the ability of giving me a raise. Maybe she felt vindicating herself was unnecessary. Well, I felt justified in confronting her.

My response to her was only one word: "Good." I had requested only what I deserved, no more and no less. From that day forward, she was careful about what she said to me, and there was never a school newspaper left in the office again. I wonder why. That did not stop me from reading the school newspapers. They were free all over campus.

I could not stand a liar, especially one affecting my livelihood.

Not long after that incident, she hired another black student assistant to work there with me. The new student assistant was nice but younger and a little naive. Maybe my boss was tired of me pointing out her untrue statements and was looking for my replacement.

One day I was asked to deliver a package to an area on campus that was a good distance from the art department. I agreed and asked if the other assistant could go as well. My boss said yes. I thought; *Great, I had someone to talk to*. The walk was long and hot; it was about 88 degrees outside. On the way back, we stopped and got ice cream cones to help cool off from the uncomfortable heat.

We were only halfway through our ice cream cones when we arrived at the art department. The other student assistant went inside, and I stayed outside the art department door for about five minutes to speak with a law student. My supervisor could see me through the glass structure. When I finished my brief conversation, I came in and went into the file room, where the other assistant had already started filing.

She whispered to me, "They're mad at us. They said we took too long to come back, so they docked my pay for an hour."

I quietly considered that accusation.; *An hour? It had taken at least forty-five minutes to walk there and back. Were we, suppose to run there?* I looked at her and said, "Calm down; you're shaking. Take a deep breath. Is that what you're nervous about?"

"They're mad," she said.

No sooner had she spoken, when in walked our boss. She asked the assistant to go into the other room. As soon as she left, our boss, looking at me in a menacing way, went on to say that we had taken too long and that she was going to dock our pay for an hour.

I cocked my head to the side and, with a "Bring it on!" expression on my face, responded, "Fine. Anything else?" She could tell by the defiance in my voice that she could not hurt me. I was not scared of her, and I was not about to apologize for an action that was not wrong. You see, none of the other workers, had wanted to walk that document to the office building in the hot, blistering heat.

Her face turned even redder, and her eyes blazed with a fury I had never seen. She asked, "What did you say?"

Slowly, but firmly, I again said, "Fine. Anything else?"

"I don't know what's gotten into you. You've changed."

"Oh, I haven't changed." Thinking to myself; *I've never liked a liar.*

I knew my response, viewed as rebellious, earned me the title of troublemaker, but I did not care. Right was right. As my mother used to say to us when we were children, "If the shoe fits, wear it."

Enraged, she turned and stomped out of the room. Her heels clacked loudly as she stormed out of the room with her dress swirling around her because she moved so fast.

A few more episodes like that one followed for the next two pay raises I sought and received. I never had a problem standing my ground and defending myself, no matter who was going against me. The following year, I let them know I would be leaving because I had a new job as a substitute teacher for the Detroit Board of Education, paying thirty-two dollars a day, much more than my $1.80 an hour. A few days after that announcement, my boss asked me what I planned to do when I graduated from Wayne State. I told her I planned on teaching for a few years and then going to law school. As I answered, I thought about my reason for wanting to go to law school. *It was to acquire the ability to stand up to anyone and have the law as a sword by my side that I could wield when necessary.*

I guess my boss thought it was in my best interest to warn me about the rigors of law school. She slipped her glasses off and said, "Oh, Leonia, law school is very, very hard. I know because my son is in law school now. It is not like undergrad. It is very difficult. I think the path of education you're on is good for you, not the one of law school."

I stood up from my desk, closed my briefcase, walked over to her, and said in a firm, unwavering voice, "I know it's hard, but I am going to law school."

"You need to think long and hard about that," she replied.

I said, "I have," and I left the room.

I left there angry that day. How dare she tell me in so many words that law school was hard and yet okay for her son but not for me? Why? Because he was white; hence presumed smart, and I was black and presumed not to be smart enough? In so many words, she was saying, "I don't think you can cut it. I don't think you're up to the rigors of law school."

By then, no form of racism was a stranger to me. For many generations, barriers had prevented people of color from entering medical schools, law schools, and other institutions of higher learning. These barriers were based solely on the applicant's skin color or gender. Our generation said, "No more."

The generation of today should learn from generations before them and understand that they can climb to any height and in any direction. No matter what barriers of societal biases exist, whether they're based on sex, race, sexual orientation, age, gender reassignment, religion, gender preference, or disability, discrimination doesn't and won't determine who you are, what direction you take in life, and what you can accomplish. Only you determine that.

I left that job and became a substitute teacher for the Detroit Board of Education. After I graduated from college, I went on to teach for the Detroit Board of Education full-time. I never forgot my boss's words, which were meant to plant seeds of doubt in me. I was supposed to accept the initial goal I set to be a teacher and be satisfied with that. However, she did not know the true me.

I did not fathom that our paths would cross again eight years later for a final encounter.

CHAPTER 5

Teaching Young Minds to Be Strong

I'VE GOT TO USE MY IMAGINATION

After graduating from college, we both landed jobs as teachers. In September 1971, I was hired to work at a highly ranked inner-city performing arts high school located in the heart of downtown Detroit: Cass Technical High. Leona was hired to teach at Redford High, located in a predominantly white area where the black kids were bused in. It was the 1970s, and a lot of people thought black kids should stay in their own neighborhoods and not infiltrate theirs.

Unlike the more established teachers, we wore Afros, jeans, turtleneck bodysuits, and miniskirts with knee-high boots. We looked so young that we were often mistaken as students. In fact, the school employees would not let us into areas restricted for teachers because they did not know we were teachers. Their suggestion for us to wear name tags fell on deaf ears. However, our youthful appearances turned out to be a favorable asset in our relationships with the children we taught. They felt we were more approachable. We taught for four years before entering law school.

Leona and I both brought our experiences in social consciousness with us when we became teachers. We believed that all people were born with the right to pursue whatever goals they set for themselves, no matter their race, sex, or gender preference. Being in two different types of schools, we had to approach teaching differently. While teaching at a predominantly white school, Leona made it her mission to lift the black students up, even if they were not in the classes she taught. She would select students she saw walking down the halls of the school to join her after-school speech activities. She found a way to include them in activities inside and outside the school that showcased the extraordinary talents of both black and white students. She was not going to let anyone cast black students aside as though they were invisible, as my high school geometry teacher had done to me. For her, all students attending that school were entitled to thrive.

Leona felt that no race was to be treated better than or different from another race, so in the school assemblies, she made sure the black national anthem was played whenever "The Star-Spangled Banner" was played. All students had to stand for both anthems. She was teaching them to respect each race's cultural differences.

Because all the students liked and respected Leona, she had no problem with any of the students; however, the parents were a different story. Leona was called into the administrative office several times due to complaints from white parents regarding their children's participation while the black anthem was being played. My sister explained in all fairness that both anthems should be played and equally respected. It was a matter of mutual respect for both races. She stood by her belief and principles. That ritual with the anthems continued until the day she stopped teaching and left for law school.

It was the early 70's and during that time there was substantial racial turmoil and in-your-face discrimination and Leona's school was no exception. One day, after drama play rehearsals, Leona got caught up in an act of violence when several of her students were ambushed and attacked at Redford High School.

After regular school hours, she and another teacher, Cheryl Mason, had just finished leading a rehearsal for a play. The students were headed to their lockers to get their coats and leave the school. The students were unaware that a group of thuggish-looking white boys who were not students at the school, dressed in black leather jackets, were lying in wait for any unsuspecting black students. While the black students were retrieving their coats from their lockers, the white boys rushed them and told the black students to get out of the school. Their plan, which they vocalized at the top of their lungs, was to beat up any black students they saw. They began hitting and pushing the black students, who started to fight back. Chairs were flying, and kids were fighting. Blood splattered the floors. The black students were scared out of their minds, so they ran to get help from Leona and Ms. Mason.

Leona and Ms. Mason immediately jumped up frantically and ran down the halls, following the crying students. When Leona arrived on the scene, she was shocked at what she witnessed. She saw a white boy with a chair in his hand, standing over a black boy. He was about to hit him in the head with it, but she intervened with a strong and powerful voice, shouting, "Put that chair down! Put it down now!" The white boy gawked at her, and she yelled out, "Put it down! I'm a teacher!" He gave her a puzzled look, probably because she looked like a student, but she sure did not sound like one. He put the chair down and ran. The rest of the trespassers backed off a little, and when a black janitor ran into the room, the boys scattered, running from the school.

Leona went to survey the other areas of combat to see what injuries the children had sustained. As she approached, she could hear the children crying. Blood was streaming from the tops of their heads, the sides of their faces, and out of their mouths. It was pandemonium. The kids were okay, although a few were bloodied; however, Leona's teacher friend Cheryl, who had gone to help the students, was pushed down a flight of stairs and badly injured her leg. She suffered from that leg injury for years, and it ultimately required surgery.

The police were called out, and Leona, Cheryl, and the students gave statements. Parents were able to talk to the police and take their injured children home.

By the evening, word had spread quickly about the afternoon incident and the next day, the black students rallied for revenge with bats and sticks in their hands. They had left their classes and gathered outside the front doors of the school. The crowd had reached a high, rowdy pitch. The black kids thought Leona had gotten hurt in the classroom ambush, because she and Cheryl Mason were absent from school that day. They were not listening to the principal. All they knew was that their favorite teachers had been hurt, along with other students, and it was payback time. Without further delay, the principal called Leona at home and pleaded with her to come to the school immediately to speak to the kids and let them see that she was all right. He was trying to prevent a race riot from breaking out. Leona, even though exhausted from the events the evening before, agreed to come and arrived at the school within thirty minutes.

Leona drove frantically to the scene of the ever-growing crowd, parked her car in a no-parking zone in front of the school, and jumped out. She could hear the anger in the voices of the students. The crowd believed in an eye for an eye. Leona proceeded quickly through the crowd, approached the steps of the school, and stared out at a sea of about a hundred angry students. She faced the principal, who said, "I am so glad you are here," as he handed her the megaphone.

Leona was cool and kept her composure. She told the students that violence on violence was not the answer. "That's exactly what they expect you to do, and it's not the answer," she said. She faced a black kid who stood with a bat in his hands and tears in his eyes, ready to fight, and with a soothing voice and reassuring smile, she asked him to give the bat to her. She had a calming effect on him. She knew his surrendering of the bat would send a message to the other students to calm down and listen as well.

With tears streaming from his eyes, he handed her the bat and said, "I thought they hurt you."

She took the bat, held his hand, and said, "No, I'm all right." She told the crowd that those boys had been caught, and she assured them that she and Ms. Mason would be in court to make sure the situation was handled correctly. Her eyes connected with the crowd as she realized the love her students had for her and Ms. Mason, and she said with urgency, "Please trust us."

The black students could feel my sister's truth, so they started cheering and then settled down. They followed her instructions and went back to class without incident. The principal sighed with relief when it was over and thanked Leona for coming. Leona had kept a near riot at bay. The principal was a smart man. He knew he had not yet earned the respect of the black students, but he knew for certain that the students loved and respected Leona.

My sister, Leona in 1972 as a Redford high school teacher

Leona knew that those children, who had been born during the civil rights movement, did not believe in turning the other cheek. If someone hit them, they had better be prepared to fight. She understood their frustration and made sure the black students felt included and had a voice in matters that were important to their high school.

My sister's rationale ran deep from the days when we had been students at Mumford and become councilwomen at our high school. As students, we had wanted our voices to be heard and our opinions to matter.

◆ Schools within the Heart of the City

In the school where I taught, we had different problems. Cass Tech High School was predominantly black; however, the school only enrolled students from Detroit who were the cream of the crop. These were children who had done well academically and scored high on the national aptitude tests. There was always a waiting list of children who wanted to enroll at the prestigious school. However, as smart as the students were, they were not immune to the societal and cultural changes going on in our country at that time. Their generation was the love generation, and at the center of it was the use of mind-altering drugs. Weed (marijuana) was a mainstay, accompanied by psychedelic drugs, such as PCP (phencyclidine, or angel dust) and LSD. These drugs were floating all around the United States, and high schools were not excluded from that explosion, including Cass Tech.

I was one of twenty-five new young teachers hired at the school that year. We were all under twenty-six years of age, so the students nicknamed us the Mod Squad (named after the TV show in which young-looking undercover cops under thirty years of age passed as students and other young people). We were a new breed of teachers, with new methods of teaching. My method of teaching was influenced by my social consciousness. For example, in my English class, I gave students an assignment to write an essay on discrimination. I instructed them to really think about it before they began writing. In order to stir their imaginations and creativity, I passed out several eight-by-ten-inch, black-and-white glossy photos of a civil rights 60's demonstration that had taken place in Birmingham, Alabama. The photos depicted young children about their age, being attacked by vicious dogs while marching. Some had had their clothes torn to shreds by massive water hoses turned on them, and some lay defenseless in the streets, using their hands to protect their faces from brutal beatings with batons and sticks. The children in my classroom looked at the pictures as we discussed the content of the photos. The next day, they were to turn in their essays. My goal was to have the students feel the injustice they saw in the pictures and then write about their feelings on discrimination.

However, it was wishful hoping on my part because the pictures did not strike a nerve. Their essays were properly structured but contained no passion or in-depth feeling; in other words, they were shallow. To wake up their passion, I decided to emulate an experiment on discrimination, done in an elementary school classroom and shown on *60 Minutes* in 1968; the show titled, *The Eye of The Storm*.

I split the students into two groups: one group that had straight hair and the other group that had Afros. I used the element of hair and not blue eyes and brown eyes, as they did on *60 Minutes*, because I only had a few students in the class with blue eyes, and I needed the groups to be as close to equal in number as possible. I physically separated the groups in the classroom. I initially treated the straight-haired group as brilliant students and praised them during the class hour. I had them make placard signs with the word *smart* on them and stand them upright on their desks all hour. They were given no homework because I indicated they were already smart, so they could go home and watch television. The children with the Afros, on the other hand, had to make placards for their desks with the word *dummy*. Their signs sat on their desks for all to see. I did not praise those students, and I told them that because they were slow, they would have homework, and it was due the next day.

When class was over, the students with straight hair strutted out grinning, but the students with Afros were frowning and scrutinizing me as if, I was the teacher they no longer knew. The next day, the students came in and had to take the same segregated seats as the day before. The straight-haired children came in smiling, pulled out their signs, and proudly placed them on their desks, but the students with the Afros came in scowling and said they could not find their signs. So, I had them make new ones. It is important to note that a few students who had worn Afros the first day came in the second day with their hair straightened, so I let them sit with the straight-haired children. They did so with glee.

Then I pulled a switch on them. I had to make it feel real. I told the children with the Afros that they had done a great job in turning in their homework promptly. Then I said, "As smart as you are, I shouldn't have given you any homework. You are, in fact, the smartest group in the room; therefore, you are not going to have homework for the next two days." At that point, the straight-haired children looked a little confused and afraid. I told the students with Afros, "When I say, 'Go,' I want you to go across the room, and change seats with a student in the straight-haired section, but leave the *dummy* signs lying face down on your desk." Then I walked over to the straight-haired children and said, "When I say, 'Go,' you are to take a seat on the opposite side of the room and lift up the sign *dummy* so I can see it. You see, I have given it much thought, and it is your group that should have been the dummy group in the first place." Then I yelled, "Go!"

The children with the Afros ran over to the other side of the room, while the straight-haired children moved slowly to the negative side of the room. I had both groups make sure the signs were visible. The children with the Afros were gleeful, holding their signs in the air for all to see, while the straight-haired children were sullen, awaiting their impending doom. I told them they were going to get twice the amount of homework the Afro group had because they needed to study to catch up.

To make sure the experiment had an effect, I continued it for the next two days with the straight-haired children as the dummies. On the fourth day, I had the students take their original seats. Then I started a discussion on discrimination. How did they feel when being discriminated against because of something as trivial as their hair? I said, "We all know your hair is not an indication of how smart you are, but no matter what, I made your hair a factor of importance that would indicate whether you were smart or not, and I treated you accordingly. How did you feel when I labeled you a dummy and treated you that way?"

Oh boy, did the hands fly up into the air. I could not get the children to stop talking about their feelings. With tears in her eyes, one girl said, "Ms. Lloyd, you are one of my favorite teachers, but I was so mad at you. I could not understand why you thought I was dumb, but you made me angry because deep down, I knew I was not dumb. I felt helpless and powerless and I had never felt that way before. You had made up your mind that because my hair was in an Afro, I was not as smart as the kids with straight hair. You were the teacher and you had all the power." I could hear her pain.

I then told the students, "For those of you with Afros who straightened your hair overnight, I want you to tell me in the essays you are about to write why you did that and what happens if you can't change the thing about yourself that you are being discriminated for, like the color of your skin."

Two days later, they turned in their essays on the theme "What Discrimination Means to Me." The experiment had touched their souls. Each one of them had been discriminated against and had heard painful and untrue statements that didn't realistically apply to them, yet Ms. Lloyd, the teacher, a person in authority, had said it about them, which had made them feel bad. They could feel the unfairness, the hopelessness and the injustice. I wanted them to recognize discrimination if they ever had to face it in the real world and to never let anyone define their value as a person by the color of their skin or any other meaningless attribute.

The second set of student essays were spectacular. The students wrote from a deep part of their hearts that had never been touched. Some were so well written that with the students' permission, I entered some of them in a national writing contest; several won awards. I used an unusual path to pull out the greatness they had inside them. I am sure they will never forget that experience in that class.

However, when a teacher goes off the traditional path, there are bound to be repercussions. I got summoned to the assistant principal's office because of the number of irate phone calls she received regarding my exercise in discrimination. I explained to the assistant principal what I had done and told her my idea had come from a documentary I saw on *60 Minutes*. She responded, "I told them I thought you were trying to teach the students a lesson, because how can she say students with Afros are dumb, when she wears her hair in an Afro every day?" The assistant principal was on point.

***

Even though the school consisted of bright students, there were always students who needed an extra push or needed attention because of the problems they were dealing with.

No matter the reason, students sought me out to listen to their questions and help guide them out of possible wrong decisions.

Being as close to the students as I was, I knew the students who had alcohol or substance abuse problems. I knew where the alcohol was stashed and the foolproof containers it was kept in. I knew the nooks and crannies of that old school, which consisted of seven floors of classrooms.

The lavatories were a common place for the distribution as well as use of drugs. Using alcohol and other substances was their way of coping with the pressures of school and of life. The behavioral patterns of students and class informants who cared about their friends made me aware of the students who had serious drug problems. It was not unusual for students still tripping from LSD they had taken three days before to run into my office scared because they thought they were dying; they were sweating profusely and felt as if they were on fire. They wanted to know what was happening to them. I explained that the LSD had not finished with them. I assured them they were not going to die and escorted them to the school nurse. However, if they were having a severe attack, I took them to the principal's office, and their parents were notified to come get them to seek emergency medical attention.

I found the best tool to use in helping students deal with the problem of using was talking—spending time with them, listening to their problems, and explaining to them that the route they were on was not the answer. Patience, time, and conversation were the best tools to use to reach the students. The more traditional older teachers saw the same problems in the school, but they wrote the students off as crazy or problem students. They focused on the students who did not give them any problems. But looking with a blind eye was not going to help the student with problems.

Years later, I came across students who thanked me for taking the time to talk with them and guide them in the right direction. Those students indicated that my help had made all the difference in the world in their lives and the decisions they made later in their lives.

◆ Love Conquers Hate

In the latter part of 1973, I was transferred from the English department to the Performing Arts department. I was ecstatic because I had minored in that area in college. However, when I got there, I soon found out there was a dark cloud hanging over the department. The department had a serious problem of negativity and hate growing among the students. The students' favorite teacher had been transferred to the English department. There was a silent protest and rebellion among the students.

However, the protest did not stay silent for long. The kids organized walkouts and decided to be outwardly rebellious in the classroom. A couple of teachers were reduced to tears because they had not bargained for that type of mental stress as teachers. It got so bad that teachers dreaded coming to school to do the thing they loved: teaching. Some of the teachers entertained the idea of quitting teaching altogether.

The department did not know what to do. I realized I had landed smack dab in the middle of a war between the students and the Performing Arts department, not to mention I was the teacher who had replaced their favorite teacher. The department needed to turn the negativity around, and they needed to do it quickly, but how?

Our department head, Mrs. Hamburger, called a meeting to discuss the problem and see if there was a possible solution. However, when she went around the room for suggestions, she saw only sad, tired faces. No one had a clue as to how to resolve the problem, which was growing like cancer. Looking around the room, I saw the hopelessness and despair in their faces. I was only twenty-three and the youngest teacher in the department, but in my short life, I had already learned some lessons about working through obstacles and not quitting, because for me, quitting was never an option. I felt we had to think outside the box and color outside the lines for a solution to the problem. I knew the only way we could fight the hatred from the students was with love. We had to show the students that we loved and appreciated them.

With that in mind, I raised my hand and stood up. "We have to make the students realize we care about them. So, I think, we need to establish a special night focused on the students and all the positive things they do for the department. We can make it an awards night, like the Oscars, where we hand out awards celebrating the outstanding work done by our students. For example, awards would go to the students for best actress, best actor, best play, best musical, best stage crew worker, and other awards for the students who work behind the scenes. We can form a group that sponsors this gala and call it the Performing Arts Guild. The setting for the event would be at a fancy but elegant dinner restaurant."

The room fell silent, and the looks they gave me spoke volumes. Their facial expressions shouted, "What the hell is she talking about?"

Our department head said it was a great idea but would take a lot of work. There was a long silence in the room and then she turned to me and asked, "Would you spearhead it". I accepted the challenge. After agreeing to do it, I saw that the other teachers were all too busy with other activities to work on it with me, so I decided to do it on my own. I was not a quitter.

I formed a guild called the Performing Arts Guild, that sponsored the event. I developed a plan for our Oscar night extravaganza that would take place in the elegant Roostertail restaurant that was positioned on the edge of the beautiful Detroit River. The kids would have to purchase tickets to the dinner to attend. However, the only way one could buy a ticket was if he or she earned a certain number of points for doing positive things in the department and presented said card to me, signed by a teacher for every set of points given for the work done. Once students acquired the requisite amount of points, they were permitted to buy tickets. In other words, I didn't just want the tickets to go on sale; I wanted the students to engage with their teachers in each of their classes by asking what they could do to help in their class or with an after-school project in exchange for points and acknowledgment by the teachers' signatures. I was indirectly forcing the kids to perform acts of positivity. I knew that was an unusual path to take in selling tickets, but I walked down my own path, the one less traveled.

My department head had already written a check for $1,500 as a deposit on a lavish dining room at the Roostertail Restaurant. She was nervous about all the money we were spending, but I felt confident that the event would be a spectacular success. Unfortunately, Mrs. Hamburger did not share my faith when it came to spending money, so I was not surprised when she came to me about the price of the dinner tickets. She was frantic. She strongly felt I should lower the price, because twenty-five dollars a ticket would be a costly mistake. I pointed out that the price I set for the tickets would cover all our costs. But confidently, I told her, "Look, these kids spend ten dollars every other day on junk food in that little store across the street from the school. It will be alright!" I was close to the students and I picked up on that type of information. but she was unaware of their daily habits.

She reluctantly relented, but only a few days later, she came running to me again in a panic. I saw it on her face. *Here we go again.* She was trying to micromanage the financial situation. With a heightened voice, she asked, "Is it true that you'll only sell tickets to the students if they present a card with points on it, signed by their teachers?"

"Yes, that's correct," I said.

The expression on her face told me this was not going to be an easy sell to her. She was insistent. "Leonia, we'll lose our money and be in the hole again. We will not sell enough tickets to cover our costs, because the kids aren't going to do this point thing. It took me five years to get this department out of the red and into the black, and now I feel we will go back into the red with this plan of yours."

"No, we won't," I insisted. "I guarantee you this will work. Look, if the tickets were easy to get, then nobody would want them, but if you make somebody earn the right to buy a ticket, then automatically that ticket has shot up in value. This says, 'We don't want your money unless you have enough points to buy the ticket,' and it says indirectly, 'I have to start working with the teachers, not against them, in order to get the points to buy the ticket.' You see, when they are indirectly forced to communicate and work with a teacher, then they will get to know that teacher. I am forcing these walls of negativity to come down."

She gawked at me as if I were crazy. Shaking her head, she threw her hands up in the air and walked away, saying, "I hope you're right."

The awards night turned out to be the formal event I had dreamed about. Girls were to come in long gowns, and the guys were to wear either a tuxedo or a suit. Students came to me right and left with index cards reflecting signatures of teachers and points earned, as late as the date of the event. It was not unusual to see a kid with five signatures on his or her card. The kids had decided this was an event they could not afford to miss. I had arranged for the restaurant to have thirty extra plates in case we sold over the amount of the tickets for the dinner.

For the night of the event, I had boxes of awards engraved for the different categories. I had certificates I signed for recognition of the work done in the department by each student. Practically every student was going to walk away with something in his or her hands that night.

In May 1974, after more than six months of working and planning, the night of the event arrived. I had butterflies in my stomach because the success of the event was riding on my bold presumption that love could conquer hate. That notion was put to the test that evening. I needed at least one hundred students to attend.

When I drove up to Detroit's beautiful Roostertail restaurant, I felt the ambiance of a tropical island. The Roostertail sat like a sparkling jewel on the blue flowing waters of the Detroit river. Dressed in my dazzling evening gown, I entered the building and walked into main dining area of the restaurant, where our event would take place, and my mouth dropped open as I gasped for air. The décor was magnificent. Crystal chandeliers suspended from the high ceilings. This premier venue resembled a page out of Hollywood. It was decorated in a style for the rich and famous. Mr. Schoenith, the owner of the establishment, with whom, I had signed a contract, had promised me a night that would be unforgettable. He provided us with a red carpet for our gala event! He pulled out all the stops and kept his promise. It was simply marvelous and far greater than my expectations.

My sister and Cheryl were there, and they were knocked out by the beautiful decor.

At seven o'clock, the kids started streaming in, dressed to the nines. They were in awe as they entered the dining room and dizzy with excitement. We had to use forty extra plates, not thirty, for the over sale of tickets, and luckily, the Roostertail was prepared for that. The evening was a huge success. The waterfall behind the stage was timed to give a colorful water-and-light show that vividly displayed all the colors of the rainbow throughout the event creating an illusion of mystique for the entire evening. It was breathtaking.

I had arranged for a recent December Cass Tech graduate, Greg Phillinganes, nicknamed Mouse, to return in May to play the theme song of each musical or play on the baby grand piano located at the side of the stage. This young man, that I entrusted to play all the famous songs from the Broadway plays and musicals was super talented. As fate would have it, years later, he went on to become a keyboardist, singer-songwriter, and sought-after musical director based in Los Angeles, California. He became one of Michael Jackson's most significant musical directors.

In the middle of the evening, Mrs. Hamburger came up to me and said, "At first, I thought you had lost your mind. I just knew we were going to lose our money, but I was wrong, and you were right. I cannot remember seeing these kids this happy. I feel nothing but love in this room tonight. So many kids came up to thank me for this event. It wasn't me; it was you." She hugged me and said, "Good job, Leonia. Good job. This was beautiful." She bounced away with her hands waving in the air again, but this time, she did so with a huge grin.

We ended up making money on the event, and more importantly, it created a positive bond between the students and the teachers. The kids left that night beaming. Some came up to me crying, saying it was the most wonderful night they had ever experienced in their lives.

Life had taught me that when people engage with each other, they have an opportunity to understand and appreciate the other person.

Only then can the walls of hatred come down. Those children had to learn that lesson. The teachers of the department learned that when things get hard, quitting is not an option. As Martin Luther King Jr. said, "Hate cannot drive out hate; only love can do that."

Once the cloud of negativity was gone, all of us were able to be the teachers we were meant to be.

◆ Forty Years Later

Fast-forward forty years later. I was having my makeup applied for a sizzle reel shoot, which is a short promotional video made for a television series or film. The makeup artist was a young lady who had just graduated from Cass Technical High School. As we chatted, she mentioned that she had majored in performing arts at Cass. I told her I had taught there many years ago in that department. She went on to tell me about the Performing Arts Guild and the big Oscar night extravaganza they recently had. Her eyes were filled with excitement as she explained that it was like the Oscars. At that moment, my heart was full of happiness and pride. With a smile on my face I told her, "I know what that night was like because I created the Performing Arts Guild and the Oscar night it sponsors back in 1974." She was stunned by that account of history.

I was amazed that after all those years, the stream of positivity had continued and was passed on to generation after generation of students. Little did she know, as she applied my makeup, she had made my heart smile.

As a teacher, I learned the lasting power of positive thinking, thinking outside the box, and encouraging individuals to take the road of positivity over negativity.

Years later, I used those instruments of positivity, love, and thinking outside the box effectively in my courtroom as a judge.

◆ Directing Plays: A Teaching Tool with a Positive Message

I elected to support another teacher as an assistant director on two of his large productions, *The Great White Hope* and the musical *Purlie*. He felt the insight of a black codirector would be helpful with the production because I would bring a different perspective to the plays as well as a different interpretation of script dialogue and the development of characters. He was right, I brought my totality of knowledge.

After those two plays, I decided to direct my own plays with my sister as my codirector and Cheryl Mason as an assistant producer. We all understood as teachers we had the important task to mold young lives. With that understanding, my sister and Cheryl drove every day across town, after their classes were finished to codirect plays with me. We chose plays that resonated a positive message of strength and hope.

In 1974, we selected the play *Black Girl*, written by J. E. Franklin. It was first produced on public television in 1969 and later adapted as a feature film released in 1972. That was when I saw the film in the theater. I could not stop the tears from cascading down my cheeks. I could feel the main character's pain. I knew when I left the theater, I was going to direct that play.

The play is a drama about a young black woman who defies the low expectations thrust upon her by her family and pursues her dream of becoming a professional dancer. The story examines the black power movement's influence on the women's liberation movement. It was important for the students, especially young women, to understand what it felt like to go against the odds and have the strength to stand alone if necessary. The play had a relevant story to tell.

The actors we selected were stellar. They could deliver the powerful emotions of the script as required. As we watched the final rehearsals, we found ourselves watching with tears flooding our eyes. I identified with the young girl in the play, a girl in high school trying to make something of herself while those around her try to hold her back. When I thought about the pain, I had experienced in my geometry class, I felt her pain. The only support the young black girl has is her grandmother, and that gives her the strength to go forward. Like her, I had only one person supporting and believing in me during my geometry drama: my mother. She gave me the strength to not give up, even if I had to go the journey alone.

I knew once the kids in the school saw the play, it would be a hit. I was right. The play had all sold-out performances and received a standing ovation from the students, as well as, the parents each time it was performed.

◆ Inner City Blues

In 1975, the next play we decided to direct was the musical *The Me Nobody Knows* by Gary William Friedman, Herb Shapiro, Bob Livingston, and Stephen Joseph, a Broadway musical set in a New York ghetto. These were children's voices from the ghetto. In their struggle lay their hope and ours. They were the voices of change. As the Broadway League noted, it was "the first Broadway hit to give voice to the sentiments of inner- city youth." As far as I was concerned, it could have taken place in any big city of America, including Detroit.

After seeing the Detroit riots, I wanted students in the school to understand that even though our city had problems, there was still hope. I wanted the students to know they were our hope and our future.

I assigned one student the onerous challenge of arranging appearances for me on television shows as advertisement and publicity for the upcoming show production before it debuted at the school. I knew that had never been done before at the school for any play, including the big yearly musical, but I followed my own path guided by myself.

She accomplished the task and arranged for the students and me to appear on three TV shows and demonstrate a choreographed performance of a song from the upcoming show. Due to our exposure on TV, every performance sold out. Our department head came to me before the start of the evening performance and said tickets for the main floor had run out, so they were using raffle tickets for the seats in the balcony. She was worried about the acoustics because they rarely sold enough tickets to need use of the balcony.

I told her we had used it during our rehearsals, so I knew it would be fine.

"That's great because the line for tickets is wrapped around the building," she said. That was another first for the Performing Arts Department. Every seat in the balcony was filled.

The students received a standing ovation for every show.

◆ The Final Curtain

A few days after the final show, the students were still glowing. One of the kids mentioned the slim chance of performing the play at the historic Music Hall Center for the Performing Arts. I did not want to dull their glow, so I said, "Why not?" I would never discourage the dreams of a student. I had my go-getter student arrange a live audition with Dr. David DiChiera, an American composer and the founding director of the Michigan Opera Theatre and the Music Hall Center. I was shocked when he agreed to the audition.

My students performed three musical numbers from the play for him, and he was knocked out. In a meeting with Leona and me afterward, he said he loved the idea of the play being done there with our kids, and to sell tickets, he would get some well-known Broadway actors to join the lineup. We shook hands, and he told us we would hear from him soon.

When Leona and I got home, she said, "Leonia, we cannot do this; we are going to law school at the end of the month, and you will have left teaching formally. You've got to break this to your kids."

I knew she was right. I did not want to burst their bubble of enthusiasm. However, I knew it had to be done quickly. The next day, I explained the positive outcome of the meeting, and the students were all excited. But then I had to tell them that June was my final month of teaching, and I would be starting law school that summer. I would not be there to pull off the performance. They were a little down at first, but one young man said, "That's okay, Ms. Lloyd. At least you got us in the door, and we know now we are good enough to perform at Music Hall, and that is good enough for me. You helped show us that, Ms. Lloyd."

I smiled. I knew if I would have stayed, I would have given it my all, but I could not do both. However, I had the satisfaction of knowing that my students were not afraid to go out into the world and step up to all challenges they might have to face. They knew they were good enough for any opportunity that came their way. The lesson I wanted them to remember was to always believe in themselves. They would remember that tryout proudly for the rest of their lives, and so would I.

Leaving a job, I loved was bittersweet. The department and the students gave me a going-away luncheon. As a departing gift, they handed me a jeweler's box, and inside was a velvet box that contained a double-sided gold star necklace. While one of the students fastened it around my neck, Mrs. Hamburger stood up and, with tears in her eyes, said, "The star symbolizes what you have been to the department and to the students." My eyes filled with tears because of the love they displayed for me. I still have that star necklace to this day; it is one of my most prized possessions.

CHAPTER 6

Law School

KEEP ON TRUCKIN', BABY

Just as Leona and I caught our breath from leaving teaching, we had to get ready to enter the world of law. It was late June 1975 when Leona and I graced the doors of Wayne State Law School. Even though we entered on a scholarship that paid our tuition for the first year, including summer classes, there was still a major adjustment because we were no longer receiving a regular paycheck.

The summer session consisted of approximately one hundred students of which twenty were minority students. The schedule consisted of two regular law classes, Torts and Criminal Law, which were taught by a white professor and a black professor. The two classes were to be completed in two months instead of a year, so we were studying all day and all night. The challenge required all our time and energy, but Leona and I had each other's back. We helped each other get through it. She was right there by my side, going through the same thing. She turned down her acceptance to UCLA School of Law (after I pleaded with her to stay) to go to Wayne

State Law School with me in Detroit. So, she stayed. Now, that was sisterly love.

Before starting law school, Leona and I attended an orientation for the black students, given by the Black Law Student Association. They tried to prepare us for the climate of racism we would face at the law school. They also pointed out that women were not welcomed there either. To support that claim, they indicated that the law school building had been built with no lavatories for women. They were added much later. That was incomprehensible to us.

Law school was going to be tough, and the Black Law Student Association tried to lay the groundwork for us. They told us to think about why we wanted to go to law school and to hold on to that thought. They said, "When you think about quitting law school, when it gets rough, go back and grab that reason why you came here in the first place. That will be the only thing that will keep you here."

They warned the new students who were thinking about getting married to wait until their second year, saying, "Your first year, you will be married to the law, and she is a jealous mistress and will have no other before her."

Well, I did not listen to their good advice: I got married during my first year of law school. That was a bad decision and the timing was not right. My husband and I knocked heads too many times; he wanted an attentive wife, and I could not give him what he needed. Law school sucked up all my time and energy. I was surviving on little sleep. The daily routine of law classes and studying was relentless. I should not have gotten married. We were divorced two years after I finished law school.

Leona and I successfully completed the summer term, and we then had to get ready for fall and a full load of classes. It was not too long before the black law students began to experience in our classes what the Black Law Student Association had warned us about. An example occurred in our writing class. The teachers were not supposed to know which students wrote which papers. Assignments were identified by our Social Security numbers. For the first four writing assignments, my sister received all grades of *B and B+'s*, while mine were in the *C* category. However, after a few months rolled by, Leona started receiving *C's*. She could not understand why her grades were different, when her writing and analytical skills were the same. She confronted the teacher about the change in grades, but he could not give her a real reason. The next year, when we asked a black professor about the difference in her grades in the writing class, she asked, "What month did the grades change?" My sister told her the month and she said, "That is the month when the teachers all received our charts with your names and your corresponding Social Security numbers. He knew who you were when he gave you the lower grades." My sister was angry, but there was nothing she could do about it. We knew then that the supposedly anonymous system was a lie.

Racism was not going to stop either of us. We leaned on each other and persevered. However, near the end of our second year of classes, the black students heard that the faculty planned to quietly terminate the minority program for the law school, beginning with next year's students. They planned to do this without allowing input from the black law students or their representative at the meeting. As a result, the Black Law School Student Association decided to block the doors of the school, forming human chains. It was the schools' second lockout protest by black law students and my second protest overall.

In the previous lockout a few years earlier, the black law students had secured the doors with real chains. With this one, the administration cut the utilities off later that afternoon, hoping that would force the students to leave, but it did not work. The black students locked arms in front of the entrance doors to the law school, preventing entry or exit. The protest was filmed live by the TV news stations, which caused an outpouring of black lawyers and black elected officials coming down to the law school to find out from the black law students what was really happening. They were supportive of the black law students. Leona and I had jobs, but Leona suggested we leave our jobs early and go back to the school while the protest was still ongoing to see if the black law students needed anything.

Food was the answer. Knowing that the protesters had been out there for several hours and must have been hungry, we went around to all the students and wrote down their food orders. One black professor stood there with a pen and pad in his hand and said to us, "You know, we're writing all your names down as participants in this. You can all kiss any future legal careers goodbye."

Leona, laser-focused on him, said, "Make sure you spell my name right."

Leona and I walked into McDonald's and started giving the food order. "I want twenty Big Macs, fifteen double cheeseburgers, and thirty orders of large fries," Leona said.

Before she could say the number of Cokes, the guy behind the counter asked, "Is this a joke?"

Leona said no and explained that the black law students were protesting to stop the law school administration from eliminating the minority programs that allowed qualified black students entrance into law school. She said, "These programs are the reason a lot of us are students there, like me."

The young guy smiled and said, "We'll throw in some extra Big Macs, fries, and desserts for free."

We returned with boxes loaded with food for the black law students. The line was not going to stop because of lack of food, not if we could help it.

A few hours after the food was delivered, the administration saw that the students were now energized and were not going anywhere. Shortly thereafter, the administration finally agreed to talk to our representative, Attorney Chokwe Lumumba, and the strike ended.

At a subsequent faculty meeting Attorney Lumumba attended, an agreement was reached. At least the minority program for the next year would continue, which would enable future black students' entrance into the law school.

Leona and I did not care about possible threats of termination. We were determined to make it through. We had left full-time careers to start new careers, and we were not going to let anyone turn us around.

◆ Our Mother's Second Nervous Breakdown

As if, law school was not enough to deal with, our mother had her second nervous breakdown during that time. Her mental health was taking a toll on our father and us.

On a warm spring day in 1976, our mother started displaying strange behavior. Our father did not pay much attention to the fact that our mother was not in the kitchen preparing food, when it was already after 5:30 p.m. That was unlike her. Instead, she was in their bedroom, taking off her clothes, sweating profusely. It was way too early for bedtime. What was she doing? And why was her hair such a mess?

Our father was reading the newspaper in his favorite wingback chair. Just as our dad went to check on her, our mom zipped past him and dashed outside naked. Yes, butt naked! Our father could not believe what he had seen. Immediately, he ran off after her.

She had reached the third house on the block when our father caught up with her, grabbed her around her waist, and lifted her straight up off the ground. He carried her back to their home and got her through the door, but he would not let go of her as she struggled to break free while yelling, "Let me go!"

Our father, although an average-sized man, was extremely strong and fast on his feet. Back when he was a young man right out of high school, he was an amateur boxer. He won a few titles, but when he suffered a blow to the face, leaving a permanent scar near his nose, that was the end of boxing. The point is, our mother did not have a chance of getting out of the hold our father had on her, no matter how she tried to wiggle out of his arms. Even though she had gained weight during their marriage and outweighed him by thirty to forty pounds, she was no match for him. When she finally stopped struggling due to exhaustion, she promised to sit down and not run. Our father placed her on the couch and slowly released her. He sat next to her in such a way that she could not take off.

Confused and distraught, our father did not understand what had just happened. He asked her, "Why did you run outside with no clothes on?" She just focused on him with an unblinking stare, tapping her foot and not uttering a word.

After a few more minutes, she faced him and said, "I want to go put some clothes on."

Our father, not trusting her, said, "Okay, but I'm coming back there with you." She went into the closet and pulled out a floor-length yellow chiffon negligee.

After she put it on, she made a dash out the bedroom door, but this time, she did not make it outside. Our father grabbed her again, and using all the strength he had, with his arms around her waist, he lifted her up again as she kicked to get free. Placing her in a chair, he made sure she could not get up. The chair was within reach of the wall phone, so he called EMS while holding her down in the chair and with desperation asked them to come get her quickly.

About twenty minutes later, an EMS truck arrived at the door. Our father had left the front door unlocked so they could enter. He explained what had happened. They asked our mother some questions, but she was huffing and puffing, trying to get out of our father's grip. She gazed at them but did not answer any of their questions. They told her to sit still and instructed our father to let her go. He followed their directions, and she immediately bolted for the door, but the EMS attendants restrained her. As they placed her in a straitjacket, tears fell from our father's eyes. He felt helpless and lost. He did not know what else he could have done.

The EMS attendants told our father they were taking her to the hospital in Lincoln Park. He knew where it was and told them he would follow behind their vehicle. Quickly, they placed our mother in their vehicle. Within ten minutes, they were gone.

While they were checking our mother into the psychiatric wing of the hospital, our father called Leona, explained what had happened, and asked us to please come as soon as we could. Leona and I were working on some law school studies in her penthouse office apartment.

"We're leaving now," she told our father.

On the way there, Leona explained to me what had happened. This time was worse than the other time she had had a nervous breakdown. Leona said, "How did this happen? What led up to this? She was fine the last time I spoke with her a few weeks ago."

I explained to Leona the missing link to the puzzle, which was the answer to her question. Our mother had called me about her last ob-gyn appointment, during which her doctor had looked at her bottles of medications and asked why she took an antidepressant. She told him it was for her nerves.

"You don't need this. You look fine to me," the doctor had said. He went on to tell her she did not need that medication anymore. That was all she wanted to hear. I tried to explain to our mother that the physician was wrong to say that to her without consulting with the doctor who had prescribed the medicine to her in the first place. I reminded her that the ob-gyn was not a psychiatrist. His giving her that advice had been pure negligence. Our mother made me a promise to keep taking all her medication.

Leona shook her head and said, "I bet she stopped taking that medication."

As we sat in the hospital waiting room, our father joined us and told us that our mother hadn't taken those pills for more than three weeks and that she'd told him, "The doctor told me to stop taking the pills, so I am." Leona's guess was correct. Because of the doctor's negligence and questionable advice, our mother was back in the hospital.

It scared us that she had never acted out like that before. We wondered how many other women that physician had told to stop taking a medicine without consulting the prescribing doctor. What had happened to our mother could have been much worse if our father had not been there. The thought of that sent chills down our spines.

I was with Leona when she called the ob-gyn to tell him that his bad advice had caused our mother to be hospitalized again. Leona was not nice about it. She threatened to sue the physician if he ever again told our mother to stop taking medication another doctor had prescribed. When we spoke to our mother's psychiatrist, he said our mother's latest episode was caused by her abruptly discontinuing the meds for depression. He indicated that patients who did so not only suffered setbacks but also risked having their conditions become worse.

It took our mother two weeks to start coming back to herself and a full thirty days before she was released to return home.

Leona and I took turns going over to our parents' house to check on her and sit with her. If we could not be there, we called and had long conversations with her. We made sure to take our parents out to dinner a few times a month because she enjoyed that. Even though it was hard to do all that, due to our classes and studying, but we had to make it work. It was hard on us but, we felt we, had to make sure our father did not carry the responsibility by himself. Some friends suggested we take a year off, but to us, that meant maybe not going back, so we were determined to stick with it and get through it, no matter what, because quitting was not an option.

We knew our mother would eventually have her annual checkup with her ob-gyn, and that day finally came. When our mother went back to her ob-gyn's office for her checkup, the medical assistant told her she had been permanently switched to one of his partners. Even though our mother liked her original doctor, we felt it was better for her to have another ob-gyn. Therefore, the same mistake would not occur again.

She followed her psychiatric doctor's orders from that day forward, and in a proper amount of time, our mother was slowly weaned off her psych meds and never had another nervous breakdown.

However, after her last breakdown, she became more hostile and belligerent toward us. In one incident, our mother and father disagreed about getting a new refrigerator. Our father said the old one worked just fine. I sided with our father, who was the only one paying the bills, and that angered our mother. *Whop!* She slapped me! My new eyeglasses flew across the room, and I ended up with a black eye. Our father physically interceded and made her sit down. The next day, she called me and was tearfully remorseful about what she had done. I forgave her. She never hit me again.

Again, the doctors said the breakdown was caused by depression. When our mother was asked what she was depressed about, she said, "I'm not depressed." If she was depressed and consciously knew what was bothering her, she was not going to tell anyone. Her therapy consisted of repeatedly asking her that question and giving her medication.

She improved and had no more nervous breakdowns, but no doctor ever drilled down to the root of her problem. Maybe, she really did not know the problem that caused her mental state. Years later, as a drug court judge, I learned that sometimes doctors couldn't get to the root of the problem with their patients when they were dealing with mental illness; however, that didn't stop treatment nor the patients' progress toward wellness.

◆ Law School Graduation

With our mother having no more episodes of anxiety or breakdowns, we continued smoothly in school. However, we were always cautious and on alert, anticipating a call from our father regarding our mother. We worried about our father's drinking, because there had been a death in the family due to the abuse of alcohol. We were worried about the health of them both. Sometimes, we felt as if we were walking on eggshells.

Before we knew it, we had completed our last year of law school, and our last day of law school arrived. I had just finished my last exam and was packing up my books, when I thought about my old boss in the art department. The law school building was across the way from the art building. I had to go that way anyway, so on a whim, I thought; *Let me see if my old boss is still working there*. Eight years had passed since I had last seen her. In that span of time, I had taught school and finished law school.

I walked into the art building and headed to the same administrative office where I had worked. The former secretaries were gone, but my old boss was still there, sitting at the same desk. Grinning, I entered and greeted her. Pouring on the charm, I said, "Hi. I do not know if you remember me. I am Leonia Lloyd. I worked here as a student assistant about eight years ago."

Slowly, she studied me with a smiling yet puzzled expression on her face. To help trigger her memory, I said, "I'm the one with the twin sister."

The smile vanished from her face as she responded, "Oh yes, I remember you."

I thought to myself; *I knew she could not forget the little spitfire.* "How are you?"

Her face turned beet red as she spoke. "I'm doing fine."

"I'm doing fine too. Before I left this job, I told you I was going to be a teacher and was contemplating going to law school. I doubt if you would remember that. Well, I accomplished the teaching goal and became a teacher at Cass Technical High School. I decided after teaching for four years to enter law school to become a lawyer. Today was my last day of law school, and when I looked across the campus and saw the art department building, I thought I would come by to say hello.

"I wasn't sure if you were still here or if you had retired, but I thought to myself; *It is such a short walk between the two buildings, so why not take a chance and go by?* After all, it was you who warned me how hard law school was going to be, and you were right; it was hard. I believe your advice stemmed from your son being in law school. But I knew I was smart and determined and could make it if I put my mind to it. Speaking of your son, how is he doing? I assume he has finished law school by now. Correct?"

Coolly, she replied, "Yes, he finished, and he's doing fine."

"Great. Glad to hear that. Maybe, one day, our paths will cross. Well, I have got to get going. I have got a lot to do to get ready for graduation. Good to see you again." Yes, it was great to see her and let her know this was one black girl that refused follow her negative advice.

She gave me a halfhearted smile as I turned to leave. With pep in my step and a smile on my face, I felt great. My generation did not let any person or group hold us back.

Instead of encouraging me to climb higher, my art department boss had told me not to try, because it might be too hard for me. No one should try to stop a person from growing and climbing. I use all negative energy and vibes in a positive manner, including hers. To all the generations of the future, as my father said to Leona and me, "No one determines what you're going to do with your life but you."

Leona and I were prepared for the big day of graduation. Our girlfriend Carol Hammock-Evers flew in from California to attend our graduation ceremony. All the people we cared about would be attending. Our only concern was our parents.

Between our father's drinking and our mother's odd behavior when she mixed alcohol with her medication, we feared there might be a scene if they came. They knew our concerns were serious and knew how much the graduation meant to us. They promised there would be no problems.

They attended and were just fine, because they were truly happy for us. Leona and I were ecstatic and feeling on top of the world. We ended the afternoon with a lunch at the revolving restaurant at the top of the Renaissance Center with all our girlfriends. We all toasted glasses of champagne to our graduation and Leona's and my upcoming future.

CHAPTER 7

Our Father's Struggle

WALK AWAY FROM LOVE

Our father, Leon, was an amazing man who had many wonderful qualities. However, during his life, he had to deal with some serious problems—problems that might have caused a lesser man to turn and run as soon as he got hit with the first round of serious issues.

He had to deal with racism, as I stated before, because it was a fact of life. Even though he happily worked as an auto body mechanic, he dreamed of having his own auto repair shop, but that never materialized. What bank would have taken a chance on him and financed an auto shop run by a black man at that time? However, no matter what blows were dealt to our father, he never let them affect how he felt about the progress of his girls and our accomplishments.

Sometimes, when we were talking to our father, he would say, "You know, I was born too early. We didn't have the opportunities you have now."

Leona and I often wondered, with the drive our father had, what career he would have selected had he been given more opportunities. What would he have become? We knew that no matter what choice he would have made, he would have been something else! But that was the hand our father had been dealt in life, and he had learned to live with it. However, our father was not prepared to deal with the multiple personalities of our mother due to her physical and mental illnesses.

When our father married our mother, there was no drinking problem. It developed after we entered college. Over time, his increased drinking coincided with the escalation of our mother's health problems. Our father was there to help our mother with her health concerns, but he was not prepared as a young man to deal with the health issues of a wife who, in time, developed three additional distinctly different personalities. These problems commenced in their fifth year of the marriage.

With each illness, she would shed her personality for a new one. He fell in love with a person who had a beautiful personality and married her, and five years later, they had my sister and me. The first change occurred after her brain hemorrhage, when my sister and I were five years old. The second and third changes occurred after her two nervous breakdowns.

My father was a man of commitment. He had no intention of leaving his wife or us, even if that meant living with a stranger for the rest of his life. His only mistake was in trying to handle all these problems by himself.

Neither he nor my mother received counseling regarding the major changes in her life due to her first brain injury. To be honest, I doubt that type of counseling was even available. Even though my mother had been a nurse and had taken care of patients with brain injuries, it was different being the patient. After the initial brain injury, my mother relied on my father for everything. She went from being a partner in the marriage to being, a dependent in the marriage.

Ten years after the first brain injury, our father felt the strain of paying bills and raising two teenage daughters. He wanted our mom to help with the bills by going back to work but she refused. Did she lack confidence in her ability to do a job due to memory problems from the brain hemorrhage? That question was never answered because no one ever had the courage to ask her.

Her nursing buddies tried to get her to return on a part-time basis and work alongside them. They would say, "It'll all come back to you."

Our mother always laughed and smiled at them but quietly answered, "No."

Her nursing friends' words were a strong indicator that they knew our mother had forgotten her training as a nurse, but they were willing to indirectly become teachers for her, hoping she would regain what the brain injury had taken. If it did affect her memory, our mother, who was a proud lady, said nothing to any of us. Maybe, she did not comprehend what had happened to her brain. However, she knew that because of the hemorrhage, she was now different and would never return to nursing.

There were times when our mother would be cleaning out her purse, and she would take out her wallet, pull out her state license as a registered nurse, and show it to Leona and me. She would say proudly, "This is my state license, and I can go back to nursing anytime I want to." But as she said those words to us, tears would well up in her eyes.

As she wiped away her tears, we would ask, "Mama, what's wrong?"

Her response was "Oh, nothing. I got something in my eye." Her facial expression would look so broken that our first response was to hug our mother tightly until she stopped crying.

It was impossible for us to understand what was really going on with her or how disappointed she must have felt, that at the young age of thirty, part of her life was gone and would never return. Maybe the reality of working as a nurse was no longer possible, but to Leona and me, she was a wonderful mother, and all our friends loved her and affectionately called her Mama.

Our mother kept her license active up until the day she died. It was symbolic of what she had earned as a person.

Our father, having no help from our mother, was left alone with all the financial burdens and trying to navigate through uncharted waters. That was when he turned to 100 proof Black Bull whiskey to temporarily erase the pressures of life.

Initially, his drinking was just a weekend thing, but eventually, he was steadily drinking during the week. With his drinking came a change in his personality and attitude. He was no longer the carefree, jovial Leon my mother had married. However, while carrying all the weight of everyone, how could he have been carefree?

We often thought if our father had received counseling about our mother's condition and how deeply rooted it was, he would have had the answers to some of his unanswered questions. He would have viewed her unwillingness to work differently. We realized that in the black community at that time, going to a counselor or psychiatrist for answers was not a usual choice for our father or most black men. However, that choice was not even presented to him.

His use of alcohol escalated with the next two nervous breakdowns our mother had. Unfortunately, our father's focus was on supporting his family and not on how the drinking was damaging him.

While in college, my sister and I had to write a paper on our family. Our mother was home, still adjusting from the hospital and the first nervous breakdown. It was evening, and our mom had turned in for bed, so Daddy had plenty of solitude in the house. Who better to interview than our father? That was when our father told us about the mother we had never known. He said we were too young to remember her. During the first ten years of their marriage, she had been full of life and a lot of fun to be around.

"Well, Daddy, the mama we knew through grade school and high school was nice and supportive of us and all the things we did as a family," I said.

"Yes, I agree, and she was a very beautiful person, but she was very different from the woman I married," he said. As he made that statement, we could see tears pool in his eyes.

We found the new information difficult to wrap our minds around. Our mother had been an entirely different lady whom everybody loved, but we had been too young to remember. Oddly, our mother could remember some things and people from her past, but her personality never changed back to the one our father and their friends had known before.

Our father had lived with our mother's four personalities, and my sister and I had lived with three. Her last personality had a mean spirit and a bad temper. No matter what our father said to her, she would argue with him and raise her voice. Most of the time, he just remained quiet and did not say a word, hoping she would quiet down, but she did not.

Her first nervous breakdown was in 1967, and the next one happened the year before we graduated from law school, in 1978. Those were the years when our father's drinking increased.

He had a scare in the latter part of 1978, when he felt numbness in his left side, and our mother called Leona and me after he drove himself home from work early. We immediately rushed over and made our father go to the doctor with us to get checked out. He had not had a stroke, but his liver was hardening up, so the doctor told him to stop drinking and gave him medication to help him get off alcohol. He did not like the way the medication made him feel, so a few weeks later, he stopped taking it. I think that change in his health was a big factor in the life choice he eventually made to move back to Memphis.

In 1979, a few weeks after Leona and I graduated from law school, our father made the final decision to walk away from the family he loved and move back to Memphis. The only reason he gave for the move was that he wanted to be in Memphis when he died. However, we thought that as he was getting older, he was getting tired of all the years of stress and saw no letup in it. He had no idea if another upheaval for our mother was around the corner. He was seeking peace and trying to survive.

In other words, he left to save himself, which took an incredible amount of strength. After all, he had raised his two girls, and he knew when he left that we were about to become lawyers. He knew Leona and I would be all right. However, when people are in survival flight mode, they may not think things through, and such was the case for our father. He later found out if he had left two months later, he would have been able to receive his pension. He had not thought out his plan and the drinking did not help.

His drinking problem, unfortunately, tagged along with him to Memphis and got worse. Even though he had a loving family in Memphis, the pain he developed from missing the family he had created in Detroit was immovable. He quickly learned the true meaning of loneliness. That loneliness accelerated his drinking. Sadness and drinking are a combustible combination. We pleaded with our father to get help to stop drinking and move into a condo or come back to stay with us, but he said no.

When I became a drug court judge, I had to handle hundreds of cases involving alcoholism. I knew it was a disease that took over the willpower of the person, so I had to use steps that made the individuals stronger. They eventually learned they could reclaim their lives without alcohol, but I explained it was going to be a hard journey, and they might want to turn back when it got hard, but I promised them I would be with them every step of the way. I made sure they got the right type of counseling and did scheduled and unannounced urine screenings every week to make them accountable.

Every time I saw the reunification of a family in my courtroom, I would smile and think of my beautiful father. The gift of firmness I needed to deal with the defendants with alcohol addictions came from my father. Because of my father, I knew that each defendant in front of me with an alcohol problem was a different person from the one he or she had been before the drinking began. My job was to help the defendants restore their lives to a new and improved version of their lives before alcohol. My father was a kind and giving man with a heart of gold who played a major role in shaping our lives, but alcohol can destroy the life you had, it does not care.

Our cousin Beverly, Daddy, and Aunt Kathryn at her home in Memphis, Tennessee

One day Aunt Kathryn called me to say our father had been taken to the hospital. The handyman who fixed things in Aunt Agnes's house had paid him an unannounced visit, mugged him, and robbed him of his money. My father was badly hurt and remained in the hospital for a while, and then later, he finished healing in a medical nursing facility for several weeks. Upon our visit we felt that was a very nice facility When he was released from the hospital, Aunt Kathryn placed him in a nice nursing home with our blessing. Leona and I flew in a week later to make sure he was settled in and all right, and he was. There was no drinking allowed in there. He lived there for eight years, and we visited him several times a year. He died in 2004 from natural causes at the age of eighty- four. He and our mother never divorced.

Leon T. Lloyd, Jr., our handsome father

CHAPTER 8

The Abandonment and Rebounding of Mattie Lloyd

I'M COMING OUT

Not long after our graduation from law school, after our father left Michigan, Leona and I had the hard task of breaking the news of his departure to our mother. We called to tell her, but before we could say anything, she told us our father had not come home the night before. We could hear the worry in her voice. She thought something horrible had happened to him. That made it even harder to tell her what really had happened.

"No, Mama," I said. "Daddy came to see us last night to say goodbye. He said he was leaving for Memphis in the morning. He said that was where he wanted to be."

Our mother was quiet at first, but then she said, "What? He didn't say anything to me."

"I don't think he wanted to argue about it," I told her. Our mother had had no idea he wanted to leave.

She said, "Fine. If that is where he wants to be, with his relatives instead of us, then fine. He can go."

Her response was surprising to us. There were no tears, but there was anger in her voice. Even though we were shocked and confused that he was doing this, we understood all the stress he had been under, and we guessed that everyone had his or her breaking point. He had reached his.

We told her he had not wanted us to call her until he left in the morning. So, we followed his wishes. He had just wanted to see his daughters before he left. We knew it would take our mother a little while to process that after thirty-five years of marriage, he was gone. It had not really sunk in for us either. Owing barely $5,000 on a house mortgage, her husband had decided to leave her with no money and no way to provide for herself and head for Memphis, Tennessee. That was a lot for her to grasp.

My sister and I were afraid that when that reality hit her, she would get depressed and have another nervous breakdown. After all, she had depended on our father to take care of her, the house, all the bills, and us. She had not worked for almost thirty years. Not only was she alone, but also, she now had to be responsible for everything. If there was ever a time when depression could hit her, now was the perfect storm. We prepared ourselves, making sure we were around her if something happened. We waited and waited, but our mother did not crack. She did not fall apart.

To our surprise, our mother regrouped. My sister and I said to each other, as they say today, "She got this." With the help of her girlfriend and neighbor Mrs. Robinson, she started figuring out what she had to do to collect her Social Security to pay her taxes and her mortgage. Yes, our mother was left with a lot of baggage, but she was not ready to throw in the towel. She called her brother and told him what had happened and her concern about losing the house. Her brother, Napoleon, paid off her house in full. My mother had no worries about her house after that. We took her grocery shopping twice a month, and sometimes she went with her neighbor down the street.

Our mother became the independent woman she had been years before and she was enjoying it. She was surprisingly pleasant with everyone. However, if people mentioned our father's name, they might get cussed out. No matter how good she was at hiding her pain regarding our father leaving, it was still there and surfaced in the form of anger when anyone mentioned his name. After about five years, her anger toward our father for leaving her died down, but she never wanted to talk to him again after he left her. At least that was what she said to us.

Socializing was a key factor on our list for our mother. We made sure she got out and went to the movies, concerts and plays with us. Before she came to live with me, she was always over at one of our houses for Thanksgiving and Christmas. She got to go to a lot of concerts, including a Dionne Warwick concert where she and Mrs. Robinson were seated in the golden circle, which allowed them to eat dinner with Ms. Warwick and the stars of her show. We got our mother and Mrs. Robinson tickets for two Ray Charles shows, which tickled her to death. Because we were in entertainment law, we had tickets to a lot of things, and we always invited our mother, who never said no to any invitation we extended. If we could not drive her, she asked her girlfriend Mrs. Robinson if she wanted to go to an event and would not mind driving. Mrs. Robinson was always ready to go with our mom to any show. She enjoyed the shows right along with our mother.

Later in life, our mother became ill and had to have her gallbladder removed. We were there with her, making sure she pulled through.

Under our orders, she had to stay with us until we felt she was well enough to go back to her house. Our mother stayed with us for months after a few of her surgeries. When she did go home, she decided to remodel her house into a smaller version of my sister's house, from the floors to the walls to the furniture and the built-in dishwasher and microwave. Our mother had not washed dishes at our houses, so she decided she was not going to start washing them in her house again either. If that meant knocking down the antiquated interior of the kitchen and rebuilding and repositioning the cabinets and sink in order to accommodate the dishwasher, then presto—it was done.

She enjoyed her newly renovated house for a while, until her health turned, and she needed dialysis treatment three times a week. She then came to stay with me. We made sure she ate at least three times a day. Leona lived only three houses down from me, so when our mother wanted to, she would call Leona and walk to her house. Nothing stopped her from being on the go.

Leona and I with Mattie, our mother, receiving three Mother of the Year awards. Our mother at my judicial investiture, 1993

She was the mother I remembered from grade school and high school. The mean streak she once had after the nervous breakdowns was gone. She was the sweet mother we remembered and loved.

Twelve years had passed since her final nervous breakdown, when her health took a turn and our mother had to have her gallbladder removed. A few weeks after she came out of the hospital, I was sworn in as a judge at my investiture ceremony. I got up to speak and thank all the people who had helped me with the election, but when I got to my mother's name, I had her stand. She was too weak to walk up the steps to the stage, but she gathered her strength to stand. She stood in front of her seat, smiling as she looked to the stage at me. I gave a tribute to her and my father. I indicated that she and my father had molded me into the type of lady I had become. I stated that they had supplied me with the love, strength, and stability I needed growing up. They were always there to encourage us to get back up if we fell. I dedicated all that I was to them. I looked at my mother with tears streaming down my face and said, "I love you." At that moment, the entire auditorium stood for her.

As far as Leona and I were concerned, she was Mother of the Year—a title she later received three awards for. Mayor Coleman Young even signed a certificate from his office recognizing her as Mother of the Year. You see, sitting in the auditorium that day of the swearing in ceremony were the Wayne County Clerk, Teola P. Hunter and the president of the Lewis College of Business, Dr. Majorie Lewis Harris, who both wrote my mother separate letters informing her that she had been selected for Mother of the Year. I felt my mother had earned those awards because she had instilled in both her daughters the ability to be winners in spite of the odds, while our father had drilled into us that no one could stop us from achieving our goals but us. Life is not perfect, and your parents aren't either because they are human, but when it came to giving us the best gifts one could give to children that would carry them for the rest of their lives, they both did a spectacular job. When I look at the strength Leona and I had as women, I do not have to look far to see where it came from.

Our mother got the chance to attend both of our judicial swearing-in ceremonies before she passed on Thanksgiving Day in 1998 at the age of seventy-six. She had undergone several procedures for an alleged blockage in her pancreatic duct, but the hospital could not find the blockage. The procedures weakened her, so at the insistence of the hospital, we allowed a tracheotomy to be done in her neck to help her breathe. They negligently placed the wrong size tube in her neck, and it popped out. The hospital could never seem to figure out how long she had been without it, but the mishap resulted in no oxygen going to her brain, and she became brain dead. The hospital replaced the tube with the correct size the next day, but they knew the gesture was not going to reverse the brain damage. They were just going through the motions to try to satisfy Leona and me. However, that was impossible. Their gross negligence killed our mother.

Our mother at home dancing with her girls as pictured in Ebony magazine, 1984

Part THREE

1979–2001

CHAPTER 9

Here We Come

DO THE HUSTLE

It was the fall of 1979. Our father had relocated to Memphis, Tennessee, and our mother had reinvented herself successfully. Both parents were doing fine with the new lives they had created for themselves.

Leona and I had graduated from law school, so now we were ready for the next chapter of our lives. Leona stayed in Detroit, but I joined my husband in Indiana, where he was attending law school. However, due to the problems that had developed in our marriage throughout my tenure in law school, my stay was short, and I returned to Detroit at the end of 1979, to the supportive arms of my twin.

My sister refused to let me wallow in self-pity; she made sure the new year of 1980 started with a bang. She quickly lined up two job interviews for me, treated me to a day at the hair salon, and took me shopping and bought me a sharp red suit. She was getting me ready for a spectacular holiday party happening my first weekend back in Detroit. She knew once I started socializing and got out on the dance floor, I would be all right. Dancing was the one thing that would cheer me up. She knew me well.

◆ Getting a Job and Taking the Bar Exam

In 1980, in the cold winter of Detroit, we both had jobs as law clerks but had to focus on passing the bar. We had so much going on that neither one of us passed the first time, so we had to find time to study for the bar and keep our jobs and a roof over our heads. It was the mother of all struggles, a real juggling act. I cannot tell you how many times we had grits and bacon for breakfast, lunch, and dinner. We got tired of the same menu, but it was all we could afford. Every morning, we exercised for one hour to get our systems pumping before studying. We had a schedule and we had to do what was necessary to get it all done.

The area where we lived was rough. Prostitutes walked the streets, drug exchanges took place all day long, and we heard gunshots at night, so we never sat near windows, because bullets have no name and do not discriminate.

We were anxious to leave that destitute area and claim a better life but felt sorry for the people in the area, especially the prostitutes, who could not see a way out. A woman had to be desperate to sell her body to anyone for money. Their profession was about survival. It seemed to me that something should have been done to help those ladies; Funding from a governmental agency could have been used to help develop special programs for them.

The images we saw never left us. I remembered those images years later when I decided to play a major role in creating a program to assist women, like the many I have seen years before.

Regardless of where we lived, Leona and I were working at upscale Detroit law firms while preparing to take the bar exam. I had secured a job at a well-known black law firm, Patmon and

Young, P.C., and Leona worked for another equally well-known black law firm, Bell and Hudson; a firm, that represented, a number of celebrities as clients.

However, securing the job as a law clerk was a difficult path I had to navigate, with a lot of curveballs being thrown at me. The Patmon and Young firm was recommended to me by a law clerk who worked at the Bell and Hudson law firm with my sister. He said Patmon and Young was one of the top black law firms in Michigan. Based on his recommendation, I decided to go there and drop off my résumé after my job interview with the defender's office.

My interview with the defender's office went well, and I was immediately offered a position as a law clerk; however, I told them I had one more possible interview with the Patmon and Young law firm, and then I would make my decision. The director of the defender's office chuckled, saying they could not compete with that firm, but if a job there did not come through for me, there was always a position waiting for me at the defender's office. Smiling, I thanked him and promised I would let him know how everything turned out.

Off I went to the offices of Patmon and Young. I was not ready for the impressive view I saw when I stepped off the elevator. The massive office seemed to span the entire floor of that building. I walked through the glass doors, and *impactful* is not a strong enough word to describe the splendor I saw. Everything from the lovely decorative plants to the uniquely designed reception area was in pristine condition. The vivid, lush carpeting was the foundation for the beautiful reception area, which was furnished with plush leather couches and chairs.

I spoke to the receptionist, who greeted me when I came in. After I told her I was looking for a position as a law clerk, she said she would contact Mr. Patmon's main secretary to have her speak with me. I took a seat, and shortly after the receptionist placed the call, a woman who appeared to be in her mid-fifties came out to greet me. I approached her and said I was looking for a job as a law clerk. Sizing me up, she peered at me through her wire-rimmed glasses and said sarcastically that they had no openings.

"Perhaps I can just leave my résumé to be placed on file in case a position for a law clerk opens up," I said.

"That won't be necessary because we won't need a law clerk, so keep your résumé."

The receptionist's woeful eyes gazed at me before she turned her attention back to her desk. I withdrew the offer of my résumé and politely said thank you. I moved back to the chair and returned my résumé to my briefcase while the secretary stood there with a smirk on her face, proud of figuratively slamming the door in my face. But at that moment, an attorney for the firm ambled through the reception area and spoke to me.

"Hi. Weren't you at a holiday party Saturday night, wearing a red suit?"

I laughed and said, "Yes." I thought; *That stunning red suit my sister bought me.*

"I saw you there. Why are you here today?"

"I wanted to submit my résumé for consideration for a law clerk position, but this lady said the firm wasn't accepting résumés."

Coming over to me, he told me to have a seat and asked for my résumé. He told me he would return shortly after showing my résumé to Mr. Patmon. With a swift glance at the secretary, he marched to the inner office. Shifting her eyes sideways at me, she followed behind him. The envy and jealousy of the secretary was coming through loud and clear. A woman had never treated me in that manner before. She had not treated me as a person with a law degree and, therefore, a brain but had scrutinized me as an attractive object, one she did not want there. Hers was an attitude that fostered stereotypes based on sex. There was no other basis for her to summarily reject me.

Well, she was overruled, because the attorney sent her back to the reception area to tell me they were going to see me for an interview in fifteen minutes.

"Thank you," I said. She rolled her eyes and left.

Not long after our initial encounter, she returned to take me to the conference room for the interview. While walking me to the conference room, the secretary told me an attorney, not Mr. Patmon, would interview me because he only interviewed lawyers, not law clerks. To my surprise, however, I was interviewed by Mr. Patmon himself and the attorney who had arranged the interview for me.

I had submitted my professional legal writings of publishable quality with my résumé. Mr. Patmon asked me a series of questions that were not typical for a law clerk position. In fact, a person with a weak personality would not have survived that interview. One of Mr. Patmon's unique questions was "Do you have blue blood running through your veins?"

Pointedly, I responded, "The last time I checked, my blood was red when I bled."

He faced his associate and rolled his eyes. Pointing at him while keeping an eye on me, Mr. Patmon said, "My associate can trace his bloodline back to royalty."

I said, "That's great, but I don't have blue blood running through my veins. My mother is a registered nurse, and my father's a body mechanic, so no, I don't have blue blood running through my veins that I know of."

Mr. Patmon threw a blank stare at me after my response.

Breaking the awkward silence, the associate said, "She's submitted some publishable-quality legal writings for us to review."

Mr. Patmon said, "I don't want to see that mess."

Then, for whatever reason, the associate added, "She also has an identical twin sister who's a law clerk for Bell and Hudson."

Mr. Patmon sat up in his chair focused pointedly at me, "Do you have a picture of the two of you"?

"No, I don't."

"Well, if you say you're the prettier of the two, you're hired."

His comment caught me off guard. I thought to myself; *I know he is not serious*, so I just squinted at him.

Again, he asked, "Which one of you looks prettier?"

"She does." That was the answer I always gave when someone asked me that stupid question, and people asked that question a lot. Leona would say I was the prettier one when she was asked that same question.

He grunted and then studied me for a moment, then stated, "I want your opinion on something."

Finally, I thought, *a legal question.*

"What do you think of body chains?"

I saw his associate turn red in the face.

He was referring to pieces of jewelry worn around the belly or waist, in open view or under clothing. Some chains attach to a navel piercing, and they are made of gold or silver, usually worn with a bikini, low-riding and hip-hugging pants, or lingerie. It was obvious the question was supposed to elicit a shocked reaction from me. I was supposed to blush and be too ashamed to answer. However, I was unashamed and did not blush nor blink. It was a sexist question, so I gave an answer he did not expect.

"Some chains look quite beautiful if worn with the right outfit; however, it's always better if the chains are made from gold, with soldered links."

With a puzzled expression, he said, "What do you mean 'soldered links'?"

"If they're real gold, the links will be soldered and therefore won't break as easily and fall off when met with friction."

His eyes stayed on me without blinking. Speechless, he did not know what to say. His only response was "I'll have you dictate your employment contract into a Dictaphone."

"Oh, I see. Another little test?" I said.

"No. Since you know how to use one, I was going to let you use it."

"Fine," I replied.

As soon as I finished dictating it, his secretary whisked in with a typed copy of my dictation for me to sign. That was my baptism into the fire.

A week later, I called Patmon's office to see if I was hired, and his associate said, "Yes. Mr. Patmon wants you to report for work December 24th at eight thirty."

I said, "That is Christmas Eve."

He informed me they worked on that day, but I would be off for Christmas Day. That was a sign of what was to come.

While clerking there, I learned quickly that some men treated women in the legal profession in a derogatory manner. Fortunately, a vast majority of men in the legal profession, were supportive of female lawyers and treated us with respect. Thank goodness.

◆ Moving Forward

Now that I had a job, it was time to straighten out the rest of my life. I had filed for and received a divorce in 1981. With all the emotionally draining divorce baggage out of the way, I could focus solely on my life. I could hang out regularly with my sister and our friends again. Just being with them helped me move on with my life. Divorce affects people in different ways. To me, divorce felt like a death, and both parties needed time to mourn. However, I kept it moving!

Leona met many famous people through her work at Bell and Hudson, which handled many famous entertainment clients. However, one that stood out was the Electrifying Mojo. At that time, he was a popular DJ on the air at the radio station WGPR in Detroit. Practically everyone in Detroit and surrounding cities listened to him as he played the latest songs, which often became national hits. However, Mojo was no ordinary DJ. He was an artist.

From 10:00 p.m. to 3:00 a.m. Monday through Friday, listeners knew they were on the right station when they heard the voice of Mojo, the captain of a spaceship. Special sound effects were heard from his spaceship traveling through space and time in the galaxy, in search of a planet called Earth. Every night, listeners followed Mojo's voice as he described his final descent to North America on planet Earth. The spaceship was called the *Mothership*. I remember the first time Leona and I heard his show; it was quite an experience.

We were in law school, and we had been busting our butts, studying all week. Friday night was the only night when we put the books down, relaxed, and joined our girlfriends, who introduced us to his show. As we sat around with glasses of wine, waiting for him to come on the air, Leona said she did not hear anything.

Our girlfriend said, "Just wait and listen. You'll see."

Then *boom*! We jumped. We heard a loud sound reminiscent of a spaceship landing, and it blew our minds. When it landed, Mojo's slow, seductive voice came on, proclaiming, "I am the Electrifying Mojo," and in his unique style, he welcomed us to the *Mothership*. After hearing him that first time, we were hooked on tuning into his show on Friday nights. The wait was worth it because there was nobody on the air like him.

He was a true hit-maker for some musicians and singers on a local and national level. He was the first DJ in the Detroit area to play Prince, the Time, Vanity 6, and many other artists. As fate would have it, several years after Leona and I first heard his show, he walked into the Bell and Hudson law office for legal representation. Leona, who was their top legal clerk at that time, was called in to help work on the matter. Leona came home that evening excited to tell me she had just met Mojo, the man we had listened to on Friday nights for at least the past two and a half years. With excitement in her voice, she said, "Leonia, guess who I met today? I met Mojo!"

I said, "*The* legendary Mojo?"

She said, "Yes, that one."

Leona successfully worked on his legal issues. Mojo got a chance to see, through Leona's hard work, how talented, dedicated, and creative she was. He could see she was not afraid to think outside the box, which resulted in Mojo coming out on top in his legal matter. Little did we know that Leona's hard work and dedication to his case would pay off a year or so later when we reconnected with Mojo.

During our years as law clerks, we were invited to lots of events. While a clerk at Bell and Hudson, Leona briefly dated an NBA basketball player, and he invited us to Magic Johnson's birthday party, which was held one night in Michigan right after the game. While socializing, we met a lot of people that night and collected dozens of business cards. Later that evening, Leona suggested that after we pass the bar, we start our own law firm. Convinced we could do it and be successful, we were determined to go it on our own. That was the long-range plan.

In the mean- time, working at Bell and Hudson was exciting, fun, and a lot of hard work for Leona, but when she did not get the raise she requested, she decided it was time to move on. Even though the firm eventually agreed to give her what she had requested, because they did not want her to leave, it was too late; Leona had made up her mind. She left that law firm and started working for the State Appellate Defender's Office and teaching a criminal law class in an undergraduate program at Wayne State University. I had also left the firm I worked for to accept an offer from Chief Judge Samuel Gardner, to work as a clerk for Recorder's Court in the judicial law clerks' office, where I drafted many judicial opinions for their judges. Those were our places of employment when we passed the bar.

◆ Executing Our Dream Plan

About a year after the Magic Johnson party, we put our plan into action, securing nice office space in Detroit. It was not easy, and there was an intervention by God to make our dream turn into a reality. We moved into the newly built twin towers of the Detroit Renaissance Center. However, the move was not easy, and miracles had to happen for the move to become a reality. We were excited about the future as we ventured forward and started our law firm,

Leona and me in our new law office in the Renaissance Center on the evening of our Grand Opening.

specializing in medical malpractice law, probate law, divorce law, and entertainment law.

CHAPTER 10

Practice of Law versus Sexism

SISTERS ARE DOING IT FOR THEMSELVES

The decision to start our own law firm was settled. Now came the task of finding office space we could afford as well as the office furniture to furnish the office.

Operating on a shoe - string budget was stressful, but we were determined to make it happen. Leona saw an ad regarding offices in the Renaissance Center that came equipped with a law office, a reception area with a receptionist, a conference room, a fully stocked legal library, client bathrooms, and a mail room. The mail room was equipped with call answering personnel. A company out of Los Angeles had created this office space. It was designed and equipped for new lawyers that would allow them to give the appearance an attorney who had been practicing for ten years. The office was on a floor that was designated to serve at least thirty lawyers. The price for that prime property was unbelievably low. I told my sister it had to be a hoax. She pointed out they had several office complexes like that in several states, including California. I told her I had to see it to believe it, so Leona set up an appointment, and two days later, we were on an elevator on our way up to the office where the suites were located.

The elevator doors opened, and we stepped out and were pleasantly surprised at what we saw. The reception area was furnished throughout with beautiful overstuffed leather couches as well as several wingback armchairs covered in beautiful oriental tapestry. Large Chinese fan palm planters strategically placed throughout the reception area gave a finishing touch to the lush green carpeting that covered the entire area like a sea of green grass. The finishing touches were two hand-painted four-panel oriental screens positioned close in proximity to the large oval-shaped receptionist desk area at the back center of the reception room area. The opulence was majestic. The view as we stepped out of the elevator was breathtaking. We had to close our mouths as we tried to focus on the voice of the receptionist who was speaking to us. Keeping our gaze on her, we said, "Sorry—we didn't hear you."

Cheerfully, she said, "I'm Christina. Can I help you?"

Our eyes met hers, and we responded, "Yes, we've come to look at your office suites." Leona showed her the ad.

She had us take a seat, and within a few minutes, a young lady came out from the mail room to attend to the reception area while Christina gave us the grand tour. We followed her, and everything listed in the ad was included with the rental office space. She showed us the inside offices, which had no windows, and the outside offices, which had windows with views of the city of Detroit or the Detroit River. With either view, you could not lose. She asked us which view we preferred, and we picked an office with a view of both the Detroit River and the City of Detroit. The view was so captivating that we wondered if we would ever get anything done. The serene view of, the Detroit River was indeed magnificent.

The office space was unreal. The price was equivalent to what someone would have paid for a windowless cubbyhole, located in older buildings in downtown Detroit, with none of the fringe benefits.

When the young lady asked if we were interested in securing an office, Leona exclaimed, "Leonia, this is it!"

I told her we were ready to sign the contracts, and I thought; *Pinch me, because I know I am dreaming.* Additionally, she let us know we had two months of free rent and no security deposit, and we could bring a check in for the first month's rent thirty days prior to the move-in date. God was giving us a miracle and showing us how great he was, and he was not finished. After seeing a billboard for used office furniture, we agreed to check it out. If the furniture was horrible, we could just leave.

◆ Office Miracle Number Two

As we entered the office furniture store, we told the salesman what we needed and gave him the dimensions of the office. We told him we were on a tight budget and needed to see the used furniture first. To make a long story short, I guess the guy liked us, because he took us to a different area of the store and said all the furniture there had been returned yesterday. A deal made by the company who had purchased the furniture had fallen through, and they never had used the furniture. Pursuant to state law, the store had allowed the furniture to be returned, but now they had to sell it as used furniture. Some of the keys to desk drawers were still taped to the inside of the furniture. He offered us a good deal.

We outfitted our entire office with furniture that still smelled brand new and had not been used, at a fraction of the cost of buying it new. The price of one of the desks, if bought brand new, would have covered the costs of all the furniture we bought from him for the whole office. God was showing off his miraculous power; because the types of things that were happening to us, do not happen by coincidence.

◆ Mojo, Our First Client

In the meantime, while looking for office space and furniture, Mojo contacted us. He came by our apartment and showed us a letter he had received from the director of the WJLB radio station, which indicated they wanted him to work for them. The note stated the terms and the salary they would give him for the job. He left the letter with us and told us he wanted us to handle it. He valued the work my sister had done for him while she was at Bell and Hudson, and he understood she was no longer with them, but he wanted her expertise. Leona indicated we were forming our own law firm and would be moving into our offices in a few months. If we were to handle his case, we would be working from home because we could not bring outside work to the offices of our current jobs. He understood, and he did not care about brick and mortar; he cared about who was handling his contract. So, we agreed to take his case. He became our first client.

We knew his case was important and could make or break us coming right out of the gate, but we were dedicated and focused and had confidence in ourselves.

Negotiating Mojo's contract was a major coup for our new law firm, but it was no easy task. What started out as a two-page contract in a personal letter format given to Mojo morphed into more than a twenty-one-page contract. We consulted with the late Attorney Carl Bolden, throughout the process. He was an experienced attorney as well as our mentor. Consulting with a more experienced attorney was what new attorneys were required to do ethically.

During the day, we were at our other legal jobs, which paid the rent and put food on our table, and in the evening, we would work on drafts of Mojo's proposed contracts. We typed our drafts on a Memorywriter, by Xerox. Leona would take the completed draft to Speedy Printing to print the number of copies she needed for the meeting. We had no formal office with a secretary to type for us, so we relied on ourselves to get everything done. Those typing lessons our father told us to take in high school proved to be especially useful. Was it hard? Yes, but we were determined, and we pushed those obstacles aside as we went forth. We were determined to do a good job for Mojo, our first and number-one client.

We developed a system. Initially, Leona handled the contract negotiation meetings by herself because as an independent contractor with the State Appellate Defender's Office, her work hours were flexible and set by her. However, in the evenings at home, we would put our heads together, to draft and redraft each contract revision, causing numerous follow up meetings. At the meetings, Leona would sit across from four older white established Ivy League attorneys who represented the radio station. To understand the gravity of what we were up against, you must look closely at the details that surrounded this negotiation. The negotiations were taking place in the early 1980s. Leona was an attractive black female attorney. Many people compared her looks to the young actress Pam Grier. I am sure these attorneys were not used to dealing with a black female attorney, particularly one like my sister. The vision of my sister gliding into the meetings like a runway model; Dressed to kill in dapper three-piece pantsuits with briefcase in tow, reminded me of the popular song by Nina Simone, "To Be Young, Gifted, and Black."

The first meeting was to be a simple lunch meeting. I am sure the radio station's lawyers thought they would meet and discuss the contract during lunch because the negotiation was going to be easy and over quickly. However, my sister, innovative and skillful, hit them with a new redraft of the original contract we had previously sent them, which was extended by ten pages. Yes, this young black female lawyer came into the meeting and caused them to lose their equilibrium. When they examined the redraft of the contract, the sea of red faces said it all. "We were going to discuss the contract during lunch, but maybe it's better if we just eat lunch and then afterwards concentrate on the new contract you just handed us," one said. Their preconceived plan flew out the window, and the ball was in our court.

My sister smiled and agreed. They were not ready for Leona or the redrafts we had prepared. The four attorneys repeatedly questioned her as if she faced a firing squad, and she handled all her rebuttals with stylish confidence and authority, like a "Boss". Yes, she was beautiful, but she was also smart—a deadly combination.

Every meeting pretty much went the same way. She would come in, and they thought they were ready to discuss changes to the latest draft. However, Leona would hit them with the newest redraft of changes. Prepared for the opposing counsel to be upset about constant last-minute changes before the meeting, Leona, in a calm and sophisticated manner, explained to them that her client had some other ideas and wanted some other types of bonuses they had not previously discussed or mentioned. The meetings reminded me of David meeting with the giant Goliath. However, the radio station's lawyers were no match for Leona and her slingshot.

Leona came to the negotiations prepared to fight and determined to win for our client. As a hit-maker in Detroit, we felt Mojo was underappreciated and had been underpaid in the radio arena. When we took over negotiating his new contract, we made sure that changed. We more than tripled the initial offer and made sure he received quarterly bonus increments tied to the Arbitron ratings of his radio show. In addition to the contract that was far along in development, we felt it would not have been complete without a signing bonus, therefore it was added.

The Arbitron ratings for radio were like the Nielsen ratings for television shows. The ratings were the audience measurement systems used to determine audience size and the composition of programming in the United States. Arbitron later became Nielsen Audio, a consumer research company that collects listener data on radio broadcast audiences. The usual numbers for deejays who played music at that time in Detroit were in the two- to five-point range, which was considered a decent rating. However, when the *Mothership* took off at 10:00 p.m. Monday through Friday on WGPR, a small minority-owned station in Detroit, Mojo's numbers would skyrocket to the twenties. His ratings were unprecedented, and so was his contract we negotiated. Leona and I considered it a work of art.

We knew that representing a man who was a DJ and artist would lend itself to a unique contract. Following what our client desired, we focused on Mojo's creative freedom to select what to play on the air and when to play it. Not to exaggerate, but this type of power for deejays, to say the least, was incomprehensible, if it even existed, anywhere else in the Detroit metropolitan area. His contract was unique and gave him freedom from the usual restrictive radio station rules. Furthermore, he was protected for the duration of his contract. The only time they had no duty to pay Mojo was if he quit. Contracts we negotiated for our clients were always tailored to their wishes.

While the negotiations were going on, we juggled all the balls in the air, without dropping one; Continuing our clerking jobs; picking, designing, and furnishing our new office; and planning our future champagne law office opening—while handling all contract negotiation meetings. Handing these negotiations over to another lawyer was out of the question, and quitting was not an option.

To add a double dose of Lloyd and Lloyd, Leona and I jointly attended the final contract negotiation meeting. However, right before we left to attend the final contract signing, Mojo called and informed us he wanted an office, equipped with specific items he needed to create his musical format for his shows. This included a twenty-five-inch TV, which was a large screen at that time. We were used to expecting the unexpected from him, so we pulled out the Memorywriter and in the speed of lightening we amended the final contract. We brought the modified contract to the final signing.

Hearing the last-minute request during the meeting of the final contract signing enraged the station manager, and she rose from her seat and said, "This is ridiculous! This meeting is over."

However, the owner of the station had her sit back down as he continued the meeting and instructed her to get on the phone with building management and obtain office space for Mojo. The additional terms were agreed upon and the modified contract was signed. It all worked out in the end. Everyone knew how talented Mojo was, not only as a deejay but also as an artist. They knew he deserved everything he requested. Attorney Carl Bolden, our mentor and friend, said he was proud of us and told us we had taken the contract to a whole different level. Those complimentary words from him meant a lot to us and made us feel proud about the job we had done.

◆ The Opening of the Lloyd and Lloyd Law Firm

A few months after Mojo's negotiation was finished, we had our champagne office opening. Excited about the future, we ventured forward and started our law firm, specializing in medical malpractice law, probate law, divorce law, and entertainment law. At our grand opening, family and friends came to celebrate our new venture. Mojo, our first client, also came to our law firm's opening. Even Mr. Patmon, my former employer, graced us with his presence. Our mother, Mattie, was there, but our father, who was still living in Memphis, could not make it. We missed him terribly and wished he could have been there.

We were concerned about our mother because she was beginning to have other physical health problems, but that evening, she had a ball with her brother from Boston, our Uncle Napoleon. He had congratulatory flowers delivered to us that morning but flew in unannounced that afternoon. That night was about fresh beginnings and the pure, joyful anticipation of what the future held for us.

Right away, we went to work trying to get clients. At the insistence of my Uncle Napoleon, we followed in his footsteps and advertised in several publications, which was historically considered a no-no for attorneys back then. However, a relatively new US Supreme Court ruling held that lawyer advertising was partially protected under the First Amendment. As my uncle said, "Advertise, advertise, advertise. How is anybody supposed to know you are here? That is how your aunt Sue and I did it. Almost every year, we put your pictures on our Christmas mailings. People all over the world knew me and the two of you. They watched you grow up through my yearly Christmas mailings. Advertise."

Following his advice, we found hundreds of clients through our ads. We did not worry about what other attorneys thought of our bold action. We selected publications, such as the *Michigan Chronicle*, Michigan's largest black newspaper, that would welcome our advertising dollars. It was not long before other attorneys started advertising their services too. Today you cannot turn on the TV without seeing attorneys announcing their services every hour all day.

The weekly newspaper advertisement of our law firm that was listed in the Michigan Chronicle

◆ Dating and Our Firm

In addition to starting our firm, whenever we had time, my sister and I both dated. We were different in our attitudes about men, but we tended to focus on one man and relationship at a time. We learned a lot through heartache, but we also knew life was short, and we had to keep it moving.

I dated several nice guys but later discovered some had problems with substances. Whether it is addiction to alcohol or a substance, it can ruin a relationship. Under the influence, personalities you thought were one-way morph into people you do not recognize or like. I learned a lot about drinking and how it changes a person from my father's alcohol use. Alcohol or drug addiction can make it difficult to sustain a stable, loving relationship, so I ended those types of relationships quickly. Besides, we were focused on building our firm. That became our number-one priority.

Us featured in Ebony Magazine, Lloyd & Lloyd Attorneys at Law at our offices in the Renaissance Center

◆ Do Not Cross the Lloyd Sisters

Leona and I had no publicists to get our names out there, but we had God. We had faith that our prayers would be answered; it did not take long. We started getting business from the ads and the attention of the media. We were featured in numerous publications, including *Ebony*, *Jet*, *People*, and the *Enquirer,* to name a few. Identical twins starting their own law firm was newsworthy.

A year after appearing in *People* magazine and *Ebony* as well as on some nationally syndicated television shows, we were rocking and rolling. We received tapes from artists all over the world.

We were off to a great start and busier than ever. As expected, when Mojo went on the air, he took WJLB to number one. He became one of the most sought-after radio personalities by merchandising companies wanting him to endorse their products. The Little Caesars pizza empire to Faygo Beverages, makers of a popular local soft drink, were among a few. The companies we negotiated product endorsement deals with on behalf of Mojo had to be amenable to giving back to the community they served.

Leona and I felt good about the WJLB contract negotiation for Mojo. We figured he had nothing to worry about for a while, and everything was fine for about a year and a half. The WJLB radio station remained at number one with Mojo at the helm of his *Mothership*. But for some reason, the station acted as though they could keep the number-one spot without Mojo, because some strange things started happening.

Was it a control issue? Jealousy? Arrogance? Did they feel that Mojo was not worth all the money they were paying him? Maybe they were afraid that if they allowed Mojo to get those perks and set that precedent, other deejays would eventually want the same thing. The station was up to something, and we were going to find out what it was. Leona and I were not about to let him and his *Mothership* crash and burn. Oh no! The Lloyd twins were tough and did not play. He was a valued client, as all our clients were, and when it was time to fight for him, we put the gloves on and hopped into the ring. We were ready for battle.

We soon discovered our suspicions were correct. Mojo found out through his friends that the station was planning to meet with him to terminate him if he did not sign their new contract. The station felt confident that if they fired Mojo, he would have nowhere else he could go. They were wrong to jump to that conclusion.

Mojo was given a written notification requesting his attendance at the upcoming meeting. The meeting occurred as expected, and Leona and me, were in attendance with our client. They passed out a new proposed contract that they wanted Mojo to sign, which would replace and cancel his original contract. The attorney for the station further stated, "If the contract is not agreed to before the end of this meeting, Mojo will be removed from his on- air duties until an agreement can be reached. The removal will start this evening". Sure enough, the rumors were true, it was a setup to take him off the air unless he agreed to sign the contract, they offered him. A deejay was already in place to replace him that evening. Mojo glanced at the contract and smirked at them as he asked who had drafted the document. One of the WJLB administrators took credit. They wanted to know why he had asked. Boldly, he responded, "They are very talented, because they have something in common with Richard Pryor and Eddie Murphy—comedy. I don't need lawyers to know that the last sentence in this agreement totally cancels any control I have over my show, regardless of the prior content contained in the rest of the agreement." With no agreement reached, they told him not to report to the station that night because he was officially off the air. This angered Mojo, after all he had taken that station to number one like he promised. The lawyer representing the radio station, indicated he would be contacting our office to continue contract negotiations. At that moment, Mojo, looked at him and said, "My attorneys are not to negotiate with you about this new contract". Following Mojo's lead, we told the attorney there would be no need to contact our office. Mojo shook their hands and we left. The three of us went out to dinner, to discuss plans for his future.

A few days after the meeting, a mysterious, unsigned notice was posted on a bulletin board at WJLB, claiming Mojo had plans to tour with Prince and had left WJLB. If that garbage had been true, the station would have had cause not to pay Mojo another dime. Luckily, an employee warned Mojo about it and gave him the copy of the posting he had pulled off the bulletin board. Mojo promptly delivered that notice to our office.

Leona and I, immediately contacted the station's attorney, told him about the false posting, and said that because of the posting, we wanted it in writing and made clear that WJLB had removed Mojo from the air. The attorneys wanted to discuss our request and call us later. We said okay, but we felt that was not a good sign. Later that afternoon, the station's attorney contacted us and said it was not in the best interest of the station to give us such a letter. So, we informed them that without a written statement from them, we would have a press conference, to make known publicly, WJLB's actions and reasons for removing Mojo from his nightly show. We reminded them that Mojo's fan club and loyal listeners would be enraged and probably picket the station. We had already advised Mojo to go to work every night so there would be no doubt he was ready to work and not on tour with Prince. They had three days to provide us with a letter or face our wrath. We knew without quick swift action from us, the problem could mushroom and result in Mojo not getting paid a salary or bonuses for a year and a half, which was close to the mid-six-figure range. That was not going to happen.

The next day was Good Friday, and all the law offices were closed, but Leona and I were in our office, catching up on legal work, when we got a call from Mojo. Within twenty minutes, Mojo arrived with an envelope in his hand. Smiling, he said, "The attorneys of WJLB called me in desperation because they couldn't reach you to give you this letter." Inside the sealed envelope was a letter, which we read aloud, indicating the date of the removal of Mojo from his on-air duties by WJLB and saying the removal would continue until contract negotiations were resolved. Mojo laughed and said, "You won." They had to play fair and straight with us and not try to undermine the contract nor their duty to pay his compensation. Mojo continued to receive his salary payments on time.

After a little more than a month, by written notification, WJLB took Mojo permanently off the air. Leona and I had been waiting for that day to arrive, and we had to act quickly. Through our contacts, we knew the stations that were interested in Mojo and just waiting for his contract to terminate. Once the termination was final, we promptly contacted several stations. The radio station, WHYT, was more than ready to scoop Mojo up with a bigger salary and perks. They knew his worth and value to the airwaves. We were in no rush because Mojo had a thirty-day noncompete clause in his contract, but once that time period was over, we quickly negotiated a new contract with WHYT.

Because our client was an artist, we had to make the contract comfortable for Mojo, yet within reason for the station. Almost three months after his termination by WJLB, Mojo officially started recording artistic promos announcing a spectacular happening that was coming and would shake up the radio world. All of Michigan, as far as the sound waves traveled, heard the promos. They did not announce his name, but the voice was undeniably Mojo's. It implied that he was coming back and landing his *Mothership*.

Leona and I heard that some of the employees at WJLB who were listening to WHYT on the evening when he landed the *Mothership* actually cheered when they heard Mojo's signature sign-on and the sounds of the *Mothership* landing at its new home at WHYT.

When deejays are fired from large radio stations, they usually cannot, obtain a job for years in the cities they were originally broadcasting from. However, that was not the case for Mojo. After the non- compete time period was finished, Mojo was free to sign with any station he desired and still receive his full salary from WJLB. An undeniably loud and clear message was sent to his former employer, just like Mojo's signature radio sign-on. The message was that Mojo was part of a dynamic team. Do not mess with the Lloyd twins!

◆ Jumping into the Music Business

It seemed everyone in the Detroit metropolitan area heard of the new radio contract we had negotiated for Mojo. New artists started calling us as music tapes poured into our office as well as Mojo's. His contract and the articles in *Ebony* and several other magazines ignited a firestorm of public interest in us.

Detroit, the home of the Motown sound, was known for its great supply of talented artists. When Motown moved its operations from Detroit to Los Angeles in 1972, the move left a void for Detroit artists who were looking for a way to be discovered. Due to our exposure in the media, we now seemed to be that new possibility for them.

Tapes poured into us not only from Detroit but from all over Michigan. There were so many tapes that we had to place them in huge containers. On Saturdays, Leona and I would come to the office, listen to the tapes, and read the letters that accompanied them. The large number of tapes we received spoke volumes to us about the desperate cry for help. Some of the artists were talented, but none of them had recording contracts from recording companies for us to negotiate for them. One Saturday in 1983, while listening to musical tapes, we decided we were going to select one artist or group out of all the tapes we received and help that person or group receive a recording contract for us to negotiate. With our love for music and our background in playing the piano, we felt we could recognize talent when we heard it.

When Mojo stopped by our office one Saturday morning, we mentioned our new project and our intention. Knowing a lot about the record business, he explained all the possible steps we would have to go through to help an artist get his or her music heard by a record company. He said they got thousands of tapes from hopefuls, and most of the record companies would not even listen to a tape unless it came from someone they knew or from a reputable source. Record companies had faced many lawsuits from artists who claimed that someone had passed their music along to another artist on a record label, changed a few things about the song they had written, and forwarded it to the company. After discussing the number of hours and possible expenses we would incur, he asked us, "So are you sure you want to still do this?"

We glared at him and said, "Yes."

He could see how determined we were, so he agreed to listen to songs we were considering and give his opinion on them. We knew he had the golden ear, so we wanted to move forward. Mojo asked about the artists we were considering and agreed to hear their music. Leona popped in a cassette tape, and he listened for about forty seconds before he told us to stop the tape. Mojo knew who the artist was and named him. He was correct, and we were amazed because we had not mentioned the name of the artist. He indicated that the artist had been around for a long time and said we needed to pick one who had star power, not just a good voice. That stunned us for a minute.

"Let me hear your other artists before you contact them. In the meantime, I get artists dropping by the radio station all the time with their tapes; if I hear an artist I think is worth your time and money, I will call you."

We said, "Okay, great." We knew he could hear hit music; after all, he had played *Prince* when the other radio stations would not. They could not hear what he heard.

There we were again, about to jump into uncharted waters. It would not be our first time accepting a challenge when it was something we believed in and wanted to do.

We really wanted to help a talented artist obtain a contract. For many, the only things stopping them were money and not having anybody behind them pushing them through the door. Too many artists had given up on their dreams too soon. If we could help the selected artist become successful, then that artist would be an example to other artists out there that they too could make it, even if Motown had left. If we did not do this, then who would step up and do so? I thought back to the lady in the cafeteria at Wayne State whom the Black Student Union had helped. I had known if we did not step up to help her, then no one would.

Several weeks rolled by since Mojo had dropped by the office, and then our phone rang in our office. On Saturdays, we answered our own phones because the people who normally answered them for us were off on weekends. It was Mojo, calling to let us know a group had dropped by the radio station the day before to play their music for him. He thought they were good, and he had complimented them as they were admiring one of the platinum records mounted on his office wall. He said they could be bigger than the group the *Time*. They knew that was a huge compliment coming from Mojo, who had played the *Time* on the air before anyone else had believed in them. The group had asked him if he could help them get a record deal, and he had said, "No, but I will give you the name and number of my lawyers. They can help you get a record deal." He told us to be ready for their call and added that they appear to be nice guys.

◆ The Call from a Group That Changed Our World

After Mojo referred the group from Flint to us, they called us, and we set up a meeting with them. At the meeting, we told them we had heard their 8-track tape but more importantly, Mojo, our client, felt their songs were hit songs and worth investing our time in. We let them know we valued Mojo's opinion when it came to music because he had an ear for music and hit songs. The group responded with smiles.

We met with them a few more times and provided them with retainer agreements, and we explained they would have a few weeks to take the agreement to their parents and any other outside lawyers for consultation. Two weeks, later they returned with their contracts signed by themselves and their parents. Once we received the retainer agreements, we financed and scheduled studio time for them in Studio A, a twenty-four-track studio, to rerecord two of their songs, one of which was titled "Tonight."

We were in the recording studio with the group, and once the songs were completed, we took them to Mojo and let him hear them. "Something's missing," he said. "They need to bring in the guy who recorded them on 8-track. He knows their sound."

We hunted that guy down. Bernard Terry was his name, and he agreed to come to Detroit to rerecord, remix, and do whatever he needed to do for the song "Tonight." Again, we were in the studio with the group and Bernard for more than five hours while they worked on the song. We took the final version to Mojo and let him hear it. We held our breath as he quietly listened. Hoping Bernard had the magic touch, we crossed our fingers. Mojo exclaimed, "It's back! What did you do?"

"We did what you said. We got the guy who recorded them originally to come do this."

With several additional songs recorded, we sent their demo tape out to several big recording companies, but they all passed on it. Mojo realized we were a little down, and he wanted to prove to us that he was right, so he said, "Let me play the song 'Tonight' one time tomorrow night and see how many people call in to hear it."

We agreed he could play it, keeping the group as mystery artists, but asked him to play it only once. We did not want any future plagiarism problems. That night he played it on air and the phones lit up like firecrackers on the Fourth of July. Mojo called us and pleaded with us to let him play it one more time because the phone request line, at the radio station, was on fire for that song. We agreed to one more time. Mojo showed the group and us that the song was a hit just waiting to happen.

The airing on the radio only supported what we felt all along and that was the song was a hit. Leona and I continued to provide support and guidance for the group. Again, in uncharted waters, we took the next step to show that the record was really a hit record; we agreed to put the record out under their own label, Blue Lake Records, which we created for them. The next hat we had to wear was the one of a temporary- manager.

◆ Looking for a Name

The group now needed a name. We hired a Virginia lawyer to check out the names selected by the group as well as one selected by us, in the United States Patent and Trademark Office located in Alexandria, Virginia. The names we submitted were all taken, so we had him secretly check out the name Ready for the World. The name came from one of the songs they had written, and it was not taken, so Ready for the World (RFTW) became their name.

The group gave us some static at first, but after a while, they fell in love with their name.

Next, we needed to set up photo shoots to obtain professional pictures of them and then have them mass-produced. We had to have them ready for autographing at record stores and local television show promotions. We were optimistic. We believed their music was hit music, and we were determined to help get it out there and prove the record companies were wrong that had passed on them and rejected them.

Once again, Leona and I refused to take no for an answer. The rejection by the record companies was an obstacle we would overcome. It made us more determined.

Kelvyn Ventour, an independent record promoter, helped by promoting the record in Michigan and New York. Kelvyn got their records played on radio, throughout Michigan as well as the local dance television shows. We had thousands of records pressed up, shipped and delivered to our office. Once the boxes arrived at our office, we notified Kelvyn and he carted them out the next day to the record stores. In a matter of a few weeks, the records started selling and flying off the shelves. With our blessing, Kelvyn set up a meeting in Washington, DC, with Jheryl Busby, the vice president of the Black Music Division at MCA Records, and flew there for the meeting. He showed him the stats on RFTW's record sales, as well as their ranking on all the stations that had played their music.

Kelvyn's hard work promoting the song paid off. He showed Mr. Busby that the song "Tonight" was already a bona fide hit throughout Michigan and New York. Kelvyn became part of the production unit because of his contribution. Mr. Busby's meeting with Kelvyn, helped solidify the deal for RFTW with MCA Records. As their legal counsel, we negotiated a major recording deal with MCA Records for them. With worldwide distribution, the song "Tonight" became a number-one hit in *Billboard Magazine*. RFTW became known throughout the world. Their first album produced three number-one songs in *Billboard Magazine* and went Gold and Platinum. Several months later, we joined RFTW and Bernard Terry, their coproducer, with the MCA record executives at the Gold Record Party celebration sponsored by MCA Records, in Flint Michigan.

With the worldwide success of RFTW, a previously unknown group from Flint, Michigan, an additional unintended but welcome blessing was that we became some of the most sought-after entertainment attorneys in the United States.

RFTW, New Edition, Leona, and me with MCA promotional personnel in 1984.

The next Detroit artist we got signed to CBS Records was Davina, and then we negotiated a contract with Arista Records for the group Kiara. Kiara consisted of two talented young men, Gregory Charley and John Winston, from Detroit, Michigan. We managed and traveled the world with Kiara as they promoted and performed their hit records. Two songs off their first album climbed to the number-one and number-two spots in *Billboard Magazine*, and two videos became number one on BET's show *Video Soul*.

Leona and me showing Gregory Charley and John Winston of Kiara their promotional sweatshirts in 1988

◆ Stepping Out on Faith

Leona and I were stepping out on faith and going into the world of entertainment, a world we did not know. A lot of lawyers saw our success and asked us how we found talented artists like the ones we worked with. I told them it was simple: we believed in them, and we put our money where our mouth was.

One attorney said, "You mean you spent your own money out of your pocket on these artists?"

"Yes," we replied.

Expressing his concern, he said, "But that was a gamble. It is like going to the casino and placing your money on a number at the roulette table. At the end of the spin, you could lose all your money."

We smiled and said, "That was a chance we were willing to take. However, the one component you left out with your example was that you didn't have us and our winning team as a key factor."

◆ Working with Icons

At that point in our lives, we were hustling like crazy, trying to stay on top of all the new clients coming to our law firm. Even though we had other entertainment clients, the first major iconic entertainment clients we landed were David Ruffin and Eddie Kendricks, formerly of the Temptations. We met them through their manager, Bruce Tucker, a man we had known since we were children. Bruce warned us that David and Eddie were hesitant to hand over management of their legal affairs to two young black female attorneys. We understood that but felt if we had a chance to talk face-to-face with them, we could change their opinion. Again, we had a background in public speaking, and we wanted a chance to use it.

Bruce made it happen. The meeting in the conference room, at our office was a success; we convinced them we were the real deal and would take care of them. If given a chance, we would earn their trust. They agreed to give us that chance, and we shook hands. As they left our office, a few lucky secretaries obtained their autographs.

Shortly after that, our first job for them was to review and redraft sections of the production contract Mr. Tommy Mottola's production company had offered them. After we overnighted several red-lined copies of the production contract to him, Mr. Mottola insisted on finishing the negotiations in his office and offered to cover all travel expenses. With the approval of David and Eddie, Leona and I flew to New York and personally met with Mr. Mottola to review and finalize the production agreement between David and Eddie and Tommy Mottola's company.

The meeting went smoothly. Mr. Mottola admitted that he had seen who we were on paper, but out of curiosity, he had wanted to meet us. He said, "I didn't know Detroit had entertainment lawyers like you two."

Smiling, we responded, "It does."

Once the meeting was completed, all that remained was the matter of getting David and Eddie to sign the agreement.

◆ The Signing of the Contracts

Due to past legal problems David and Eddie had had early in their careers, they wanted us to hand the contracts directly to them for their signatures. That was no problem, except they were in New York, and we were in Detroit, so their request meant we had to change our calendars and reschedule meetings with other clients as well as make sure we had no court appearances that couldn't be changed. Once we had jumped through all those hoops, per their request, we flew back to New York to present them with the final documentation to sign with Tommy Mottola's production company.

Time was of the essence, so we had to interrupt their rehearsal with pop stars Hall and Oates to have them sign their contracts. No problem. They happily finalized the deal. It was done. While we were there, Leona and I took a photo with them and Hall and Oates sitting on the steps of the Apollo Theater in New York. We pulled a guy off the street to take that picture. Hey, what can I say? Things moved at a fast pace, but that was one of the most rewarding days in our lives. We convinced two artists we had idolized for years as little girls, to trust us with their careers.

Eddie Kendricks and David Ruffin signing their contracts on the steps of the Apollo Theater, New York

Not long after all contracts were executed, Mr. Mottola became the head of Sony Music Entertainment, parent company of the Columbia label, which David's and Eddie's contracts were assigned to, per their agreement.

Gwen, Leona, and Davina with Eddie Kendricks and David Ruffin.

Davina, me, Leona and Eddie Kendricks backstage before their concert in Sterling Heights, Michigan

Shortly after that, on our birthday, they called and sang a sweet birthday greeting for us on our answering machine. What attorneys get a greeting like that from two of the biggest recording stars in history?

◆ Greed Is What Gets People in Trouble

With all those things happening to us in the entertainment world, we were sought after as speakers for many events. Because we were twin attorneys in the entertainment arena, many articles were written about us, and we were featured on many TV informational shows. All that attention and coverage made us instantly recognizable. Being approached at airports, malls, and clubs was something we got used to.

Unfortunately, sometimes, with that type of exposure, you can draw the wrong attention. We had appointments for consultations all the time regarding the entertainment business. One appointment was made with two men who wanted to talk to us about the music industry. We were not prepared for the two men who entered our office. They looked like gangsters, dressed in all black from their hats down to their shoes, except for their white ties. As they introduced themselves, we noticed their accents and knew they had not been born in the United States. If I had closed my eyes, I could have sworn we were in a *Godfather* movie.

They indicated that their purpose for coming to talk to us was to discuss how they could help us in the entertainment business with promotions or finding new recording artists. To say we felt uncomfortable would be just touching the surface. We explained that we were not a record company; we were only interested in helping and discovering new talent. They insisted, "We want to help you with that. We want to be part of that with you. How much money do you need to help develop your artists?"

We were not born yesterday. You must pay the piper, if you dance to his music. We understood that taking money from an entity like that would mean someone else would own us. We had worked too hard to earn the freedom to do the types of things we wanted to do without reporting to anyone or getting approval from anyone. Becoming connected in business to two people and their unknown organization was not anything we were interested in, so we turned down their offer.

They would not take no for an answer. They assumed money could buy anything and anyone. They did not know it could not buy us. "Everyone could use money. You could move into larger suites," one of them said as he pulled out a checkbook from his suit pocket. "So how much will it take?" They were willing to write a check that day for any amount we stated. I guess they felt that money talked louder than they could. Again, we turned down their offer and said we did not want their money because we were doing just fine. When they realized we were not interested, the man put his checkbook back into the inside pocket of his suit jacket, and they left. That was the first time we had ever had a meeting with someone who left us with chills going down our backs. We were relieved when they left.

◆ The Telephone Warning

Shortly after that meeting, we received an anonymous message on our phone service saying, "You'd better be careful. You're getting too big too fast." After that call and the office visit by the two men dressed in black, a little fear set in. We decided to have security with us when we went out to large gatherings or traveled in a limo. We told the limo owners, Dan and Otto, who were our friends, about our strange meeting and calls. They volunteered to handle our long-distance transportation. We knew we were safe when we were with them; they would not let anything happen to us.

Greed is what gets people in trouble. My father used to say, "You don't get something for nothing." That statement our father made to us as little girls, was a rule we followed our entire lives, even as judges. We saw examples of greed all the time. People who want money without earning it are subject to the high price it will cost them. That was a price we were never willing to pay. All money ain't good money!

CHAPTER 11

My Election for Judge

HERE COMES THE JUDGE

As independent lawyers, Leona and I took meetings with high-ranking music execs and moguls. The Lloyd sisters were making it happen for themselves and other artists. We had moved up to a "deluxe apartment in the sky," just like the theme song from *The Jeffersons* TV show. We were living on the twenty-seventh and twenty-eighth floors of the Trolley Plaza, in a beautiful two-story penthouse that had a breathtaking view of the downtown Detroit skyline. For eight years, we made that our home. We were on top of the world.

That period in our lives was fun and exciting, but something inside me yearned for more. I wanted to make more of a difference in people's lives. That was when I started thinking about running for a judicial office. I knew as a judge, I would make important decisions that would have a direct, immediate impact on the lives of everyday people. I felt that litigants would have a fair opportunity to be heard as well as receive an opportunity to change their lives.

When I first mentioned the idea to my sister, she did not think I was serious. Our dreams had come true, so why would I change anything? However, after a long discussion with her, she understood and was totally on board. She instantly became my campaign manager.

In 1992, I decided to run for a judgeship seat. There were ten incumbent judges running, plus two other challengers, which made thirteen of us running for ten seats. Whew! I knew it was going to be a lot of work, but I was confident I was ready for it. Leona and I rolled up our sleeves and dug in. We had our crew of people working with us, and our "Don't quit" mantra rang true again. Sure, it was a huge challenge, and I was in uncharted waters once again, but we had faced several challenges with hidden obstacles before and still come through.

Running for office is not for the weary or weak of heart. It involves nonstop talking; being seen; and meeting with neighborhood groups, parents, church congregations, and political groups. You are on the go at a rapid pace all the time, except when you sleep, even then your mind is racing.

Then there were other pressures. The automobile lobby in Detroit was huge. In the Motor City, it was almost impossible to win an election without the support of the auto labor unions. They would be up in arms if they saw a candidate driving a foreign car. If one were not driving an American automobile, the winds would shift quickly. At that time, we owned a Lincoln Continental and a Ford Probe.

Politics can be an ugly monster. The singing group Undisputed Truth had a hit song in the 1970s called "Smiling Faces," which sums up politics: "Smiling faces sometimes tell lies." People get vicious and downright ruthless in their pursuit of winning a political race. Winning is almost ingrained in us as Americans. We grow up wanting to beat our competitors. If we lose, we try to be good sports about the loss, but everyone wants to win. No one competes to lose.

The incumbent judges did not want me to run. Fear, jealously, unwillingness to give up their seats, and the costs of a reelection campaign were issues that all came into play. Leona and I hustled as if our lives depended on it. We had long days and longer nights. I did not have a large budget for mailings, so we did everything ourselves, including trips to the post office.

Our mother, who was staying with us because of her health, got involved in the campaign. She put stamps on hundreds of absentee voter literature mailers. We were happy our mother had improved mentally. The personality Leona and I had known as kids had returned. Our mother rolled up her sleeves to help as much as her physical health would permit. Believe it or not, she was having a ball.

My friends and I stuffed large duffel mailbags with my absentee voter literature. I personally transported the bags, which felt as if they weighed a ton, to the post office delivery ramp from my car. The man at the loading dock whose job was to receive incoming mail grabbed my bags of mail, opened them, looked at the picture of me on my literature, and asked me, "Is this you?"

Full of enthusiasm, I answered, "Yes, it is."

He said he had never seen a candidate bring his or her own bags of mail in before.

"Well, now you have. Low funds will make you hustle."

With understanding eyes, he grabbed the oversized bags and yelled to the workers to mark them for delivery the next day.

"I'll be bringing more shortly," I told him.

He said, "I'll be here." Gwen, one of our most reliable friends; along with Leona and me, stacked our cars with the huge US Postal bags of literature mailers, returned to the docks, and dropped them off with the same guy. There must have been more than twenty thousand pieces of literature in those bags. Hard work was our middle name. I did not let the fact that I could not afford to have mailers laser-printed with labels and postage stop my mailers from going out.

◆ You Don't Get Something for Nothing

Speaking of hard work, fundraisers are the lifeblood of a campaign, but they take a tremendous amount of work. After I had held more than a dozen successful fundraisers, one night, a fundraiser was given for me that had a disappointing turnout due to poor planning. I was sitting at the bar of the establishment where the fundraiser was held, waiting for my sister, when a man approached me with my campaign literature in his hand. He said he wanted to support me in my run for office. I thanked him and told him I would count on his vote. However, I soon learned that was not the kind of support he meant.

"Well, I know campaigns are expensive, and all candidates can use money. I'm willing to donate ten thousand dollars to you, but there is one thing I will ask from you."

Making direct eye contact, I waited for him to continue.

"One day—I don't know when, but one day—I'll need a favor. I do not know what the favor might be, but I will expect you to help me with my request. I have helped other judicial candidates before with the same exchange terms."

I glared at the man and told him, "I might need money for my campaign, but I don't need money that badly. No, thank you! I will be just fine. Whatever I raise is what I will use. I am not interested in your proposal." I got up from my stool, told him it had been nice meeting him, and left. Somewhere in the back of my mind, I could have sworn his words were something from another *Godfather* movie. Was that déjà vu? Leona and I had been down that path before. The only thing missing this time was him pulling out his checkbook.

As I said before, all money *ain't* good money, and to quote my father once again, "You don't get something for nothing." What price would that favor have cost me? I did not know, and I did not want to find out. People who accepted an exchange like that would have a pressure hovering over them every day they went to work. That, to me, would have been insanity.

It was the last week in October 1992, and the election was drawing near an end. I had a few large churches left to visit, and Hartford Memorial Baptist Church was one of them. Reverend Charles G. Adams, the pastor of Hartford Memorial Baptist Church, a historic black Baptist church in Detroit, was sponsoring a candidate forum. Reverend Adams had been a close friend and mentee of my uncle Napoleon when he lived in Boston.

I had been informed of all the stringent rules of the candidate forum. However, at the last minute, I decided to go to the event at the encouragement of my committee members in defiance of the unfair rules.

I realized it was the Sunday before the election, and I had been campaigning hard nonstop for several months and was weary and drained. In addition, I had received calls at my law office from members of that church telling me if I planned on coming to the event, there were things I could not do. I could not speak, I could not pass out literature in the church, and I could not sit on the stage. Only the members of the church that were candidates, could sit on the stage. In other words, the three candidates who were members of their church would be very visible, and I would not be. After explaining the guidelines to me, they asked me if I was still coming, and I answered, "I already knew this, and yes, I will be attending."

So, you can see why I was not motivated to go. But one of my committee members, Reverend Fallins, who drove me to the church, had faith that everything would be okay.

When Reverend Fallins dropped me off, he said he and some other committee members were going to form a prayer circle and pray for me. Based on my facial expression and lack of enthusiasm, I guess he thought I needed it. I smiled and said, "Okay, it can only help. I'll see you back here after church," and I went inside the church.

I knew Linda Feigens, a member of my committee and my church facilitator, had written a letter to Reverend Adams to let him know who I was, what my relationship with my uncle Napoleon was, and that I would be attending the forum as a judicial candidate running for office. However, when I heard in the early morning worship service that the pastor had just flown in on a red-eye flight from Somalia, Africa, that morning, I figured he would have been too tired to go through a bunch of mail on his desk on the same morning he flew in. I thought; *Oh well, so much for Linda's letter. At least she tried.*

◆ A Miracle

The early morning service was over, and it was about nine o'clock, when Reverend Adams took to the stage for the candidates' forum. Food had been served, so everybody was sitting and eating. I had a plate of fried chicken, my favorite food. As I was eating a chicken leg, Reverend Adams stood on stage, scanning the audience. He called out my name, asking, "Is Attorney Leonia Lloyd here?"

Startled, I almost choked on the chicken I was swallowing. I placed my chicken leg down and raised my hand. He spotted me and said, "No, darling, I want you up here sitting next to me."

As I stood up with a big smile on my face, I thought; *He must have read Linda's letter. That is why he called out my name.*

I went up to the stage and walked toward him. He hugged me and had me stand next to him as he personally introduced me to the audience. He proceeded to state that my uncle Napoleon had been like a father to him when he had moved to Boston as a young man, who did not know anyone there. He said he had watched my sister and me grow up through the pictures on my uncle's Christmas cards mailed out over the years and added, "She is part of my family. She will sit up here next to me. I'll let the candidates who are members of the church on the stage speak first, and then we will hear from Attorney Lloyd." My brain was alert, and excitement was now pumping through my veins because I was no longer invisible. In fact, I was being showcased.

When it was my turn to speak, I felt a shot of adrenaline race through my body. I gave the crowd a rousing speech. It was dynamite! Reverend Adams gave me a big hug after I finished. He let me leave early with his blessing so I could attend the other churches that morning, which he explained to the congregation.

He gave the church audience his personal endorsement for me at that candidates' forum, and at his 11:30 a.m. service, he had the members of the church write my name down on the church political action committee (PAC) list that was in the church program. I could not believe it! A former deacon of Hartford pointed out to me, there were ten thousand members who belonged to that church, and with the two services on Sunday, they usually had an active attendance of five thousand people. When the final votes were in for the election that following Tuesday night, I had won by a margin of 1,900 votes. I feel in my heart that Hartford church made a difference for me and Linda's letter made it all possible.

◆ Waking Up to Election Results

The morning after the election, I awoke in the early hours of the morning when the phone rang. It was my campaign promoter, the late Mr. James Houze. Leona answered the phone, and he asked, "May I speak to Judge Lloyd?"

My sister paused for a minute and then said, "What did you say?"

He laughed and repeated the question again.

At that point, Leona screamed, "Yes!" and she dropped the phone and came running into my bedroom, screaming at the top of her voice. "You won! You won!"

Dressed in the campaign T-shirt I had worn to bed the night before—I had been too exhausted to change into nightclothes—I got up, and we both jumped around in excitement. I then said, "I think Mr. Houze is still on the phone." We laughed, and I ran back to speak with him because he was indeed still there.

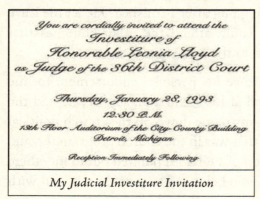

My Judicial Investiture Invitation

Can God do it? Yes, he can! To my readers, even when everyone counts you out, remember who you are and whose you are. I was God's child. Have confidence in yourself, and remember, it is not over until it is over.

◆ The Swearing-In Ceremony

I was sworn in as a judge in January 1993 with my mother, sister, minister and Gwen by my side. Our father, still living in Memphis at that time, was unable to physically be there, but we felt he was there in spirit.

Initially, in the ceremony, when a judge is given her robe, it is called the robing. Assisted by Gwen, Leona placed her gift of the robe on my shoulders and handed me my new gavel, which she had had engraved with my name.

Chief Judge Allen swore me in, as my minister and sister jointly held the Bible for the placement of my hand.

Leona gave a heartwarming introduction for me. When she finished, there was not a dry eye in the whole auditorium. I hugged her and then took to the podium. Nervous and emotional, I was barely able to speak. Tears gushed down my face throughout my acceptance speech because memories of the sacrifices made by so many people, who refused to give up on me flooded my brain. My sister, realizing what I was experiencing, ran up onto the stage and handed me tissues she pulled out of her purse, so I could finish my speech.

As I mentioned earlier, I had our mother stand, as she was too weak to climb the steps onto the stage. I gave a tribute to her and our father for being there for Leona and me when we needed them.

At the end of my speech, my sister presented me, stating, "I now present to you the newly elected judge of the Thirty-Sixth District Court, Judge Leonia Lloyd, a twin for justice." She held my hand up with hers in victory. The crowd stood and cheered. It was a momentous occasion and one I will never forget.

◆ My New Chambers

It was January 1993 when I quickly settled into my new office, my chambers. My court reporter, Florence Dunklin, helped me decorate the office. As in our law offices, I had one wall I called the wall of pain. On that wall were all the degrees I had earned and my certificate of Admission to the Bar in Michigan. Additionally, the wall showed all court certifications allowing me to practice before several courts, including the United States Supreme Court. The other wall was called the wall of fame. That wall consisted of individual as well as joint awards, framed national news articles about us, and the framed gold records presented to me. One was from Ready for the World and the other was from Eddie Kendricks and David Ruffin when they recorded an album live at the Apollo with Hall and Oates. Leona and I had requested separate gold records.

Little did I know that would earn me my first nickname, the Rock 'n Roll Judge. Quite often court personnel asked Florence for permission to come in and view my chamber walls. Giggling, she would give them a brief tour.

After the exhilarating swearing-in ceremony and decoration of my judicial chambers came my first day on the bench. It went from exciting to sad because of the many young people, ages seventeen to twenty-five years old, who came in front of me. Most of them had dropped out of school. At such a young age, they had decided to quit on life with no plans for what they would do with their futures. Many troubled teens had lost their way and begun skipping school and using drugs. Their parents, who felt helpless, had become distraught and worried about them.

As a judge, I felt I had to do something to motivate them. After all, the desire to help others was what had driven me to run for judge in the first place. I had to let them see that they could achieve anything if they worked at it. The motivation I provided was in the form of a dismissal of their tickets for non-assaultive crimes if they raised their grades by the next report card or if they studied for and passed the GED test. For many, the next step forward was to apply to a four- year college, a community college, or a trade school to get certified in a skilled job.

One method I used when I felt I needed to, was to call the young people up to the bench and look at them directly face-to-face. I always pointed out how talented and special they were and asked them what they wanted to do with their lives. Often, I asked about their grades, their grade point average and did their grades reflect their best efforts. They almost always responded with a no. They said their best efforts would result in them getting, *A's and B's*. My reaction was, "I will hold you to the grade point average you indicated was possible for you to achieve." Countless times, I made pacts with them, to bring their report cards for each school card marking on their scheduled return court date. Oftentimes, young people needed to be held accountable and encouraged in order to change. I was like the second parent, except I was a judge, a person of authority cheering for them, encouraging them, and anticipating change. I praised them to success. Simultaneously, they paid their debt to society and changed the trajectory of their lives.

I knew encouragement from the bench made a huge difference for young people. I had two large cabinet drawers filled with copies of GED certificates, letters of acceptance to colleges or trade schools, and report cards reflecting vast improvements in grades. Many times, when I was satisfied with the improvement of young defendants and was about to dismiss the tickets, the parents asked me to keep their children longer and not dismiss the cases yet because they had never seen their kids improve their grades to such a high level of performance. Smiling, I would agree, and then I would look at the defendant, who usually smiled as he or she said, "See you next time, Judge." That was the kind of impact I wanted to make. That was why I became a judge.

Becoming a judge did not mean I had to stop being me. In fact, the job suited me perfectly. I realized that even though I was firm, I maintained my sense of humor and style. I had always been a girlie girl, and some referred to me as the Rhinestone Judge, my second nickname, because of the rhinestones on my reading glasses, gavel, robe, and fingernails.

In my courtroom, I wanted the defendants I interacted with to have a positive experience to remember, so I started using an applause button—a gift from my girlfriend and fellow judge, Miriam Martin Clark—and other musical sounds to amplify and emphasize my decisions. When a defendant made great strides or successfully finished a training program or when a teenager received great grades or graduated from high school, I pushed my applause button, and it always elicited smiles. Sometimes a little levity is needed to break the seriousness of being in court. Some people who visited my courtroom did not want to leave. They wanted to see what was coming next.

I enjoyed cases in which the outcome for the defendant was a positive learning experience. However, the reality was that not all cases were rosy, and not all had positive results. Many cases involving young people tore at my heart, particularly cases of young people who made bad decisions that landed them in front of me and that could not be taken back. Many of those cases involved violence. Violence is a given in big cities, and Detroit was no different. I had to confront it in my courtroom every day. Purse snatchings, home invasions, carjackings, burglaries, and murders were no stranger to my court docket. Sometimes the violence was brutal.

I took a hard stance on violent cases, even if they involved offenses committed by minors. One case that was particularly disturbing involved a group of teenage boys who skipped school to smoke marijuana, drink, and get high. The boys were visiting a twenty-five-year-old man they knew. They were playing their music loudly, and an upstairs neighbor knocked on the door and asked them to keep the music down, as he had to go to work later that evening. The boys said they would lower the volume of the music and the man returned to his unit upstairs. However, the music continued to blast and pound. The man went downstairs to talk to them again. At the direction of the older man, the boys attacked him; beating and kicking him so badly that his face swelled to almost three times its normal size.

The boys then tried to put him in the incinerator, but he was too large, and they could not get him into it. At the same time, the man's little boy, who was about five years old, came downstairs, looking for his father. He sat on the steps as he watched the boys trying to toss his father down into the incinerator. His father died that day.

At the hearing, I could not with a good conscience give any of those boys a personal or low bond. Their lawyers pointed out the parents of the boys, who were seated in the courtroom, to illustrate that they all came from good homes, but I reminded them that a man's life had been taken, and his child had witnessed part of the killing. I let them know that if the boys had been in school, where they were supposed to be, the dead man would still have been alive. Now those kids would get an education of a different kind. Some of the boys cried as they heard my words, but it was too little too late. A life had been snuffed out because of them. They had to pay the price for taking a life. I had to make sure the public was safe from that type of behavior and that no one else would be subjected to that type of violence from them. The case was remanded to the Circuit Court for further disposition.

The variety of cases I had as a judge prepared me for the long difficult journey, I would take on the bench in the next ten years.

CHAPTER 12

Leona's Election For Judge

Ain't No Stopping Us Now

Leona ran for judge two years after I became a judge. Believe it or not, I had to convince her to run. Every time I asked her about running, she always responded the same way: "Leonia, I feel like I have already run." I realized she was tired after helping me, but I knew she would be a much-needed addition to the bench. I knew if she joined me on the bench, there would be at least one more person who felt the same way I did about using the law in a positive way to help people as well as to dispense justice fairly.

She would not mind doing the extra work to accomplish that result. We could make a double impact. It took many months to wear her down, but with her final nod to proceed, the race was on.

The campaign signs read, "Vote for Leona Lloyd—A Twin for Justice." Once again, we took to the streets and community to get her elected. At one point, at a community forum, a man asked why the people should elect Leona. He asked if people were supposed to elect her just because her twin sister was a judge. But Leona had a definitive response for him. As a lawyer for the City of Detroit, Leona told him she had a 98 percent win rate in all the appeals she'd filed, which meant that of all the cases the city had previously lost at trial, Leona had been able to get those cases reversed on appeal. The reversals she had won, meant the City of Detroit had avoided paying out millions and millions of taxpayer dollars. It was a win for the citizens of Detroit. She informed him she had practiced in the Michigan Third Circuit Court, the Michigan Court of Appeals, the Michigan Supreme Court, and the US Supreme Court. She said, "Don't vote for me because my sister is a judge. Vote for me because I am the best qualified, and I want to make a difference." No way was she riding on my coattails.

A history making moment in 1995. Me swearing my sister in as a Thirty-Sixth District Court judge at her Investiture while our mother held the Bible

Endorsements of a candidate from major groups and organizations are important during an election. Members of those organizations often vote for the candidates supported by their organizations. The more endorsements a candidate receives, the more exposure and votes he or she can capture. However, if your opponent has powerful people supporting them, it is possible they will receive more endorsements based on that leverage.

When I was campaigning, I had a lot of endorsements, however Leona received only two endorsements when she ran. Notwithstanding, they were major: Michigan's Fourteenth Congressional District and the Eastside Slate. Both of those organizations were grassroots organizations that had the manpower to help push their political slates to the voters of the City of Detroit before the election and on the day of the election at the polls. However, Leona was not relying on just the endorsements; she took her campaign to the people. She hit the streets with a caravan of cars decorated with her signs. In large neighborhoods she went door to door with her literature and lawn signs. Her lawn signs as well as poster boards for stores were plastered all over Detroit. For a powerful visual message, she had a slew of billboards strategically placed around the entire city.

In November 1994, my sister was elected judge by a landslide, winning by a margin of more than forty thousand votes. At that time, we were the only identical twins to serve as judges on the same bench at the same time in the United States. Our courtrooms were next to each other. We really were the Twins for Justice.

Leona's Oath of office sworn in by me on December 16, 1994

◆ Her First Day on the Bench

My sister was prepared for her first day on the bench because of our discussions prior to her taking the bench. A month and a half before formal judicial training started for the newly elected judges, she came into my courtroom daily to watch, listen, and study my actions and procedures. Leona knew she would see hundreds of young people who were lost and needed guidance. She was ready to tackle those issues.

In addition to her monitoring my courtroom as a training tool, I felt she needed something more. I needed to prepare some written guidelines that would assist her or any new judge taking the bench.

At the time my sister became a judge, there were no manuals or written guidelines for judges to follow regarding Thirty-Sixth District

Court procedures, so I developed two workbooks for Leona to use as guidelines for a new judge. One consisted of forms and procedures involved in handling various misdemeanor cases. The second manual consisted of written procedural guidelines and Michigan statutes to be used in the courtroom during criminal examinations. With the written materials and her courtroom preparation, she was armed and ready. She hit the ground running on her first day as a judge, assigned to the criminal examination docket.

I gave the guideline book on criminal examinations I initially created for Leona to new judges in training who sat with me during my tenure. They all said it was extremely helpful to them. The only thing I asked of them was to help any new judges they train by giving them copies of their training materials.

They must have kept their word, because that handbook was handed down to new judges from that point on; as years went by, some judges added more information to it as new laws were created. The book became an unofficial training guide for newly elected judges; today, it is called the holy grail.

Leona did a great job on the bench. Sadly, she and I worked at the same time, so I never saw her in action, but I knew my sister. The attorneys who had practiced many times in front of me were curious as to how my sister was going to be on the bench. That was the big question for them. They had their answer after her first month on the bench. Many attorneys came into my courtroom and said, "We all wondered how she was going to be as a judge. Well, after listening to her and watching how she handles cases, it seems she sounds and acts just like you. She even makes the same types of jokes on the bench. If we closed our eyes, we wouldn't know which one we were in front of."

I just laughed. If either one of us was absent, the lawyers would come to the other twin's courtroom and ask for their case to be heard there instead of adjourning it to another day. One lawyer said, "We already know the two of you will come out the same way on the case, so I might as well get it handled today."

Yes, we were similar in our thinking, but from the things she relayed to me about her handling of some of her cases, I thought she displayed more humor. As a judge, Leona heard a variety of cases and was in a position to make a difference. So, it was not surprising to me when she stopped by my house after work and told me about a case of transformation in her courtroom that day. The lady in front of her had pleaded guilty in a drug paraphernalia case. My sister was aware that the defendant was in the sex trade, or prostitution. As she listened to her, Leona remembered the ladies she had seen from her apartment balcony as a college student and in other neighborhoods we had lived in. She vividly remembered seeing them strolling up and down the street, selling their bodies. She had not been able to do anything to help them then, but she could now. During sentencing, she had a discussion with the defendant, asking her, "Do you know how beautiful you are?"

The defendant turned and looked around the courtroom because she was puzzled. "Are you talking to me?" she asked my sister.

"Yes. Let me help you help yourself. I know how beautiful you are, but you must see it too. Will you let me help you? Will you go and remain in the treatment program I put you in today if I order it?"

Shocked, the defendant replied, "Wow, nobody's ever said I was beautiful before." She wiped tears from her face and said, "Yes, yes. I'll go today." The defendant glared at the man who had brought her to court. "You might as well leave because I'm going to the program the judge is putting me in today. Bye."

Turning back around, the defendant cracked a smile at my sister. She took a seat in the front of the courtroom and waited for the probation officer to come get her. Having a caring person in authority really look at a person and reach him or her, by have a life-changing discussion with them is monumental.

Leona changed that lady's life; that story had a great impact on me and my decision later to partner with the Wayne County Sheriff's program Project Fresh Start, which focused on rehabilitation for drug-addicted prostitutes.

There are many areas in which a judge's sentencing style could have great and lasting effects on the lives of many individuals. However, my sister and I felt that one of the strongest impacts we had was with young people, especially teenagers. Because of our style on the bench, teachers would request an opportunity to bring their classes to our courtrooms to watch cases and learn.

◆ Reaching the Youth

Leona had a unique way of connecting with young visitors who came to visit her courtroom. She would start off with a direct personal greeting: "I see we have some special guests in the courtroom today." The children were fascinated and animated, and their eyes immediately grew large as a result of the special attention she gave them. She made a point of asking each child to stand and state his or her name and what he or she wanted to do in life after high school. If someone said he or she wanted to become an attorney or judge, she would ask that student to come sit with her on the bench. As they approached the bench, the children in the audience would ooh and aah. When court was completed for the day, she would ask the children what they had seen and learned in the courtroom. Hands would fly up into the air. In order to have closer interaction with the young people, she would step off the bench in her robe and speak one on one to them. She was close enough that they could reach out and touch her—yes, she was real. Leona enjoyed having young people come into her courtroom.

Every so often, we both had requests from parents to allow their children to come to court to watch the proceedings. Sometimes the parents wanted to scare their children into being better students, or sometimes the children were interested in going into the legal field. Regardless of the reason, we always permitted them to come watch.

However, Leona would go the additional step of letting them sit with her on the bench. While a child was up there with her, she would explain the case to the young person, what she was going to do as a judge, and the result she was looking for. The child was engaged in the process. Afterward, it was not unusual for Leona to receive letters from parents thanking her and saying what a difference the experience had made in the child's behavior. Many children wrote to her, indicating their new interest in becoming a judge to affect the lives of people in a positive manner, as they had seen her do. That was precisely why I had needed her to join me on the bench. She was doing what I had known she would automatically do.

That direct-contact method with young people was something I learned from Leona. I adopted that style and used it until I retired from the bench.

As judges, we were both called to speak at many events, and because we were twins, the event organizers often wanted us to speak on the same topic. They realized that having the two of us come to speak would be fascinating to their audience. The only problem was that Leona and I felt the same way about a lot of things, so for us to speak on the same topic, we had to go the extra mile to make sure our speeches were different. To guarantee the individuality of our speeches, we would write them away from each other. Once we were done, we would get together to hear the speech of the other one to make sure there was no inadvertent duplicity. I always wanted her to speak first because I knew she would stir up the audience. It did not matter if the audience was young or old; she was an ever-ready bunny and truly a force to be reckoned with. She had a bubbly personality and a gift for speaking. She could get a crowd riled up in a hurry. Even though I liked for her to speak first to warm up the audience, I never wanted to follow her after she spoke. I know—it sounds crazy, right? One day she laughed at me and said, "Leonia, you're the only one who can follow me and get a standing ovation."

Her dynamic speaking style led her to help others who ran for office when they requested her assistance. With adjustments, she would elevate their speeches. She enjoyed lending her support to well-qualified candidates. Everyone knew how vociferous she could be. Once, the minister of a church invited Leona to be the guest speaker and deliver the sermon for that morning. By the time Leona finished speaking, she had the whole church, including a row of deacons, up on their feet. When she opened the doors to the church and welcomed people to come down to the front of the church to join as new members, more than twenty people marched down the aisle to join. The response astonished the minister. She was dynamic in any arena.

In a jovial voice, the minister told his congregation, "I knew judges wore black robes too, but I didn't know they could preach like that." Clearly, he was not prepared for my sister.

Twins for Justice Photo Credit: Victor A. Toliva

Part FOUR

2001–2009

CHAPTER 13

A Day That Changed My Life Forever

My Whole World Ended the Moment You Left Me

One particularly hot, sticky, and uncomfortable day in June, Leona and I were on our way to talk to a group of junior high school kids at Hope Academy in Detroit. It was their graduation day, and we were the commencement speakers. Leona and I had spoken at school graduations many times before, both separately and together.

Despite the stifling heat, Leona wanted us to wear our majestic judicial robes with the doctoral hoods and velvet tams. I told her they were too heavy and hot for the weather, but she said, "I know, but the sight of the black judicial robes on two twin judges will grab their attention and will be unforgettable."

As soon as we walked out, we heard the kids ooh and aah and then burst into applause. As hot as I was, I knew from their response that Leona had been right.

We felt the excitement of the young people as they jumped up from their seats clapping. Leona leaned over and whispered, "I told you."

Watching and feeling the enthusiasm of the kids sparked a flame inside me. As Leona stepped up to speak first, I watched the enthralled faces of the young people. Leona was animated and knew how to get a crowd to respond to her over-the-top statements. As Leona spoke, the kids spontaneously burst out clapping. Their faces beamed with excitement. Leona told them they could be anything they set their minds to be. They just had to set a goal and develop the steps that would take them to that goal, and it could happen.

I watched their bright young faces as Leona spoke. They did not even notice the heat. All they heard was her speaking. As I sat there waiting to speak next, I thought to myself; *Maybe, some of these children, by listening to us, will think, I too can become a judge, lawyer, or doctor. Look at them. If they did it, I can too.*

I was next. I was determined to keep the fire Leona had started going. As I spoke, I let them know that after they had set their goals, they had to ignore the naysayers who would tell them they couldn't do it, they weren't good enough, or it would be a waste of their time to try to achieve their dreams. I told them to keep dreaming and working toward their dreams and not to let anyone turn them around. Then I had them repeat after me, a phrase from an old black spiritual and they had to say it like they meant it; "I ain't gonna let no one turn me around! I ain't gonna let no one turn me around! I ain't gonna let no one turn me around!" I ended with a "Thank you." At that moment, the young people, their parents, and even the teachers rose to their feet, clapping. The crowd of more than three hundred people cheered. The children were energized.

Leona stepped up next to me, and we took a bow. Two boys came up to us at that moment and handed each of us a bouquet of flowers. We looked out at the crowd and bowed one more time.

Afterward, the parents came up to us to shake our hands and take pictures with us. They were as excited as their kids. One parent told us, "The two of you said what our kids needed to hear. In fact, us grown folks needed to hear the message you delivered today. We know you spoke to motivate our kids, but to be truthful, your words motivated some of us adults as well. I know you moved me, and I plan to change some things in my life. Like you said, it is not too late to dream and move on that dream. Thanks to both of you for waking me up this evening." The woman smiled, shook our hands, and then walked away.

We wanted to effect change and motivate the students, and we felt we had accomplished that. Inspiring and empowering some of the parents to reignite their lives was a bonus.

The evening had gone great, just as we had planned, and now it was time for us to go home and wind down. I had no inkling of the horrific evening that was waiting for us.

As we entered our residential community that evening, we talked about the excitement of the kids and how motivated they were. I dropped Leona off at her house, and she reminded me that it was our movie night. Leona and I lived just a few doors from each other and treated ourselves to a DVD movie a couple of nights a month. This time, our movie night was at Leona's house. I told her that as soon as I changed clothes, I would come to her house to see the movie. I had chosen a race car movie; *Gone in 60 Seconds*, as Leona liked sleek, fast cars and had owned a few in the past.

After being delayed on a phone call, I finally arrived at Leona's house. Gwen, one of our dearest friends that we considered a play cousin, arrived shortly after I did and joined us. We all settled in with popcorn and sodas.

"This movie is supposed to be really good," I said enthusiastically.

Leona and I were seated on opposite ends of the love seat. I started the movie, but Gwen and Leona kept cackling back and forth, so I had to restart the movie three times before they settled down to watch it. The movie had played for only fifteen minutes, when Leona kicked me.

Glancing at her, I asked, "Why did you kick me?" but she did not answer. Then I noticed her eyes looked dull and half closed. I called out "Leona! Leona!" She still did not answer me.

My anxiety heightened and my heart rate quickened each time I spoke to her. I kept calling her name but got no response. I scrambled off the love seat and called 911. Gwen and I got her on the floor and administered CPR but still got no response. I stayed on the phone, following the operator's instructions, until the paramedics arrived. I kept doing chest compressions. It felt as if the ambulance was taking forever to get to the house. When the ambulance finally got there, they parked in the wrong cul-de-sac, so we told them to run across the yard, which they did. Once they came in, one of the EMTs took over the chest compressions; the other got the stretcher ready. They put Leona on the stretcher and, running, carried her to the ambulance.

I jumped into the back of the ambulance to be with Leona. As the ambulance sped down the streets with her, the paramedics had her hooked up to a large machine that kept going up and down while compressing her chest, but her eyes were still blank and lifeless. I thought; *God, what does all this mean? Is my sister breathing? They are not saying anything.*

I asked if she was going to be all right, and one of the paramedics just stared at me and said, "I don't know." We arrived at the emergency entrance to the hospital, and they rushed my sister inside. I quickly followed.

At the hospital, the staff wheeled Leona into a room, where they immediately began working on her. In a state of confusion, I kept crying. I did not know what the hell was going on. No one was saying anything to me. I jumped up from the chair, I could not stay still. I paced back and forth. Gwen tried to console me, but nothing could do that.

Finally, the doctor came out. I saw the grim expression on his face. He was not smiling. He took off his gloves as he walked over to me and said, "I'm sorry. She is gone. Her heart stopped. We did everything we could do for her. She never regained consciousness."

In shock, I asked Gwen, "What did he just say to me? Did he say my sister was gone? Gone where? She is not gone; she is still here. She cannot be gone. We were just laughing and playing around fifteen minutes ago."

With tears in my eyes, I demanded to see my sister. They took me into the room. She just lay there. I yelled her name and laid my head on her side. As I did, the attendant who had taken all her jewelry off her said, "Here are her belongings. They appear to be expensive, so I thought I would give them to you."

With a swollen red face, I replied, "Thank you."

That night, June 8, 2001, God called my sister to heaven. I never got to say goodbye, but I held her hand that night and hugged her because I did not want to let her go. I had lost my best friend and confidante. We would never laugh or cry together again. Never again would she be able to console me in my darkest hours of insecurity or uncertainty. She was gone. Her death became a wound I would struggle to heal from.

◆ On the Night Leona Died, She Returned

That evening, people started coming to my house, but no people were allowed into my bedroom, which was located on the first floor, where I rested. I came out from time to time to greet people. Cliff, my sister's last former boyfriend, overwhelmed with grief, came over and wanted to give me an eight-by-ten framed picture of Leona he had taken the week before with his new digital camera. I thanked him, and Gwen and I placed her beautiful portrait on the black-and-white marble end table in the great room. Her portrait would be the first thing anyone saw when coming through the front door. There was a small framed picture of me and a male friend of mine on the same table, which I moved behind the large portrait of Leona. Before Gwen left to go down the street to Leona's house, where she had resided for several years, she came into my bedroom to make sure I was okay before she left.

She sat on the chair by my bed, talking to me, when I noticed something odd. I told Gwen, "Look at the black Chinese diorama. Do you notice anything different?"

Gwen turned, studied it, and said, "Yes, it's facing the window." The three-dimensional Chinese tableau consisted of lifelike sculpted figures of pagoda houses and panda bears made of cork, encased in a glass case within a black lacquered frame. Leona had bought two of them, one for herself and one for me. The one she had bought me sat on my black dresser in my bedroom, and it was always facing me.

Black lacquer gathers dust over time. I usually dusted the piece a few times a year. It had not been dusted for a long time, but strangely, as Gwen had said, it was no longer facing me. I asked Gwen, "Did you turn it toward the window?"

She said, "No."

We exchanged perplexed looks. I said, "Well, no one else has been in this room but you and me, and it can't turn by itself." I got up off the bed to examine the black frame. Gwen came over to look as well. The frame had a thick coat of dust on it, but there were no fingerprints on it, which would have been evidence that someone had turned it or moved it.

Gwen said, "Wow, there are no fingerprints—nothing—but it can't turn by itself."

"I know, but I didn't touch it."

"Neither did I."

I immediately thought of my sister. I had heard stories of the spirits of loved ones who had died coming back shortly after their deaths and doing something like that. They sometimes left an important personal item behind for others to find, signaling to their loved ones that they were all right and helping to relieve worry.

I said, "Gwen, this has got to be Leona." I smiled, and a tear rolled down my cheek. "This is a sign from her. She is saying she is okay. She doesn't want me to worry about her."

Gwen cried as she left my room.

I was restless, but every time I lay across my bed and closed my eyes, I saw my sister with her eyes half open. It was like a video playing in my head of me trying to help her with CPR compressions. I could not block that vision from my head. That image made it impossible for me to rest.

Later that night, when people had stopped coming to my home, I quietly made a final retreat to my bedroom. I lay across my bed, staring blankly at the television screen, trying desperately to make sense of what had just happened that evening, when suddenly, I heard Leona's name announced on the TV. I focused on the screen. It was the eleven o'clock news, and Leona's picture flashed across the screen as her death was announced. I saw it, but I was in a fog. I heard the news anchor say, "She was a judge well loved by many and will truly be missed." A few days later, I heard that all the parents and kids we had taken pictures with earlier that day were shocked, stunned, and overwhelmed with grief at the news of her death. No matter how many times I said to myself, "This can't be real," the TV announcement was a shock back into reality.

The only thing that gave me solace was the message Leona had left me by moving the artwork. I ended up weeping through the night, hoping to see another sign from her. Little did I know I would soon get my wish.

◆ Second Sign/ The Next Morning

Remember the portrait of her displayed on the marble end table? Well, the next morning, when Gwen came over, she said, "Leonia, the picture of Leona was moved last night. Someone changed how we placed it on the table. I saw the change in the placement of the pictures as I was leaving out the front door. You were so happy about Leona's message to you with the Chinese artwork last night that I figured the movement of the pictures could wait until the morning. But now I see you placed them back to the positions they were in. The small picture is once again behind her portrait."

Laughing, I said, "I didn't even know it had been moved. Well, I did not move it." She smiled and said, "If you did not move them, then I bet that was Leona. Leona must have moved it."

Knowingly, Gwen and I exchanged looks. The smile in my heart glowed because once again, I felt it was a sign that Leona was okay. Little did I realize that this would not be the last contact I had with Leona. Even death could not break our bond!

Those two forms of communication made me feel that Leona was all right; however, I still missed her. I missed hearing her voice.

Confirming my belief about the pictures, later that evening, the man who was in the small framed picture with me asked, "Who changed the pictures back? Last night, I changed them around, and I placed the small picture in front of the big picture because you could not see the little picture. It was in the shadow of the big picture of Leona."

I laughed at him and answered, "Leona moved it."

◆ The Next Day

For the remainder of the next day, I felt tired and discombobulated, as if I had not slept at all.

Leona's death had been so sudden and was therefore hard for me to comprehend. I went through several alternating mood changes that came in stages. I immediately felt sadness and then anger, pain, shock, and numbness. Eventually, I felt denial, as if it had not happened. I did not understand at the time that those were all the symptoms of grief. I would sit at the side of my bed and, after moments passed, try to get up, but the grip of depression pulled me back to the mattress. The voice in my head said, *"Why get up? For what"*?

The sadness ran so deep that it consumed me. Something that all-encompassing was never going to pass, I thought. As I walked around in a fog, numb to anything and everything, the tears flowing from my eyes would not stop. I did not know how to react to losing Leona.

In 1998, we had lost our mother, but her loss was different; it just was. Besides, Leona was with me and we had gone through the pain of our loss together. Now it was two and half years later and I was alone.

The day after her death, the doorbell rang nonstop. There were people all around me who loved me, but I still felt I was facing Leona's death alone.

People streamed into my house all day; continuously delivering food and giving their condolences. People were very kind. Gwen and my court reporter, Florence, helped greet the people who came to pay their respects. Chief Judge Atkins came to speak to me about the funeral arrangements. She indicated she was going to handle the location and selections for the memorial and the funeral and discuss them with my pastor, Reverend Lester. She agreed to discuss any other matters with my funeral committee consisting of friends.

To be honest, I was such a mess; I could not have done the funeral preparations without their love and support.

After speaking with my guests, I retreated to my bedroom for most of the day. I came out only a few times; I was not ready to handle a constant flow of people and see the worry-laden expressions on their faces. In the back of my mind, I knew these people loved me and were worried about me. Because grief had struck me so hard, they wondered what was going to happen to me.

◆ He Sent an Angel

As I lay across the bed, looking up at the ceiling, with the TV blaring in the background, I heard a knock on my bedroom door. *Who is it now?* I silently thought.

"Come in," I said wearily.

There stood my ex–marital counselor, Dr. Margaret Bennett. Her unannounced visit was a surprise. My somber eyes met hers, and she seemed to read my mind, answering my question before I could ask it.

"I saw the announcement about Leona's death on the eleven o'clock news last night, and I felt you needed me, so I came this morning."

Tears rolled down my face, as I thought; *I know she helped me before when I went through my divorce, but can she save me now?* I hoped so because I felt lost. Again, without a question from me, she informed me she was licensed to also counsel on grief and loss, not just marital issues.

She gently sat down at the end of the bed. She could see from my swollen, tear-stained face that I had not slept all night. To confirm what she suspected, she asked me if I had slept or eaten anything, and I responded, "No." She insisted I had to get sleep, and I had to eat, even if I wasn't hungry. I quietly nodded in agreement.

"Have someone call your medical doctor to explain about the death of your sister. The doctor will call you in a prescription, to help you sleep." Then she proceeded to ask me some additional questions.

Fighting back tears, I answered her questions. With my answers in mind, she proceeded to explain to me the meaning of grief. The explanation was to help me understand what I was feeling and going through. She knew how close Leona and I were. That was why she had felt she had to come over right away.

I expressed my feelings of emptiness and told her how different I felt—that I did not think I would ever stop crying. She kept assuring me that what I felt was normal and that I was going through the stages of grief. After talking to me for a little more than an hour, she told me she would be back the next day. For some reason, talking with her helped lift the gloomy cloud hanging over me.

Dr. Bennett, as promised, came over every day for a week. I knew she cared about me, because coming over to clients' houses to counsel them was not something she was known to do. She normally had clients scheduled back-to-back, so for her to do that for me meant canceling or changing her clients' appointments in order to see me, which was nothing less than amazing.

I felt God must have sent her to help me, because in one week of talking to me, she had me out of the bed. I began to greet people who came to the house. She had worked a miracle for me at a time in my life when I felt as if the bottom of my world had just dropped out. Dr. Bennett provided guidance and strength for me.

I was glad she came. I started sleeping and nibbling on food again after taking the medication, as she had directed. I looked forward to talking to Dr. Bennett, who seemed to know exactly what to say to help me understand the upheaval I was going through. Only God and she knew what I was going through; I did not. I told her that when my mother had died, the loss had not felt like this, and she explained that the bond Leona and I had had was much different from the one I had with my mother. She also explained that it did not mean I had loved my mother less, just differently.

After that first week, I told her I would come over to her office after the funeral. We agreed we would start out by meeting three days a week, and as I got stronger, we would adjust the schedule to two days a week. She wrote a letter to the chief judge of our court, explaining what I was going through and the counseling plan she had for me and its duration. She indicated she would contact the court if she felt an extension was necessary.

Dr. Bennett was my lifeline. Without her intervening so quickly in my life, I easily could have slipped into a serious form of depression, which is like grief on steroids. My visits with Dr. Bennett made me stronger and stronger. She helped me through the funeral and helped me mourn and heal. She gave me the tools I needed to cope with the grief I was experiencing. With her assistance, I was able to acknowledge and not deny the impact Leona's death was having on me. When I acknowledged it, she helped me deal with it. She explained that the pain I was going through was part of the grieving process and was going to take some time to work through.

"You have to let the grief work," she said.

She saw me for the next three months every week. In addition to seeing her, with Dr. Bennett's blessing, I joined a support group organized by the hospital where Leona had died. I discovered that talking with people who were facing similar challenges and experiences with loss made me feel connected to them and not isolated. Some members of the group had good, practical advice they offered to me.

Being lucky enough to have counseling at my disposal prevented me from freefalling into the world of depression. Instead, I was strong enough, with the assistance of Attorney Carl Bolden, to set up the Judges Leona and Leonia Lloyd Twins for Justice Endowment

Scholarship Fund at Wayne State University Law School in my sister's honor before I returned to work. I simultaneously set up an identical endowment scholarship fund in the urban affairs department for undergraduate students at Wayne State University.

Me presenting the first, "Twins For Justice Scholarship" to Ms. Colina Roberts at WSU Law School Honors Convocation. Photo Credit: Michigan Chronicle

After I completed my three months of counseling, Dr. Bennett refused to take any money from me for her services. What would I pay to someone like Dr. Bennett, who saved my life? There was not enough money in Fort Knox to pay her. I want you to understand, I was lost, I had absolutely nothing left to fight with, and all my hope was gone. As the words to the song, *I Look To You*, as sung by Whitney Houston, perfectly captured my state of mind, following my sister's death: *"After all I had been through, who on earth can I turn to, when all my strength was gone, I looked to you"*. That person I looked to was Dr. Margaret Bennett. She was the angel that God had sent to me. While writing this book Dr Bennett passed away. However, I got a chance to let her know I had written about her and how she had saved my life. With a lovely smile she responded, "Oh my!". I am eternally grateful to her.

Dr. Margaret Bennett, PhD, and Leona at the Barristers' Ball

◆ Passing on the Lesson

Dr. Bennett taught me the importance of immediate counseling. When people are at the end of their rope and their world has caved in, you cannot put them on hold while seeking out help for them. You must act quickly because their lives might depend on it.

Grief, loss, and depression are emergency calls that must be answered right away. As a judge in veterans' treatment court and drug treatment court, I followed the lessons of Dr. Bennett. In urgent situations, I arranged for immediate counseling by cutting through the red tape. I found that immediate help restored hope in people's lives, and they found new reasons to live. That process had worked for me in my life and I made sure to make it work in the lives of others.

CHAPTER 14

The Funeral—for Whom?

THE END OF THE ROAD

It was six o'clock in the morning on June 16. The sun had already come out. My alarm buzzed, but I hit the button to turn it off because I was already awake. I lay there thinking about the memorial service held at New Greater Grace Church the day before; Leona had received plaques from many elected dignitaries honoring her work in the community as a teacher, attorney, and judge. The reality hit me that it was the second day of the two-day ceremony; it was also the day of the funeral. I just lay there with thoughts flying through my head. Within a few minutes, Gwen came in to wake me up, only to find me staring at the walls of my room.

I told her I was already awake and had slept for only a couple of hours. She retreated to the kitchen. If it had not been for the medication the doctor had ordered for me, I would not have slept those few hours.

I glanced at my silent phone. Normally, Leona called me to make sure my butt was up, but there would be no call that morning. It was the day I would bury Leona, my twin sister. I knew I was supposed to get up and get ready, but my legs would not move. I turned on the TV in my room just to have some noise. It did not matter which station the TV was on as long as the noise drowned out the voices in my head that kept repeating the same questions; *Why her? Why now? God, why did you call her to you? Why now? Dear Lord, she was doing your work here on Earth. She was your tool, your instrument—one who was helping guide young people away from dangerous paths and who gave older people hope and new reasons to live. So why take her now? Why? She was your servant. Why take her?*

I did not want to hear the questions in my head because I knew I would get no answers. I knew I was not supposed to ask God why, but I could not help it because his taking her did not make any sense to me. I had to ask. My head could not stop asking. I picked up my heart-shaped gold locket from the nightstand. I pushed the button, and it opened. Leona had insisted we get matching lockets shortly after our mother passed. I looked at the picture of my mother on one side of the locket, and on the other side was a picture of Leona and me in our judicial robes.

The Twins for Justice. I started to cry because that was who we had been, and that was what people had called us. *But who am I now? She is gone, so who am I?* Tears fell down my cheeks as I stared at our picture and called out my sister's name; "Leona, who am I now? When you left, a part of me left too, so who am I?" Leona always had had an answer for every question, but that morning, all I could hear was the TV, which was not doing a good job of blocking out the unending questions in my head. I kept thinking her passing was not just her death but also the death of my life as I knew it. That day, there would be two funerals.

Returning to my room, Gwen knocked on the door and entered to tell me to come get some breakfast. I told her I was not hungry. She sat next to me on the bed and said, "It's going to be all right, Leonia. I'm here, and I'm not going anywhere." She hugged me and handed me some tissues to wipe my eyes.

I mustered a half smile and said, "I'll get some coffee, but I don't want any food because my stomach may flip."

I went into the kitchen and got a cup of coffee. I half listened to my aunt Kathryn, engaged in a conversation about things to take my mind off the funeral, but I was in such a fog that I did not really hear what she was saying.

After a few sips of coffee, I went back to my room to get dressed. I had picked out a white suit with lapels embellished with sequins and beads. I thought; *Leona would have liked this suit. I wonder if she can see it.* The tears started to flow again.

I laid out all my clothes and then sat at the bottom of my bed and said: "*This is the day I am to bury my sister, my twin, my partner in life. But I cannot wrap my brain around this. It does not seem real. I am not ready to say goodbye to her, because I do not want her to go. She cannot leave me here alone. Leona, what am I supposed to do without you?*"

At that moment, Aunt Kathryn came in and said, "Baby, I know that burying your sister today is going to be the hardest thing you are ever going to have to do in life, but I want you to remember one thing: God always leaves the strongest one behind because he knows you are strong and will be all right."

Wiping my eyes and shaking my head, I said, "I don't feel strong."

"But you are, and God knows it too," she said. With that, she hugged me, got up from my bed, and added, "Remember what I said."

I nodded. "Yes."

◆ The Procession

I finished getting dressed and joined the people who had gathered in the great room of my home. As soon as I entered the room, everyone became silent. What could they have said to make the situation better? Nothing.

I eased to the kitchen and took the medicine the doctor had given me. Then I stepped into the limo waiting outside the front door. As I walked to the car, I kept thinking; *I have not talked to my sister all week.* None of it felt real; yet I felt alone. I could not get it out of my head that I had not talked to my sister that morning. That refrain was like a broken record playing over and over in my brain.

In the limo, I heard people talking, but I did not know what they were saying. I did not tune in to any of them. Before I knew it, we were at Calvary Baptist Church for the funeral. I slowly got out of the limo, when my eyes gazed at the police motorcade that stood ready to accompany us to the burial grounds, just as they had done for our mother. The situation was becoming too real for me. I looked at them and said silently; *You cannot be here for her. No! Leona cannot be leaving here.*

Someone held my hand and arm, guiding me into the church. The grip was strong as I inched down the aisle toward the casket. Things seemed to be moving in slow motion. I knew people were with me, but I felt alone.

As I walked, I looked to the right and saw a sea of black judicial robes—ninety judges paying their last respects to Leona. I walked to the front of the church, where the casket was positioned. Next to the casket was Leona's judicial robe mounted on a stand. My eyes slowly shifted from the robe to my sister. She was dressed in the red suit trimmed in red fox that she liked so much. I went up to the casket and started talking to her as I fixed her hair on her forehead.

"Ona, you can't go and leave me. Ona, I love you. I did not get the chance to say goodbye because I did not know you were going to leave, and I was right there. Ona, I love you."

My sister appeared to be asleep, but she did not answer me. My sister was gone. She was really gone.

The service started, and so did the tears. I looked back at the judges, and I saw our good friend Miriam's tear-stained face. Yes, this was real. As the service continued, people got up to speak, but I focused on my sister. My body ached with pain I had never experienced before. My brain kept screaming; *This is real! She is gone! She will never talk to me again. She will never be there to give me advice. Ona is gone.*

My body trembled and rocked as I sat there, listening to my brain speak to me. The family was told to come up and say their last goodbyes before they closed the casket. The thought of that casket closing on Ona was almost unbearable. I screamed inside; *Do not cover up my sister! Do not close that casket! Please do not close it. She will be all alone, and so will I.* I closed my eyes for a few seconds as they locked the casket. Then they pulled my blanket of red roses over the top of the casket. The service went on, but I was fixated on the casket that my Ona was in.

I remembered the night my mother died in the hospital. I came home that night and stared at the sofa, where she normally would have been sitting while watching TV. When I would come through the door, she would always say, "Hi, baby." But that night, there was no greeting, because our mother was gone. I screamed at the top of my lungs, as I sat on the sofa.

That was what I felt like doing at that moment at Leona's funeral. Maybe that would have helped to release this pain I felt paralyzing my whole body.

When the service was over and it was time to leave, I followed the casket as the pallbearers lifted it and carried it on their shoulders. I could not take my eyes off the casket. I did not want to leave her alone. We had never been separated to the point of being unable to contact each other.

Following the casket with Judge Craig Strong leading the way

◆ The Drive to the Mausoleum

The funeral procession drove by the Thirty-Sixth District Court, our workplace. Outside, lined up in front and down the side of the court building, were the Thirty-Sixth District Court bailiffs. They saluted my sister as she passed by one final time. Tears streamed down my cheeks at the show of respect for her. I thought; *Ona, this is for you.*

The 36th District Court Bailiffs saluting Leona's casket in front of the Court

We soon arrived at the mausoleum, where Reverend Lester had arranged for a saxophonist to play beautiful music. My minister said a prayer, and as they lifted and placed Leona's casket in the crypt next to our mother's crypt, Reverend Lester released a cage full of white doves. I looked up to the glass ceiling in the mausoleum, where the blue sky was showing, and I said in my mind; *Are you here with me, Leona? Do you see this, Leona? They are placing you next to Mama, but you know that already. Give Mama a hug for me, and please watch over me.*

Leona and I had come there many times to talk to our mother's spirit, and now I knew where to come to talk to my sister.

After the funeral, in addition to my question about my identity now that my twin was gone, there was a second question still nagging me: What had happened to my sister?

Where had she gone? She seemed to have disappeared into thin air.

Late in the afternoon, as I was driven home from the funeral, all I could think about was that I was thankful to have Dr. Bennett to turn to, because I knew it was impossible for me to get through this loss on my own. She was my saving grace.

Life was never the same after I lost my twin sister. She used to call me every morning to make sure I was up, and in the evening, we called each other to make sure we were both watching the hottest TV shows. After her death, the phone became deadly silent because our calls had ended. The list of things that no longer took place between us daily was a long one. My twin sister was gone, and a part of me was gone also. I knew that recovering from grief and removing the weight of pain and depression I was under was not going to be easy. In fact, to be honest, I did not believe it was even possible, because we had come to the end of the road, and I could not let go.

It was Dr. Bennett's counseling sessions that got me ready to deal with my new life and all the hurdles I would have to overcome. I did not know what that life would be like, but she prepared me to walk into it.

◆ The Autopsy

I had to wait six weeks to get the results of an autopsy from the medical examiner's office. It was six weeks later to the day when I sat with my minister, Reverend Lester and placed a call to the medical examiner. I found out that the cause of death had been a plaque buildup in the main artery of her heart causing a hardening of the arterial walls. It had closed off the blood flow to her heart, which had caused her heart to stop beating. It was called "sudden death." I asked the medical examiner if the hyperthyroid condition she had dealt with for the last eleven years of her life had a direct effect on the cause of her death? He responded, "It would have been a major contributing factor to the plaque buildup in the arterial walls of her heart". I did not have a thyroid condition, so I had escaped having the same malady. Unknown to her, she had a chronic disease called arteriosclerosis. At least I finally knew the cause of her death.

CHAPTER 15

Returning to the Courtroom

ORDER MY STEPS IN YOUR WORD

It was getting close to the time for me to return to my job. With all of Dr. Bennett's help, I was ready. However, there was one thing I had to do first. I explained to my therapist that it was important for me to place a portrait of my sister and me, as well as a solo picture of her, in my courtroom before I returned to the bench. Dr. Bennett thought that was a wonderful idea.

On a crisp day in October, the Friday of the week before I was to return, I had some of my friends accompany me to my courtroom and assist me in hanging the large airbrushed portrait of Leona and me. Word traveled fast that I was in the building. Upon hearing of my return, Chief Judge Atkins came immediately to my courtroom to greet me. She saw what we were doing, grabbed a hammer, and helped us hang it. She amazed me with her skills.

After the pictures were hung, I sat in the gallery of the courtroom and gazed at them. Even though I had tears in my eyes, I felt an unexplainable peacefulness with her picture there in my courtroom. I knew every time I entered that room, I would walk past her, and that made me feel good inside. I had Leona's picture positioned in my courtroom where I could always see it. It was a constant reminder and statement to all who saw it of our loving bond as identical twins. She was gone in the flesh, but I could hold on to her spirit and memories. I believed glancing at an image of her face gave me a sense of security that she was watching over me as my guardian angel. I could feel her spirit.

The following Monday morning, which marked three and a half months after Leona's death, I returned to work. I knew it was going to be difficult. Just the ride into work was going to be hard. Most mornings, we would ride to work together and soulfully sing songs in the car at the top of our lungs. Can you picture two rock-and-roll judges bouncing their heads and singing at the top of their lungs to "I'm a Survivor" or "Bootylicious" by Destiny's Child while driving to work at 7:45 a.m.? Or singing to "Stomp" by Kirk Franklin and God's Property? Well, that was us. Now the car would remain half empty and silent. Her courtroom was next door to mine, and so were her judicial chambers; now they would be empty. There would be no more morning coffee sips in her office before we took the bench and no more lunches together either. Now I would eat alone. Everything would be drastically different and painful for me. But my therapist and I believed after three months of group counseling and individual therapy, I was ready to resume my duties as a judge.

Under Dr. Bennett's directive, I would hold court for only half a day for the first thirty days. She knew that sitting on the bench was going to feel like an out-of-body experience for me now that Leona was gone. She did not want it to overwhelm me.

With time restrictions and all, I still finished my docket, even if it meant staying an extra hour. I could not let people sit and wait for another judge to come handle my remaining cases. That was just how I was.

A week after I returned to work, unbeknownst to me, a man came to my courtroom and sat for two days. On the second day, I granted his request to speak to me. He walked up to the podium and introduced himself. He told me that Leona had brought his daughter up to the bench to sit with her when her high school class visited her courtroom several years ago. He wanted me to know how impactful that visit had been, because his daughter, now in law school, had been inspired to study law after her courtroom visit as a high school senior. He wanted to remind me that my sister had not died in vain. He said Leona had a huge, inspirational impact on young people like his daughter.

"That's her legacy and yours," he said.

With tears welling in my eyes, I motioned with my hands for him to approach the bench. I shook his hands and I gratefully thanked him for coming to deliver that beautiful message in person. He truly touched my heart.

Sometimes, after dealing with defendants and finishing a difficult case, I would glance at my sister's solo portrait, smile, and think about what Leona would have done. I would think about the legacy she left. All the pictures of Leona remained on the walls of my courtroom until I retired as a judge.

Our favorite portrait that was displayed in my courtroom until I retired
Photo credit: Victor A. Toliva

◆ God's Plan for My Rebirth as a Drug Court Judge

Shortly after I returned to work, I went back to handling the dockets that had previously been assigned to me. I felt God was eventually going to reveal to me what he wanted from me and exactly who I was going to be now that he had taken Leona. Not long after returning to work, I was approached and asked if I would work in the drug treatment court at Thirty-Sixth District Court, the same specialty court Leona had been invited to join right before her death. I knew Leona had wanted to handle the drug court docket to help defendants with their drug addictions and she adamantly had wanted me to team up with her to do it. She had felt that together we could increase the enrollment in drug treatment court.

Since her request for me to be allowed to join her in the drug court was denied, Leona had turned down the offer for drug court. When the offer was made to me after her death, I felt Leona would have wanted me to work in the drug court, because that way, I could continue to help the drug-addicted defendants we were already helping in our individual courtrooms. Additionally, that was what we both had wanted to do in the first place. But now I would be doing it on a much wider scale and with more resources. I accepted the position in drug treatment court.

In January 2002, I became a drug court judge. It felt like a smooth transition from the monitoring of misdemeanor cases involving drug- or alcohol-addicted defendants to the monitoring done in drug treatment court. It was similar.

The focus and dedication I put into helping the defendants in that program, by God's grace, took the focus off my own grief and loss.

After working in drug court for the first six months and helping it to expand to include many more people who needed help, I received my answer from God.

My courtroom became an empowerment zone for the people in my drug treatment court. Empowerment of the defendants was clearly what Leona had envisioned. God had ordered my steps, as my sister often had said. While presiding over that court, I helped the homeless, the destitute, and people who had been beaten up and beaten down by life. I helped those who practiced the act of prostitution in order to supply their drug addictions, as well as veterans, men and women who had put their lives on the line for this country. Many vets felt the country had turned its back on them when they came home with addictions as their souvenirs from their time in the service.

However, walking down the path called drug treatment court, I learned just how deep the roots of deception can grow in a person with an addiction. When you place those persons in drug court, the roots grow even deeper. My drug court team and I felt as if we were in an exhausting car chase with the defendants. We tried to cut through all the lies and deception to discover the truth and then reach out and throw them a life preserver so they would not drown in a sea of drugs, alcohol, and lies.

◆ The Many Smiling Faces and Forms of Deception

When defendants are ordered to drug treatment court, they are aware they are having a serious problem with drugs and/or alcohol. Drug court is the last resort and the last chance a judge gives a defendant as an alternative to jail.

In drug treatment court, defendants knew their usage of drugs had to stop. However, even understanding that, many defendants came with their own plans. It did not matter that they signed a drug court contract agreeing to stop the usage of alcohol and drugs, go to counseling several times a week, and do a maximum of three random urine drops per week, they were looking for a loop hole. They knew that if urine screenings exposed any drug or alcohol use by them, they would face sanctions for violating the terms of the contract. However, some defendants decided they were not going to stop using. They felt they just had to figure out a way to get around the screens. Thus, the deception games began.

Having been prewarned by their previous probation officers that they would have to give a urine screen on the first day, some came in game-playing right out of the gate.

Some came in with pill bottles filled with urine from persons they knew to be clean, such as a young child. They would keep the bottles in their underwear, whether men or women. They did not understand that urine brought in from the outside was not going to be body temperature, so the paper cups they handed the lab techs would be cold to the touch, indicating the samples hadn't come from the defendants. Those defendants were busted on their first day.

Some defendants were a little more sophisticated and came in wearing a Whizzinator, which is a device that consists of a fake flesh-colored penis, available in several skin tones, filled with previously collected clean urine or synthetic urine. It is used to fool the tester with a urine sample that is not fresh but contains no drugs. Some of the devices come with a motor or heat pack to keep the urine at body temperature. The ones I saw in my courtroom had no motors or packs, and the urine from the device was not body temperature. Busted! However, I need to point out that the use of a device of this nature evidences a high level of deception. Today, Whizzinator kits are very obtainable and can be bought online and delivered to your front door.

Many defendants were caught with false urine. Some admitted they were prepared to come to each status hearing with a vial of false urine because they had a refrigerator full of previously purchased urine. They had gotten away with it in other courts, so they thought it would work in mine.

One defendant in court was adamant that there must have been a mistake with our machines because she was clean and had not used heroin for months. I looked at her, smiled, and said, "Are you sure about that?"

She replied, "Yes." However, the test came back positive for cocaine, not heroin.

When she came back from her jail sanction, she decided to be honest with the court and said that the person she had gotten the urine from had told her he had never done heroin; however, the individual had failed to tell her he had used cocaine. She could not believe she had gone to jail for another person's usage. I said, "You went to jail for also giving a failed test because it tested positive for cocaine, even though that was not your drug of choice. I believe, if we had tested urine from you, the same day you gave us the false sample, we probably would have seen a dirty screen for heroin."

"You're right," she replied.

"If you only had told the truth about using drugs, your sanction would have been reduced by half."

She agreed with me.

In dealing with the faces and forms of deception, I had to focus on getting to the truth. But oh, what a wrestling match: them versus me. They would ask themselves, "Do I tell her the truth, or do I tell her this foolproof, surefire, undetectable bet-your-bottom-dollar lie?" It was obvious in their courtroom testimony that they had worked hard at crafting their lies. That was why they prepared answers for questions they were never asked. I heard all kinds of crazy reasons why drugs or large amounts of alcohol were found in a urine screen, including the possibility of finding crushed cocaine residue dust or opiates in unwashed dirty cups, glasses, or thermoses; going to parties and unknowingly drinking spiked beverages from a punch bowl prepared by other people; or drinking from a large juice bottle in a refrigerator in someone's house that didn't belong to the defendant. The ankle tethers the defendants wore would tell me when they began drinking, how much they drank, and when they finally stopped drinking. The numbers did not lie. As time passed, I could see the alcohol amounts rise on the tether graphs. After being caught, many would ask for permission to comment, and I would grant it. The defendants anxiously waiting in the courtroom for their case to be heard would say, "Hey, man [or girl], you are wasting our time and the court's time. It is obvious you are lying. But hey, just tell the truth, because this court will break you some slack if you tell the truth. I know I wish I had told the truth, but I had to learn the hard way. Do not let her smile fool you. Man, she will send you to jail."

That response from drug treatment court participants was heard often. They knew if a defendant continued to lie, he or she would receive a jail sanction. Many defendants returning from a jail sanction, discovered that the truth was the best future route to take. Listening to the defendants in drug treatment court was always a teachable moment for everyone.

While playing the deception game with defendants, I heard stories that made me laugh so hard tears rolled down my cheeks. I heard stories about strong liquor in fruit balls floating in large bowls filled with punch. The balls were guaranteed to give all who drank the liquid a punch and based on the high alcohol numbers produced, they did not disappoint. That applied as well to the unbelievable stories about Jell-O shots, which were cubes of Jell-O that had liquor injected into them. Then there were stories of aftershave men placed on themselves before they went out for the evening. Those were fun for me to dissect. I loved explaining how quickly aftershave numbers dissipated from the register, while the numbers for alcohol consumed orally would stick around for quite a while and increase. Yeah, I enjoyed how creative the defendants were, but I enjoyed it even more when they finally learned they were wasting their time and their breath.

A great illustration of how the drug treatment court participants learned the value of truth was shown when one young man's case was called. His case followed the case of a defendant who had just been locked up for the large number of positive screens he had acquired the prior month. He knew the previous guy had been lying, and the tests showed he had boozed it up all month. When it was the second man's turn for his case to be heard, he said, "Judge, I am not going to waste your time or the court's time by lying to you about my two positive screens. You have heard enough lies told in here today. My screens were positive because I used, and there was another time I used that did not show up in my monthly screen, but I want to be honest. I am here in this program for help, but if I keep lying, I am just wasting my time, so I am being honest. Also, I want to point out to the court I have six months clean, but this month, I had some weak moments. However, you can see that the following three weeks, I was clean, and I did not have any missed screens. I knew when I went to be tested, they were going to find the two positive screens, but I went and got tested anyway. I wanted to be honest and responsible for my actions. Please take that into consideration when you give me my sanction."

When a defendant spoke his truth, as that young man did, even while understanding that the truth could hurt him, I always took that truth into consideration. Unlike other defendants who had sweat rolling down their foreheads as they stated their lies, that young man was quick, to the point, and truthful. He received no jail time for that sanction. Instead, he received intensified counseling to strengthen his reserve and community service to be performed at a place that would remind him he was on the right track. My drug treatment court participants seemingly learned wisdom quickly, because I heard truthful confessions like his more than four hundred times. They learned that truth was the cornerstone to recovery. Our motto in drug court was generated from a religious song, "We Fall Down, but We Get Up." They had to learn they may fall, but to win, they had to get back up, dust themselves off, and learn from their mistakes.

My team and I learned that the defendants' addictions made them lie to their families and friends for many years, and now it was time to lie to the court. Being honest is a hard pill to swallow for a chronic liar, but soon every defendant in drug treatment court who started out lying had to decide as to whether he or she could or could not do the program. Simply stated, they could tell no more lies unless they wanted to go to jail and do their time.

In the beginning of my tenure as a drug treatment court judge, the majority lied at first. They ended up sitting in a cold jail for several days with no homies (friends) visiting them, only the parents, and no money to spend in the commissary, because it took a long time to process spendable cash, and usually the defendants were released before they got a chance to spend it.

After experiencing that wonderful vacation, the participants quickly learned that lies did not win in drug treatment court; that jail was not a place they wanted to be. No drug was worth their freedom.

CHAPTER 16

A Story from a Drug Court Graduate

◆ Introduction to Ernest Black

In the cat-and-mouse deception game defendants played when they first entered drug court, as the judge, I had to balance out the treatment with the punishment for defendants who had their heart set on beating the system. Unlike with regular judicial dockets, I had my hands full.

Below is a story told in the defendant's own words and from his perspective. This story shows the dramatic change in one defendant from his initial defiance to the program to his 180-degree turn around to acceptance, growth, and a new life. When you read his story, know the frustration I went through and the emotional toll it took on me as a judge to try to make him see the light. I had him go back and forth, speaking with me and then the case manager; I had him watch drug court to learn about its benefits; and then he came back in front of me again. That went on for a few hours because I refused to give up on him quickly. No matter how frustrating the statements he made to me were, I could see something good in him, and I was not going to give up on him, even if he wanted me to. He was butting heads with a stubborn, determined judge who refused to give up.

I had to try everything I knew, including outside help, to reach him. By the end of my time with him in drug court, he became a positive role model whom all the members of drug court, including the entire team, looked up to. The young man turned his life around, and he continues to this day to help prepare food for Mariner's Inn, a treatment facility, on the weekends. Mariner's Inn is the treatment facility that helped him when he was in my program.

Today Mr. Black has a busy schedule restoring historic homes to their pristine beauty in Detroit as well as all throughout Michigan. His work has a sense of spirituality in it, and that is probably why it is so lovely and highly sought after. Even though he is extremely busy, he still makes time to give back to those in need. I am sure just his presence at Mariner's Inn is an indirect message to the men who are going through situations they feel are hopeless. Hopefully, they think to themselves; *If Mr. Black can do it, then maybe I can do it too.* The hundred-watt smile that radiates from Mr. Black, lets others know that his faith is strong, and nothing is going to turn him around. His life exemplifies faith, hope, truth, compassion, and leadership.

Breaking and Entering Life

ERNEST BLACK

I was arrested for breaking and entering inside of the Michigan Consolidated Gas building near the Motor City Casino. I was taken to the Thirty-Sixth District Court. The judge asked me why I was in the building. And I told her I was scrapping to support my drug habit. The judge asked me if I wanted to straighten my life out. I said I did. She said that her friend was in charge of drug court and that she would send me to her. She then told me, "If it were up to me, I'd lock your ass up. It's people like you who make it bad for the city." I decided to go to drug court. I did not want to go to jail because of my addiction, but I also did not want to give up my habit. So, it was either go to jail or go to drug court.

My next stop was Judge Lloyd's drug court. There, I watched her give people an opportunity to get their lives together through treatment. I was resistant because I had never been to treatment before. After fifteen years on the streets, there was no way I was going to let that judge restrict me! When it was my turn at the podium, I made up my mind not to go to treatment. She could send me to the Dickerson Jail. It was overcrowded anyway, so the longest I would be there was ninety days. So, when she said I had two choices, either I would go to jail or to treatment, I didn't mind going to jail. The most I would get was ninety days. Jail was something I knew about and it definitely sounded better than treatment. Free bed and board for a few months at an overcrowded jail worked for me.

Judge Lloyd and my case manager debated off and on the record with me for about a total of two hours about treatment. I told her, "No, I'm not going." My probation officer, Ms. Brimage, couldn't do anything but shake her head at my stubbornness.

Judge Lloyd tried to tell me about the benefits of treatment and being clean. I just told her to send me to jail. She said, "Okay, I'm going to lock you up, but I'm bringing you back in three days. Then you can tell me if you still want to stay there." Sure enough, she brought me back and asked me again: Did I want to go to treatment, or did I still want to go to jail?

I said, "You can lock me back up." The way I saw it, I had three days served.

But then Judge Lloyd told me, "Mr. Black, have a seat in the back of my courtroom. Whether you believe me or not, I see a lot of good in you. I am not going to just let you slip through the cracks. I'm going to have someone talk to you."

The guy's name was Benjamin T. We stepped out of the courtroom into the hallway. My first question to him was "What are you going to tell me that she didn't?"

He confided, "I know what you're going through. I've been where you are, Ernest. Just talk to me."

"If I were to go into treatment, where would I go after that? I'll just be turned back on the street with nowhere to go," I insisted.

He said, "No, that's not true. There is something called transitional housing. It's a place you can go after treatment, so you don't have to go back on the street." He went on to say he'd been through drug court, and Judge Lloyd was only looking out for my best interest.

"Slow down, and give yourself a break," he suggested.

"If I go to treatment, I'm going to need some money for cigarettes. I'm gonna need some money for phone calls and such," I told him.

He promised me he would bring me the things I needed, and he promised he would be there if I ever needed someone to talk to. I could call him anytime. At first, I didn't believe him. He was just trying to talk me into drug court.

I thought about it for a minute and decided maybe it wouldn't be a bad thing for me after all, but what choice did I have? I did not want to go to jail for years; I was actually tired of being on the streets. So, I told Benjamin, "Okay, I'm ready to go back in." He seemed to be genuine, so after I walked back in, I decided to take his advice and try treatment.

Judge Lloyd brought me back in front of the podium and asked me again, "Do you want to go to treatment, or do you want to go to jail?"

My response was "Okay, I'll try treatment."

Two days later, I was in Sobriety House. It wasn't such a bad place, but it wasn't easy.

I was real nervous my first day in treatment. I did not know what to expect. More importantly, I did not think anyone could really help me beat my addiction. I was up all night, thinking about leaving the next morning, but I gave my word that I would stay. That next morning, I woke up to didactics, something I had never heard of before. It was in that didactics class that I began to learn about the twelve-step program and myself. To admit I was powerless over my addiction and that my life had become unmanageable. It was the first step on my road of recovery.

After realizing that my life could be different and that my addiction did not have total control of my life, I began to see there was another way. Opening up in groups and being totally honest with myself, I came to understand that I couldn't do this alone and that I needed the help of Narcotics Anonymous.

For the first time in a long time, I did not feel alone. I met a lot of people I could relate to—people who had the same background I did. There were so many people willing to reach out to me and pull me out of the darkness I was in. It humbled me to know people truly cared and that I could also care in return. And as promised, Benjamin kept his word. He brought me the two things I asked for, and he stayed to visit with me for numerous weeks on end. We made a bond that lasted for years.

Days turned into weeks, and weeks turned into months. I saw myself growing and learning every day, and I was able to see a pathway for a better life for myself. I was no longer afraid of the hard work it would take to stay sober. As a matter of fact, I welcomed the challenge. It made me stronger. I was determined to see this all the way to the end. I kept thinking about what the judge had told me—*that she saw good in me*—and that also kept me moving forward because I eventually started to see the good in myself.

Ninety days were quickly approaching. All I could think about was how grateful I was for making the best choice in my life. I never thought my life would turn out this way. Clean and sober for the first time in years.

Once I completed the treatment program, I went into transitional housing, where I gained employment as a dishwasher. While there, I took a culinary cooking course they offered and enjoyed it. I found that cooking was something I loved to do. From there, I moved on, with the help of one of the employees, to the position of a cook. Then I worked for DRRM (Detroit Recovery Rescue Mission) for three years, holding down the position of cook until the restaurant I worked in closed. Afterward, I got a job with a construction company working in Brush Park, building new homes. I go back from time to time to DRRM to volunteer where it all started, just to stay connected.

I thank Judge Lloyd for believing in me and for helping me become a productive member of society. I never thought my life would turn out this way, to live a life without the use of drugs. I am eternally grateful to her and DRRM.

CHAPTER 17

Project Fresh Start: A Way Out of the World of Prostitution

A BRIDGE OVER TROUBLED WATERS

My colleagues and I had to deal with prostitution cases in our courtrooms all the time. After all, prostitution has been described as "the world's oldest profession"; it is as old as Father Time himself. The ladies and men who practiced the commercial sex trade were creatures of the nightlife and lived in abandoned buildings or on the streets. It was not unusual to find them eating out of garbage cans if they had used up their money on drugs. Their way of life was a means of survival. Some of the ladies came from well-to-do or middle-class families, and others came from poverty. Some were educated, and some were not. They came from all walks of life. Those who participated in prostitution were given tickets and ended up in our overcrowded jails.

The activity of prostitution crept out of the inner city to the beautiful residential neighborhoods. Those neighborhoods complained with loud voices to the mayor's office. They wanted him to do something about the problem because it was getting out of control. They complained it was not unusual to see women performing sex in broad daylight in cars while young children were coming home from school and could view the acts. The ladies were addicted to drugs and only cared about making money for that next fix or that rock. Their drug addiction had reduced them to their lowest existence. Selling their bodies was a means to an end to get the money they needed to fuel their drug habit and avoid being dope sick.

The problem of prostitution often goes hand in hand with street-level drug trafficking. It is seen daily in most large cities, and Detroit was no different. In the past, our sheriff's department and police department had done a good job of picking up people, giving them tickets, and locking them up, but that was not working. The ladies would be released and back out on the streets before the end of the day. In the past, drug court had always dealt with drug issues but not ones specifically targeted toward prostitutes. Well, all that changed.

It changed in April 2004 with a program called Project Fresh Start (PFS). PFS was a program that reached out to commercial sex workers who worked on the streets to get them into treatment to improve their lives and change their patterns of behavior. The program gave them a choice to pay a fine or go to jail or to grab this lifeline for another chance at a better life. Addressing the massive problem took the collaboration of the sheriff's department; the Thirty-Sixth District Drug Court; and the Bureau of Substance Abuse, Prevention, Treatment, and Recovery (BSAPTR). The three entities came together to form a powerful team that created a strong community response to the problem of prostitution. The Detroit

Police Department joined our team a few years later. The team was a bridge over troubled waters.

The program not only saved taxpayer dollars but also helped people change their lives and break the bondage of addiction. As the late Dr. Calvin Trent, the former director of BSAPTR, said, "I love Project Fresh Start because when you save a man, you save a person, but when you save a woman, you save a community." According to the Hazelden Betty Ford Foundation, the National Association of Drug Court Professionals states that the average recidivism rate for drug court graduates is between 4 and 29 percent, as compared to 48 percent for nonparticipants. They also point out that drug courts save money. It costs between $20,000 and $50,000 per person per year to incarcerate a drug-using offender, whereas a comprehensive drug court system typically costs between $2,500 and $4,000 annually for each offender.[1] The state of Oregon saved taxpayers $10,223,532 over a two-year period. Furthermore, Oregon taxpayers saved ten dollars for every dollar spent on drug courts. Similar savings exist in other states.[2]

Judge Patricia Jefferson and I were the drug court judges presiding over PFS participants. When we were asked to join the team, I immediately thought about the women Leona and I had seen on the streets when we were in college. Now I had a unique opportunity to help restore lives.

Society changes every day, and those changes affect the lives of many people. With the advent of AIDS and the transference of that disease through prostitution, many innocent parties can unknowingly be harmed. An unsuspecting wife, girlfriend, husband, or boyfriend can have his or her life permanently changed through the transference of the disease.

---

[1] httpd://www.hazalden.org>ade60612.
[2] "Where Miracles Can Happen," www.americanbar.org/groups/crsjj/.

I felt that as a judge, I could no longer sit on the sidelines of life; I had to get in the game, so without hesitation, Judge Jefferson and I said yes to Sheriff Warren C. Evan's proposal.

Everything life had taught me had prepared me for that moment. The PFS program presented the court with a novel and innovative approach to an age-old problem. Even though I had no idea what to expect, I knew I had to help be the change that was needed in the lives of those ladies and men imprisoned by drugs and prostitution. For those types of crimes, justice was about saving and changing lives, not just about locking people up and throwing away the key.

In order to make the program work, Judge Jefferson and I requested that the participants sign our drug court contract, which had a length of time of fifteen to twenty-four months instead of the ninety days stated in the sheriff's initial contract. The team agreed to the change, and soon thereafter, the drug court contract replaced the sheriff's contract. The PFS participants were now drug court participants under the PFS track, and they were treated no differently from the other participants of drug court.

The PFS program not only helped defendants become and remain drug free but also helped them obtain an education, job training, employment, and permanent living accommodations. PFS created an avenue for those who wanted to get out of that situation and change their lives. Before the creation of this program, for many, that possibility was something they dreamed about but never thought could happen.

Despite the great things the program had to offer, it was no cakewalk. If the ladies truly wanted a new life, this was their opportunity. This was a chance they had never been offered before and might never have again.

In order to place possible participants in the program, a sweep had to be done of the Detroit streets in the early morning hours, before the crack of dawn. The officers would go out canvassing the area and pick up women and men whom they caught in the act of solicitation for sex or who had drug paraphernalia on them. They would also check to see if the people arrested had outstanding warrants. Usually, they had many outstanding warrants. One young lady had fifty outstanding warrants on tickets for possession of drug paraphernalia. Well, this was her chance to earn a clean slate, but she would have to work for it.

After about a year, word spread quickly about me and my specialized court, which initially created fear in prostitution circles on the street.

Some of the ladies, when arrested and placed in the back of police squad cars, would go to desperate measures not to be brought to me. Some tried to hurt themselves while in the backseat of the officers' patrol cars so they could be taken to the hospital and left there unsupervised, because the officers could not stay. When that happened, the ladies ran.

One example illustrating the degree of fear and resistance that existed out there among the ladies occurred on a typical day, when another judge had a young lady in handcuffs transferred to me. While being brought into my courtroom, she was barely through the door, when she started screaming and hollering. She was pulling and tugging, trying to get away from the officer. I looked up from the bench, in the middle of a case I was handling, when I heard her scream, "No, I don't want that judge! I know who she is! No, take me to a different judge."

Peering over my glasses, I asked, "Do I know you?"

"No, but I know who you are."

"Place her in the jury box; it's empty," I demanded. Watching her, I said, "Sit down, be quiet, and act like you have some sense. I am going to tell you like my mother told me when I was a child: I haven't given you anything to cry about yet!"

Reacting to the tone of my voice, she calmed down. I knew she knew who I was. To her, I was the judge who would take her away from the drugs and the street life she was addicted to. All the signs were there that she would run.

As I gazed at her, I reflected on another young lady in the program, whom I had warned about running from the treatment center I was about to send her to. She'd blurted out, "Where am I going to go? You got all of us. There is no one out there that I could connect with to help me if I ran. I would be by myself."

Laughing, I had said, "I don't have all of you."

"Yes, you do," she had said. "When I go to an NA meeting, I see women that I haven't seen for a year. I just thought they were dead, because you know, that stuff happens. But I asked them why they were going to these meetings, and they said they were in Judge Lloyd's program. Everywhere you send me, I see more and more women I thought had disappeared, but they had not; they were with you. So, when I say you got all of us, I mean you got all of us."

Her words had been music to my ears. As I looked at her, I smiled; *maybe she is right*. Then I remembered, the truthfulness in a statement Dr. Trent had given when answering the question "Is there a real possibility of getting rid of prostitution?" while a panelist at a seminar. He had responded without hesitation, "Yes, we can get rid of the majority of prostitution that is drug-related with more drug court programs like Project Fresh Start and judges like Judge Lloyd."

Now I turned my attention to the lady in the box. Even though the screaming lady had heard about me, she joined drug court. However, shortly after joining and placed in treatment, she ran, just as I had predicted. The Sherriff's picked her up a few weeks later, and I sent her to jail as a sanction.

When she returned to drug court, she promised she would not run anymore and begged for a second chance. I looked in her eyes, and I could see something had changed in her during her jail stay. I gave her a second chance with a stern warning. She kept her word and never ran again. In fact, she did well and graduated from drug court.

Eight years later, she surprised me when she came to a drug court graduation with a group of former drug court graduates, who were all doing exceptionally well. She informed me she was working as a practical nurse and was about to graduate with a bachelor's degree in social work. She later went on to study for a master's degree in social work, which would enable her to advance and expand the work she was doing as a counselor with drug-addicted clients.

Even though her story had a beautiful ending, usually, the journey to the finish line was a rough one. When the participants in either drug treatment court or PFS took that frightening journey in the program, they did not take the journey alone. I was there, along with my team, hitting every bump, pothole, and detour in the road with them. As a judge, I wanted them to make it and I was pulling for them. It took a lot within me to go on those journeys with the ladies. So much so, that I did not have any energy left when I returned home to sulk about my loss. I had used it all in my drug court and my PFS program; that turned out to be a blessing in disguise.

More than one thousand people have graduated from the drug court I presided over, including 150 women and 2 men from the PFS drug court program. My collaborative team consisting of the Sherriff's Department, the Detroit Police Department, case managers, treatment providers, lab technicians, court staff and court administrators were proud of the strides the graduates made.

The probation department kept recidivism records on the graduates of the program. Fewer than 25 percent of the graduates of PFS reoffended within five years after graduation, which was better than the national stats.

The Project Fresh Start program made large inroads in the world of prostitution in Detroit. I got calls from other states in the United States and as far away as the United Kingdom inquiring about the possibility of starting a similar program to handle their prostitution problems.

I will never forget a special evening in Lansing, Michigan, at the State Capitol, when I was asked to stand and be recognized in a state address by Michigan Supreme Court Justice Marilyn Kelly, for our innovative, outstanding work with the PFS program. That type of recognition does not happen often.

My advice to courts and their administrations who want to make a difference in their communities is to start thinking outside the box. In order to have a program as innovative as ours was, partners, such as BSAPTR, and a creative sheriff's or police department are necessary. In addition, court team members with a change-the-world mind-set and a strong administration that trusts its' judge to work in the best interest of the court and community are essential. I was lucky because I had all the above.

◆ All Money Ain't Good Money: A PFS Court Story

Project Fresh Start was no joke. Drug court was a piece of cake compared to what I had to deal with in PFS. That program really tested my inner strength because it took everything in me, to help participants find their strength to break the shackles of addiction. However, once the shackles were broken, the next nagging question I asked myself was, "Will they go back and put the shackles on again?"

When dealing with PFS participants, I never knew what to expect when the sheriff brought the young ladies in, but I did know that as long as they were living on the streets and addicted to drugs, life for them would continue to be a rough ride to hell.

Things had been moving right along with the PFS program, when one day, the sheriff brought in a new set of young ladies from a sweep the night before. Quite a few of the young ladies the sheriff had spoken to while they were in lockup wanted to participate in the program, including a young lady who was different from the rest of the group.

Her name was Claudia. She was shabbily dressed. When her case was called, she quietly came up. Because she had been sitting in jail for ten days, waiting for her pretrial date, she was at that moment free from cocaine, her drug of choice. With no drugs in her system, I was able to talk to the real Claudia.

I asked her if she wanted to change her life or continue out there in the streets, going in and out of jail.

Claudia's eyes targeted me as she spoke. "Judge, I want to change my life. I am tired of living the way I do. I need to do this for me." She slowly pulled back the hair covering her left eye and added, "This is what happened to me out there in the streets."

The case manager said, "Her pimp gouged her eye out."

"I hate the way I look. I used to look cute, but I stopped caring how I look after this happened. Drugs not only made me feel better about myself but also helped me forget about my eye. I know that's no excuse to use, but we are keeping it real, right?"

I agreed. "Right."

"I have to change," she said. "Please give me a chance to join your program. I know it works; I recognized a couple of the ladies in the courtroom today. They used to run the streets with me. I had not seen them for a while. To be honest with you, I thought they were dead, but I saw them in here this morning, and I thought, *Wow, I hardly recognize them.*

"They hugged me and said, 'Join the program. It will give you a new life. Look at us.' I saw what your program did for them. Please, Judge, I need this program. I want to get my life together too, and looking at them, I know it is possible. Please, I want—no, I need—this program." Her body shook as tears flowed down her face.

The arresting sheriff directed her attention toward me and asked if she could approach and speak to me off the record, which I agreed to. "Judge, after I arrested this young lady, I spent the next ten days talking to her about her life and the program. Not only does she need this program, but I feel she really wants the program. Judge, I hope you give her a chance to enter the program, because I really feel that without your program, she will die soon out there."

She quietly stepped back. As a special officer for the PFS project and a person who also had helped initiate the program, I knew she had real in-depth conversations with the ladies in lockup and acquired a lot of information about their personal lives that could not be divulged on the record in the courtroom, so her opinion was invaluable to me.

As if taking on addiction and its issues was not enough, I knew taking on that young lady was going to be a real challenge. She would need intensive counseling in addition to dealing with the restoration of her eye. I would have to ask my case managers to step outside what they normally did to help make a miracle happen. It would be challenging for us all, but they knew the word *can't* wasn't in my vocabulary.

Knowing the extra work my team and I would have to do in her case, I told her, "This program can help you get your life together, but you have to give me a one thousand percent effort, because it will take that to turn your life around. But you cannot run; if you do, trust and believe I will send officers out there to find you and bring you back to me. However, if you stick around and stay, I promise you we will provide a cosmetic fix for your eye; you will not have to cover your eye or hold your head down in shame anymore. I want you to be able to look in the mirror and like what you see, inside and out. I do not want you to see the ravages of the past every time you are brave enough to look in a mirror. So, do I have your word? Will you stick and stay?"

Showing a huge grin, she said in a loud, determined voice, "Yes, I will." With that answer, I granted her entry into the program.

I immediately placed her in an inpatient treatment program, which would provide her with the individualized counseling she needed. Additionally, the group sessions would help her bond with others and realize she was not alone in her journey.

For the first two months, things appeared to be going well for Claudia as she experienced the same growing pains as the other ladies. However, one day she decided to run from the facility. Fortunately, she knew it was the wrong thing to do and, surprisingly, had a friend bring her back to court.

Claudia apologized for running away. However, she knew a sanction was coming her way. The sanction was going to be a sit-down in my jail hotel suite. The sit-down would be long enough to be disruptive and irritating to the defendant but not long enough for her to get used to it. Before she left, she acknowledged that she had been wrong. She knew she had to deal with the consequences of her actions.

When Claudia returned from jail, she said she had had several discussions with the sheriff about what she had done. She felt those talks had helped her, and she was ready to start over again. She was remorseful and continued to apologize for what she had done. I reminded her that she had to stay strong and focused and move forward.

As time passed, she made great strides in the program. During Claudia's first Christmas in the program, the court required stringent drug testing for all participants. Claudia passed the tests with flying colors.

Claudia was doing so well that she qualified for and was moved into residential treatment housing. There she had her own apartment. Because of her health issues, she received medical assistance from the government. However, that assistance did not cover a prosthetic eye. Ms. Brimage, her case manager, did some research and found a medical facility that was willing to donate their services and accept her into their program to provide her with a prosthetic eye.

At Claudia's March status hearing, I glanced up and saw Claudia flash her two bright, shining eyes; she was smiling as if she had won the lottery. No longer was her hair covering her eye. She said she felt whole again. She looked like a different person. Claudia now took pride in how she looked. I noticed makeup, lipstick, and beautiful earrings now framed her face. Never again did she comb her hair over her eye when she appeared in court.

I knew that the restoration of her eye had given her back a part of her heart and soul that had been taken from her. Her joy was restored, and I could see it in her every time she bounced into the courtroom.

Claudia moved forward with her life and applied for Supplemental Security Income (SSI) disability benefits. She was initially rejected, so she applied again. However, she would not get the results of her appeal until after she graduated from the program.

She felt that SSI owed her unpaid back funds. If correct, the amount she would receive would be a lot more money than she was used to handling. In a situation like that, I preferred she receive all funds, including back funds owed to her, while she was still a participant in drug court. That way, we could monitor her to make sure she did not spend her funds the wrong way. Money is one of the biggest triggers for an addict. Unfortunately, I had no control over the timing of an SSI payment to a defendant.

Before I knew it, the second Christmas holiday season for Claudia was approaching, and so was Claudia's graduation day. Graduations were always in January, after the holidays; I had learned that graduating the participants before the holidays was asking for trouble. Holidays were the hardest time for participants to stay clean, especially around relatives who were getting high and wanting them to join the celebration. Being in drug court helped them get through the holidays drug free. No one wanted a post-holiday trip to my hotel.

Up to that point, everything had been going great for Claudia. However, during that holiday season, I received two calls regarding Claudia. Since the court was closed, I did not get them until the court reopened after the holidays.

After I returned, I listened to my messages, including the alarming messages regarding Claudia. An anonymous caller talked of suspicious behavior regarding Claudia but was not specific about what Claudia had done. Then, a few days later, the same caller called and left another message, saying she had overreacted and was sorry. Despite what the second message said, I still had a suspicion that something was wrong. At the next status hearing I questioned her about the phone calls, but she assured me she had done nothing wrong.

Since there were no more incidents regarding Claudia, she proceeded to graduation. She had completed all the requirements of drug court and then some, with no positive or missing urine screens, but I still had a nagging doubt that something was wrong. I could not shake that feeling.

When graduation day came, I gave Claudia a big hug, handed her the diploma, and let her know, "If you ever need me for anything, don't hesitate to call me or come in. You know where and how to find me. I mean it!"

She smiled at me and said, "Okay."

I always threw out a lifeline to someone if I thought that one day, he or she might need it and I felt she might.

Well, fast-forward four months after graduation. I received an urgent call stating that no one had seen Claudia. My case manager informed me that Claudia had received her SSI check, including a back payment of several thousand dollars and no one had seen her since she received the money, which had been three weeks ago.

She was reported missing to the police. Subsequent, to the report being filed, the police found the deceased body of Claudia in her apartment. There were a lot of used drugs found in the apartment. The body had decomposed, but she was identified by her prosthetic eye. Since she was no longer in drug court, we had no authority to request her death certificate, which would have shown her cause of death.

I had sensed at her graduation that there might have been something going on in her life; that was why I had told her to contact me if she ever needed me. But sometimes, drugs overpower a person's willpower.

From that day forward, I directed my case managers to assist the ladies early if they felt they had back payments owed to them by SSI. That way, we could monitor and guide their spending while they were still in drug court.

Even though Claudia had succeeded in drug court and PFS, her life ended about four months after her graduation. Fortunately, that type of event never happened again to any of my participants in drug court or the specialized PFS-track programs.

CHAPTER 18

A Story from a Graduate of PFS

◆ **Introduction to Lynne Williams**

In this chapter, I am sharing a story told by a former PFS drug court graduate, Lynn Williams, in her own words about her life before and after drug court. Her case truly touched the depths of my heart.

As a judge, when I read the case background on this young lady when she first entered my courtroom, I knew that most judges would have looked at the amount of time she had been out there in the streets and passed on her; however, when I looked in her eyes in the courtroom, I saw a small glimmer of light. That light told me that, despite her past life, I had to give her another chance. I do not know why or how, but I could tell she was different. I could not say no to her and close her door of opportunity, because I knew she might not ever get another chance. I just prayed she would be stronger than the lure of the streets or drugs and would stay and participate in the program.

Month after month went by, and I watched Lynne blossom in front of my eyes. She was smart and had a talent for writing that had been ignored for years while she was out in the streets. I got an opportunity to see that talent and watch it reignite and grow anew.

When Lynne graduated from drug court, she only had two years to go to complete her bachelor's degree at Wayne State University. When I handed her the graduation diploma from drug court, I said, "I know you are going to finish college, so when you do, come back and give me a ticket to your graduation, and I will be there."

Her face brightened as she said, "Okay, I will."

She kept her word, and so did I. Mr. Al Cooper, her case manager, and I attended her graduation.

Lynne went on to become a counselor at the Salvation Army, where she helped straighten out the lives of young ladies who were lost because of their addiction to drugs. She appeared in my courtroom, representing the ladies from the treatment center at the Salvation Army. Every lady she helped in my program went on to be successful and live a happy, joyous life. Lynne was dedicated to helping people, and it showed as she appeared in front of my courtroom as a counselor. Lynne went on to be promoted to the administrative ranks at the Salvation Army. Recently, she received her master's degree, in Organizational Leadership at the Nazarene University on May 9, 2020. To say I am proud of her would not come close to expressing my feelings about this marvelous lady.

They Thought I Was Worth Saving

LYNNE A. WILLIAMS

Words are inadequate when I try to describe the impact of Judge Lloyd and drug treatment court on my life. God brought her to rescue me, and I have not been the same since. I began getting high at the age of fifteen. I went to my uncle's house to babysit, and he asked me if I wanted to smoke a joint. That was my beginning.

It was fun at first because I did not know any better. I got high on marijuana and drank into my early twenties. At that point, nothing was too terribly unmanageable in my life. I danced, partied, and played fairly innocent. Then, at one of those parties, I was introduced to cocaine.

I thought I was in love. I couldn't get enough of it. The highs from alcohol and weed paled in comparison, but I still used it all. I wanted to be as high as possible. I was an addict then, but I didn't know it. I fancied myself a young, naive girl who was enjoying life with no hard or fast rules.

The trouble was, there were hard and fast rules. I just chose to ignore them. My rule was "Die young; stay pretty." I thought I was on the journey to self-discovery. I explored this self-discovery by letting men explore me. Confused, I equated sex with the love I so desperately wanted.

In 1983, I was introduced to freebasing cocaine. Even the first time, I just wanted to do more and more. I was waiting tables at the time, and I wanted all my money to go toward drugs. It was at this point in my life that I began to know better. I knew there was something wrong with my getting high. It was no longer social or part-time. I had to get high.

I started having trouble keeping up with my habit. My desire to use had begun to far outweigh my ability to pay for it and to get up for work in the morning. My nights of drugging emptied into my days at work, and my appearance and performance showed it. It was the beginning of the unmanageability of my life.

On March 13, 1987, I was standing in the heart of Cass Corridor in Detroit, searching desperately for my car. I had rented it to the drug dealer so I could stay in an abandoned building smoking crack all night. I was tired, I was scared, I was alone, and yet I still wanted to get high. But I knew the party was over. So, after several years of getting high, I decided to give staying clean a chance.

I am telling you I gave staying clean a chance, but not God. I thought I could do this my way.

I went to meetings regularly for ten years straight. I helped make coffee. I did open talks. I got and used a sponsor, for a period of time. And I began to get my life back in order. I gave birth to two daughters, got married, started school, and began a successful career. I managed to accumulate all kinds of things. But with all the stuff I accumulated, I made no room for God. I thought I could handle life and managed to put together seventeen years of clean time. Yet I had no concept of recovery.

I thought I had graduated from the disease of addiction. I was making $130,000 a year, driving a Cadillac Escalade, living in a half-million-dollar home, and traveling extensively, and I maintained a 3.95 GPA in college. But without God and with very few coping skills, I was lonely and miserable. I was merely staying clean and abandoned all twelve-step meetings. My spiritual walk with God was nonexistent. And after seventeen years clean, all the stuff I had accumulated fit conveniently right back into a crack pipe.

This time, I fell so rapidly I was scared to stop and reflect on anything I was doing. I was on a self-destruct mission, and the cost was exceedingly great.

Eventually, the money ran out. I began watching the prostitutes working up and down the streets and decided to give it a go. I added heroin to my drug use. Things I said I would never do for drugs—turning tricks, shooting up, and letting men beat me—became part of everyday survival.

As a prostitute, I was raped numerous times, forced to perform sex acts at gunpoint, and beaten when I tried to get away. One day, while I was working the streets, it seemed rather slow. The Salvation Army bed-and-breakfast truck stopped to give me a sandwich, and when they handed it to me, they wished me a merry Christmas. I was so lost I didn't even realize I was working the streets on Christmas.

I relinquished complete custody of my daughters to my ex-husband. Having never been arrested, I caught six felonies in six months, along with several misdemeanors. I was on and off probation and in and out of jails, able to bond myself out at first but not even having a dollar for snacks in the end. After a five-year run in and out of the legal system, I was homeless. I had become a derelict with only the clothes on my back, and prostitution had become my job. I truly believed that would be the way I would die. I didn't think I had a choice in the matter.

But God is merciful. Sometimes, we don't know we've got God until God is all we've got!

In 2010, God rescued me. He arrested me and my addiction. He led me to court-ordered treatment through drug court at Sacred Heart New Life Home for Women. I remember when I was referred to Judge Lloyd by another Thirty-Sixth District Court judge in May of 2010. I had heard horror stories of a two-year drug court program that involved treatment centers and urine drops, and I had never met anyone who had completed her program. Of course, that was because I had never left the hood, so the only girls I knew in drug court were those on the run, those who were still in the streets and had no intention of completing her program, which was called at the time Project Fresh Start. In the Narcotics Anonymous fellowship, one might say they weren't ready.

I must confess that in May 2010, I didn't believe I was ready either. Nevertheless, on May 25, 2010, I signed my contract with Judge Lloyd and was remanded to the Wayne County Jail until my next court date, June 30, 2010.

I had every intention of running from treatment too. I had been living under warrants, felonies and absconded probations, for the majority of the five years prior to May 2010, so being on the run was nothing new to me. As soon as I saw a door I could open to the outside, I planned to be out of there and on my way back to the hood, the drugs, and the lifestyle.

But God is a good God, and he must have really wanted to keep me, for while I was incarcerated, I was put in a cell next to a girl named Helen. Helen shared with me that she was a Judge Lloyd Project Fresh Start girl who had run twice from treatment centers she had been sent to by the court. On this second absconding, she had caught a new case, a retail fraud felony, and unrelated to Project Fresh Start, she was sentenced to one to five years in the state penitentiary. When I asked her if the program was really so bad that she'd felt the need to run a second time after having been given a second chance by Judge Lloyd to go to treatment, she confessed that she really had had no reason to run; the treatment center she had been placed in was good to her. She had accumulated a little money and gained some self-respect. She had just left on a fluke—a painful emotion or unprocessed urge and a subsequent poor decision.

I pulled my mattress to the iron doors of my unit at Wayne County Jail on June 30, 2010, at 5:00 a.m. As I waited for them to slide open, I heard Helen's quiet, regret-filled voice call out to me: "Lynne, just give it a chance. Do not make the mistake I made. Just give it a chance."

I knew those were not only her words but the words of God.

That day, I went to court and was assessed for treatment. I had nothing and was still in county greens. When I was asked by the Substance Abuse Bureau if I had a preference as to where to go for treatment, I said, "Somewhere nice." They referred me to Sacred Heart New Life Home for Women, and that is where I went after I changed from my county greens into the outfit that was brought to me from the treatment center.

To say that was the turning point in my life would be an understatement. I began to participate in drug court and actually began to see some benefits of staying clean. I began writing again. It was a coping mechanism and a gift that had followed me in life. Writing became my passion, and Judge Lloyd helped nourish and cultivate that. I would go to monthly check-ins at court, and Judge Lloyd would ask me to share something I had written with the court. I would spend a great deal of time preparing for those days, as I wanted so badly for those in the courtroom to connect with my words. I was going through what they were going through, and I wanted to share some hope.

When I got to New Life, the other women there, as well as, signs along the wall said, "Don't leave before the miracle happens." I didn't really know what that meant at the time, but it sure sounded like Helen's voice saying, "Lynne, just give it a chance." So, I did. I know that God speaks through other people to get his message across, and he told me he was keeping me for a reason and that I should sit still and give it a chance. By all accounts, I should have been dead like so many of those with whom I got high, but instead, I decided to find out why God kept me and what his purpose is for me. Because of Project Fresh Start, I can say I did not leave before the miracle happened.

I owe a debt of gratitude to Judge Lloyd and the Thirty-Sixth District Drug Court, and there will never be anything they could ask of me that I would not do for them. If I can return in any way even a small part of what this program has given me or help another in this program, even if it is merely whispering to them to give it a chance, I would be honored. Project Fresh Start put the necessary steps in place for me to change my life and provided encouragement and strength that helped keep me going.

My boyfriend at the time was battling his own addiction and had been court-stipulated to the Salvation Army Adult Rehabilitation Center (ARC) men's campus. What a pair we were—both court-ordered to rehabilitation, both beaten down, and both homeless. But God was at work, doing for us what we could not do for ourselves. I got a pass to go to church at the ARC to see my boyfriend on Sunday, August 1, 2010. When I got there, the church was talking about recovery from addiction, singing about a new way of life through Jesus Christ. God brought me home. I began attending church there regularly and became a Salvation Army soldier in 2011.

God began to turn my life around. I graduated Judge Lloyd's drug court on September 29, 2011 and was invited to be the honored graduate speaker at that graduation. I returned to my studies at Wayne State University in Detroit. In May of 2013, I graduated summa cum laude with a bachelor's degree in English with honors. Judge Lloyd was there at my graduation, as was my case manager.

I remember giving her tickets to the graduation at Ford Field and thinking, *I will never know if she does come.* But God put them right in my path that morning. It meant so much that she made a point to be there for me. I never forgot that.

I began to work joyfully at the women's campus of the ARC as a spiritual and addictions counselor, part of God's perfect will for me, for I am now able to give back what was so freely given to me. Judge Lloyd began sending women to the center I was working at and requesting me as their counselor. The irony was not lost on me as I stood before her again, no longer pleading my own case but speaking on behalf of the women for whom she had charged to my care.

Now, about that boyfriend. His name is Johnnie Williams. We were married at the Salvation Army in January of 2012. He has been clean and sober ever since he got to rehabilitation. We each have over eight years clean.

Today I know that God kept me through the storm of active addiction because he had a plan for me. I was kept on purpose for his purpose. My addiction intended to harm me, but God has used it for good, to accomplish what is now being done: helping to bring lives to him and helping other addicts find a new way to live. He used drug treatment court and Judge Lloyd to help start me on the road to transformation.

I am now the director of rehabilitation services for the Salvation Army, overseeing both the men's and women's campuses, and a productive member of society. I thank God that he saw fit to keep me and that he has worked it all together for good. I am forever indebted to and appreciative of the intimate care and concern that was shown to me by Judge Leonia J. Lloyd and her court. She is now my friend, and we continue to work together to help people.

Me speaking at a drug court graduation. Attended by Dr. Trent and City Council members, and case managers; Allen Black and Dominique Clements

Receiving the Second Best Drug Court in the Nation award with my staff, Officer Robert Ball, Deborah Burks and Florence Dunklin

My outstanding Drug treatment court team at the NADCP conference in Washington D. C. From right to left, me, Youniqua Coleman, Chyonna Cooper, Jasmine Brimage and Al Cooper

Pictured with Lynne Williams at her graduation from Wayne State University

◆ Helping Transgender Populations: "I Gotta' Be Me"

Drug and alcohol addictions do not discriminate. They will invade all segments of society. Whether you are a man or a woman or are straight, gay, an MSM (man having sex with other men), gender fluid, or transgender, Mr. Addiction will welcome you.

However, based on which category you are in, you might not get the treatment you need. Discrimination often plays a big factor in who receives treatment. The PFS participants, as well as, my drug court team and I, participated in a live taping of a meeting held by the Partnership against Drugs Organization, led by Dr. Calvin Trent. The ladies of the PFS program gave their own personal testimonies of success.

At the end of the meeting, as I was walking out, I was stopped by a group of transgender women (AMAB: assigned male at birth). The spokesperson for the group said, "Judge Lloyd, I'm glad your Project Fresh Start program is working out well, but do you have any room in your drug court program for people like us? I'm transgender, and I have a drug addiction problem, but everywhere we go, they turn us away and say they don't have placements for us."

As she talked to me, tears filled her eyes, and the other transgender women nodded in agreement. I gazed into her sullen eyes and said, "I wish I could say yes, but I can't. But I can tell you that I am working on it. I know you have unique issues that need counseling, and that's where the problem lies, but I am working on it."

They thanked me and slowly walked out of the room. I knew I did not have the answer they wanted to hear, and I was disappointed that I could not give them a better, more hopeful answer.

On my drive back home, I could not get her voice out of my head: "Do you have any room in your drug court program for people like *us*?" That question never left me.

Not long after that, at a drug court status hearing, the silent cry for help went out again. A treatment provider's counselor stood at the podium with his client, ready to give his status report. My court officer handed me a note from the defendant in front of me. The letter was a cry for help from the defendant. She wrote that they had discontinued her drugs for her gender transition and forbidden her from wearing her clothes she had originally wore into jail: a skirt and sweater. She said in the letter, "Please get me out of here! If you can't I'm afraid I'll run." I could hear her voice bounce off the page. I put the letter down to hear the case.

When I asked for the status report on the defendant, the counselor said, "Well, Judge, he's doing okay; we just have to get the devil out of him first. He needs Jesus."

The response startled me, so I asked, "What do you mean?"

"You know, we've got to get him on the right path. That's why he's dressed differently."

I quickly replied, "You're here to help the defendants with their drug addictions, not to try to define what gender they should be or take them to church. That's not your job or mine." I was upset with the tenor of the whole case.

As they prepared to leave the courtroom, the defendant's sad eyes met mine, and she said softly, "Thank you, Judge. I know you wanted to help me."

Those words haunted me. Yes, I wanted to help her, but placing her at that facility was not the answer because it did not fit her special needs. A few days later, I heard she had run away. Days after that, I received another letter from her, letting me know she had run because she could not take staying there anymore. They would not let her be true to herself, so she had run. She wanted me to know why she had run and that she was thankful for what I had tried to do.

That was not the first time I had placed a transgender woman in a male facility only to find out quickly that the arrangement was unsuccessful. The defendant had absconded, this happened over and over again.

However, that day, I immediately called Dr. Trent, reported that case as well as others to him, and impressed upon him the urgent need for the Bureau of Substance Abuse to develop a facility where transgender women could go, feel relaxed, and not feel threatened or condemned by staff or other people who were there for treatment. I explained that I had had another transgender woman at a facility for HIV-positive men and gay men. Within three days, I had received a call from the facility begging me to remove her from the facility and take her back. I had asked why.

The facility counselor had told me, "The men around the facility are smitten with her. I saw her kissing one of the men, and I immediately stopped it. By law, I cannot disclose any of their medical conditions to her, so it's best if you just remove her."

I learned quickly that some transgender women were so beautiful that the men could not take their hands off them. The fascination, mystery, and beauty caused the men to break all the rules.

"Where can I place her for inpatient treatment?" I had asked.

His suggestion was the women's treatment facility. I had her picked up and taken to the female facility. They agreed to the transfer, knowing that she was a transgender woman. She stayed for one day; I received a call, asking me to remove her immediately because they could not guarantee her safety. Those same traits of beauty were about to cause all hell to break out. They had been unable to give her twenty-four-hour protection and feared fights endangering her health and welfare would occur. Unable to guarantee the safety of my transgender female defendant caused swift action on my part.

I had removed her quickly, but there had been no inpatient facility I could send her to for the help she needed with her addiction. Outpatient treatment had been my only option left. I used that option, but it did not work out. She heard the call of her addiction to drugs, street life, and the lure of money, pulling her back to the streets. This result was not uncommon.

Once again, I cried the blues to Dr. Trent and told him of all my failed attempts at treatment placements for transgender women. He reassured me that he was working on the issue. I beseeched him to hurry.

Dr. Trent kept his word and directed me to a facility that I could send gay men or transgender women. I sent several transgender women to the facility, which was called Jabez Recovery. Mr. Edward Aniapam, the CEO and head of the Jabez Recovery Center, had created a program within his treatment center for transgender women. In the courtroom, at the status hearings, I asked him questions about the transgender women at his facility. I could see he really cared about the safety and well-being of the individuals I had sent there. He explained the extra measures taken at the facility to help all the groups get along. Group sessions orchestrated by him were geared toward each group understanding and respecting their differences in lifestyle choices.

It was obvious to me at the status hearings that the defendants I had sent there were thriving. They smiled when I asked them how they liked the facility. Finally, there was a place where they could feel safe and get counseled by people who accepted them as they were. They could focus on their addiction issues. They were in good hands.

Several of my transgender women who attended and graduated from the Jabez Recovery facility also graduated from drug court. Some of those graduates went on to college and graduated with bachelor's degrees.

After leaving the bench, I visited the Jabez Recovery Treatment Center. I spoke to Mr. Aniapam to see how things were going. He assured me they were still treating transgender women. He knew of no other place that welcomed them. I asked about medications for them, and the service coordinator, Lisa Burton, assured me they all had their medications covered by insurance, whether private insurance, city or state insurance, Medicaid, or block grants. She said an organization named Community Health Awareness Group (CHAG) covered HIV medication as well as HIV preventative medication. CHAG is the largest minority AIDS service organization in Michigan and is committed to reducing the transmission of HIV.

When I asked about the transgender women who were placed in jail, Mr. Aniapam informed me, that the Wayne County jails were now making sure the defendants were allowed, to continue their medications for their sex transitions. However, they had to provide proof of their last prescription and of counseling they had received prior to being locked up that qualified them for the hormone therapy medication.

I was pleased to hear that and said, "Great, because two years ago, they weren't giving them anything for their hormone therapy medication. A transgender woman would walk in one way—feminine—but ten days later, they had to give her different clothes to wear because her facial hair had grown out due to lack of the continuation of the hormone medication."

I emphasized to Mr. Aniapam, my belief that there should be a separate facility for transgender women because they had issues and problems to discuss that were different from those of the other men. I explained the danger some of my defendants had experienced when ordered to go to a regular treatment facility. He said he always wondered if placing them in regular facilities without a specialized program for them could work, but I showed him example after example, of how it did not work out for those individuals. Leaving them in regular facilities and hoping everything would work out, had led to some disastrous results. I could not take that chance, I told him.

"Those treatment agencies failed to address any of the unique issues of the transgender woman," I said.

After several hours of discussion, I agreed to help his agency bring about positive change for transgender women and transgender men in any way I could. I left him with my contact information.

I believe everyone has a right to receive treatment and get the help he or she needs to become drug free. This is true regardless of the gender identity people wear. Sammy Davis Jr. expressed in his song "Gotta Be Me," recorded in 1968, that people, need to be free, to be who they are. That message is even stronger today.

◆ Heartfelt Appreciation

I knew that the things I asked of the drug court defendants were difficult. In fact, for some, drug court might have been the hardest thing they had ever done in their lives. I would recognize their hardships, when I spoke to them at their graduation in my commencement speech:

"Looking at your beaming faces, I know it has taken a lot of hard work for you to be here this morning. Some of you have shed many tears, and some have asked yourselves, if you had the strength to keep going in the program. Some did not know if they could stand the pain, and many got fed up with the endless rejections they received as they looked for a job in this new life. Some found that in this new reality, the rose-colored glasses had to come off and you had to be responsible for not only yourselves but also others who depended on you. Many of you who are sitting here today did not let fear of the unknown, rejection, loneliness, or pain stop you from continuing down this road of success you are on. You were finally where you were supposed to be in life, and you were not going to let anything turn you around. Graduating this program has shown you, that you indeed have what it takes to succeed at anything you set your mind to."

Filled with extreme joy and triumph the graduates burst into wild applause and tears.

As required, my graduates would write letters to me at the time of their graduation, letting me know if the program had helped them. They explained how hard it had been for them, the changes they'd had to go through, and all the hoops they'd had to jump through to get to graduation day. I did not expect the expressions of endearment shown in those letters. Those emotional, heartfelt statements went straight to my heart. The pain of the loss of my sister and the difficulty of seeing how I would ever work through her loss stayed with me, but as I concentrated on the people who stood in front of me, many in life-and-death situations and in need of help, my concentration was 100 percent on them and not on myself. The bonus for me was that their heartfelt letters helped lessen my anguish around my sister's death.

The following are just a few examples of one-liners from their letters:

> *Drug court was the force I needed to finally get sober and straighten out my life.*
>
> *God reached into his endless supply of miracles, and then you happened, Judge Lloyd.*
>
> *If you want a second chance at life, pray, and maybe God will send you to Judge Lloyd.*
>
> *Thank you for helping to save my life and the lives of so many military veterans.*
>
> *Do I think drug court is good for a person who wants to change? I say hell yes, with love, though—if they want a better chance at life. They should pray to God, and if it is not too late, he will send them to you, Judge Lloyd. These were the best two years of my life. My lesson actually turned into a blessing.*

I received the following letter eight years after this drug court participant's graduation:

> *Judge Lloyd,*
>
> *I just want you to know you truly saved my life and others as well. This sits with me every day of my life. I am forever grateful for you, and I carry your name forever. I talk of you all the time. My kids, my friends, and my family know you. I could have been one of those people behind bars who killed someone or a family. I cannot stress it enough to people to stop drinking and driving.*
>
> *So, I thank you and forever love you. 1/2019*

◆ Remarks from Court Personnel

Below are some comments I received from court personnel I worked with over the years while serving as a judge:

> You were the one who shaped the lives of so many through drug court. Your impact will be felt for many generations to come for many families. You are not told enough but thank you. On a personal note, you brought me into prosecutions for drug court and taught me how to transform lives through it, and I am forever grateful.
>
> —Shannon Walker
> Supervising assistant corporation counsel
> (supervising prosecutor for the City of Detroit Law Department)
> 2019

A Statement from Leona's court reporter:

> I am so glad that I was her court reporter to the end. I can remember times when she would uplift some of the ladies who came to court for their hearings who had no self-esteem at all. She would tell them that they were pretty and had so much to live for. One mother came to court with her daughter and started shouting as if she were in church, thanking Judge Lloyd for saving her daughter, shouting, "Thank you, Jesus! Thank you, Judge Lloyd, for saving my daughter!" Her daughter had gotten off drugs. I am so glad that I had a chance to make some of her campaign material when she ran again. Twins for Justice.
>
> —Helen Brown, June 8, 2019

◆ Court Accolades

Our drug court received numerous accolades over the years. In 2005–2006, the National Drug Court Professionals Association selected us as the second-best drug court in the country. At that time, there were at least 1,262 drug courts in the nation, and 575 drug courts were in the planning stages. Several were stationed outside the United States. Our court had a 75 percent success rate, which meant our former graduates from drug court had not been convicted of any drug- or alcohol-related cases for a period of at least three years following their graduation.

A television documentary was made about Project Fresh Start. Not only was it informative but the television station received a Detroit Emmy for the documentary.

Project Fresh Start also drew the attention of one of the two major newspapers in Detroit. A reporter wanted to write a special piece on the program, but she wanted to be able to follow a certain number of young ladies. I approved her request, and I had the girls who wanted to volunteer sign waivers for the project. I explained to them that they did not have to participate in the project at all. Their response was that they wanted people out there to know there was a program like Project Fresh Start that reached out and cared about the ladies on the street who had been addicted and often homeless for many years. They said the program was changing their lives, and they wanted people to know change was possible.

The young ladies selected were followed for more than a year. The reporter showed up unannounced at many events the girls participated in. She visited the living quarters of the ladies, with very little prior notice. She wanted to see the ladies as they really were, not a version of their lives that was dressed up for the press. With no fanfare or announcement, the story about Project Fresh Start appeared in the headlines of the paper two days in a row. A special pictorial section was dedicated to the story about ladies who were changing their lives. The story was unprecedented. My courtroom received a lot of calls from parents and spouses asking for help and guidance for their loved ones. They now had hope that no matter what, people could really change.

Those of us who are lucky enough to grow up with loving parents are blessed. If your parents taught you to reach for the stars and made you feel you could accomplish anything, you are doubly blessed. But people, like many in drug court, who are not lucky enough to have loving, supportive parents can overcome and live productive lives. They can become the loving parents for their children that they did not have. If people who practiced the act of prostitution and other drug-addicted individuals can start over again, anyone with a determined spirit and a supportive team can do the same.

When I look back, I know that many of the graduates of my drug court and veterans' court were brought to my courtroom through divine intervention. It was no accident. But deep down inside, the defendants had to believe they deserved a better life, a second chance. I was the vehicle through which they received that second chance.

In the beginning of this book, I included John Greenleaf Whittier's poem "Don't Quit" because it became a life motto, as well as, the underlying soundtrack for my life and now theirs.

When you are down and out, do not quit. When you feel you cannot go on another day, do not quit. Determination, a can-do spirit, positive energy, and hard work, are all it takes to turn a life around. Believe me, you are worth it!

CHAPTER 19

Paying It Forward

NEVER WOULD'VE MADE IT

While being a drug and veterans' treatment court judge, I paid forward what Dr. Bennett had graciously given to me. I saw many situations in my courtroom in which the participants had lost a loved one but had never received any grief counseling. In those situations, grief morphed into depression, and they began to use drugs or alcohol to deal with the pain of their loss. That choice got them into legal trouble, which then led them to me.

One woman who appeared before me had developed a severe drug problem after her daughter's death.

She said, "Judge, my little girl and I were sitting at a bus stop. We were talking and laughing; when out of nowhere, my daughter was shot by a stray bullet. She slumped over on me, and I screamed as I held her while she died in my arms. I haven't been able to get that vision of her out of my head—the picture of her lying there in my arms dead as we sat at the bus stop."

She told me the incident had happened five years ago. When I asked if she had received any grief counseling, she said no because she did not like talking to anyone about the incident.

"I understand. Most people I have seen in my courtroom say the same thing, because it is painful, but I know you have not really properly grieved your daughter's death; now it's caused other problems for you. I am going to order you into intensive grief counseling, something you should have had a long time ago." Sharing my personal struggle with grief with her, I said, "When my sister died, I participated in grief counseling, both individual and group, and I can't even begin to tell you the world of difference it made for me."

Glaring at me with watery red eyes, she said, "Okay, I'll go."

A month later, at her status hearing, she marched up to the podium, appearing much stronger, and said, "Judge, I'm so glad you made me go to grief counseling. I am now dealing with my daughter's death much differently. I've joined a mothers' organization that fights against gun violence; I want to help stop this type of senseless violence from happening to someone else's child."

I was proud of her. I suggested she do something to honor the memory of her daughter, such as lighting a candle at church or at home, making a scrapbook of her life, planting a tree, having one planted, or wearing her favorite perfume.

Smiling, she responded, "I will, Judge. I'll let you know what I've done next month."

That was the first time I saw her smile, because the dark cloud of depression had lifted. It was my counseling experience that allowed me to share my story of loss with her and some PFS participants. Some PFS defendants used drugs in order to numb the pain from the loss of a child. Many veterans turned to drugs because of the violent deaths of friends who had served alongside them in active military duty. Those wounds of loss had to be addressed through counseling, or what I like to call "talk therapy." Seeing the positive effects on those I ordered into specialized counseling for depression was like night and day. I wanted them to rediscover who they were and escape the world of darkness they had been living in. Depression had such a tight grip on them that some of them tried to commit suicide before being brought to my courtroom.

Depression can happen to anyone, men, women, young and old. I had many defendants suffering from depression come to drug court. Many came with freshly bandaged wrists evidencing their failed attempt at suicide. In the eyes of all those defendants, I saw sadness and emptiness. What they had in common was a deflated facial expression that said, "Life is hell and not worth living." Every time I saw that look, I would call the defendants up to the bench where I sat, have them place their hands in mine, and tell them to listen to what I was about to tell them. I would say, "I know you feel like your future is without hope and that life is so painful it is just not worth living but trust me when I say it is. You do not feel like that right now, but that feeling is going to change. I too have felt the bottom of my world fall away and devastation set in, but I promise you it will not stay. I am putting you into intensive counseling to help pull you out of your depression. I promise you I will be there every step of the way, but you must promise me that you will follow the plan we create for you. Do I have your promise?"

The energy of hope was flowing from my hands to theirs. I never let go of those hands attached to the bandaged wrists, until I heard their voices say, "Yes," as they wiped the tears from their eyes.

Month after month, with constant encouragement and reinforcement from the bench and the drug court team, a lot of changes occurred. The defendants went to work on themselves. Some obtained great jobs; jump-started educational careers; and obtained cars, apartments, or houses. The defendants reinvented their lives; their tears were replaced with smiles. Their lives were back on track, and drugs were in the rearview mirror of their lives.

When I think about the term *depression*, I cannot help but think about the subarachnoid hemorrhage my mother had, which today is considered a bleeding stroke in the brain. Most people suffering from that type of brain injury experience depression shortly afterward. In many cases, the depression comes from the fear of realizing that your whole world has changed and that you no longer can do the things you did before.

Today people are treated immediately at the first sign of depression. They do not have to feel alone. They can receive help and learn how to reprogram themselves for the new lives they are living. However, back in the 1950s, it was different.

My mother learned to function with her depression. However, the underlying depression began to worsen, leading her to a nervous breakdown, while we were in high school.

Today, when a person has trouble remembering, learning new things, concentrating or making decisions that affect their ever day life, there are tests they can take to determine if their cognitive impairment is mild or severe. Mental health professionals have come a long way with testing and treatment for brain injury.

Defendants who participated in my programs came in with all kinds of mental health issues, such as anxiety, depression, manic depression, bipolar disorder, nervous breakdowns, and schizophrenia. No matter what condition they had, I knew that immediate medical and mental health diagnosis and treatment were crucial. That was the only way they would have a fighting chance to become productive individuals. Under my watch, that was what they received.

My sister's death and the effect it had on me caused me to delve into the area of mental conditions, a world I knew little about. Because of my loss and my sessions with Dr. Bennett, I came to understand grief and depression. I knew immediate attention to those conditions could be the difference between life and death.

Unfortunately, I was too young to connect the dots in time to help my mother but learning about her helped me connect the dots in time to help those in drug treatment court and veterans' treatment court. With that knowledge and the connection, I had with a team of medical and mental health experts, I could help participants navigate successfully through their newly created lives.

CHAPTER 20

Amazing Grace: A Bond That Death Could Not Break

MISSING YOU

The bond between my twin sister and me, was strong—so strong that she managed to connect with me shortly after her death. As I said before, one message came through the movement of a work of art in my bedroom, and the other was in the movement of her picture. Those messages had let me know she was all right, and I was okay with that. I carry my sister's spirit in my heart, so she is always there. However, I was not prepared for the next three connections I was about to receive from her.

The next occurrence happened in 2006, about five years following my sister's passing. I was driving my court reporter, Florence, home from a late drug court graduation, that was held two weeks before

Christmas. (I had not developed my rule about no graduations in December yet.) I knew her husband was not home, so I offered her a ride.

The roads were horrible, covered with many days' worth of snow buildup. When I drove down Florence's residential street, it was obvious the snow had not been shoveled at all; I did not park when I stopped in front of her house, for fear of getting stuck. Instead, I shifted the car into the drive position and let the car sit in the grooves of the snow in the middle of the street, with my foot on the brake, as I watched Florence step up to her porch and into the house. She had a pin in her ankle from a previous operation, so I wanted to make sure she did not fall in the snow, afraid she would not be able to get up.

As I went to grab my cell phone, I sensed a strong, overpowering feeling to turn my head toward the driver's-side window. I immediately saw two young boys, and one was holding what appeared to be a nine-millimeter Glock, a semiautomatic pistol. It was pointed directly at my head through the driver's window.

My reflexes kicked in, and I placed my hand to the left side of my face and hit the accelerator on my Mercedes 500 G Wagon. The car was supposed to be able to drive in mountainous terrain. Well, I was about to find out how well it performed on snow-covered Detroit streets.

Florence was looking out the window. She told me later that there was so much snow kicking up from the back of my wagon, that she was confused as to what had just happened. Once my car was gone and the spray of snow settled, she saw two boys that were kicking snow after my car.

Opening her front door, Florence asked them in a stern voice, "What did you say to her?"

"If you don't want anything to happen to your ass, you better get inside that house," one of them responded. She slammed her door.

I called her when I was a safe distance away and told her to call 911 to report an attempted carjacking but I warned her that she should not open her door, because they had guns.

The next day, I reported the incident to Chief Judge Atkins. With laser-focused eyes, she said, "I don't know why you aren't dead. We have these types of cases all the time."

Wearily, I said, "I know."

As tears welled up in her eyes, she said, "It must have been your sister protecting you. There's no other logical explanation."

Without blinking, I said, "When Leona died, I asked God to make her my guardian angel. Well, I just got his reply last night!"

Since that horrific yet miraculous evening, many times, I have thought long and hard about the outcome of that evening. It has played in my brain, over and over. There are many ways that evening could have gone south. I knew because my sister and I had attended funerals of people who had been shot through the windows of their cars with no way of escaping, not to mention the number of cases we both had heard in our courtrooms that mirrored my situation. For many weeks following my scenario, I heard reports on television about carjackings, in which victims gave up their keys and personal items but were shot anyway.

It could have been me, but it was not, because a strong power in that car had made me turn my head. A power, a spirit, had pulled my head to look out my driver's window, because there had been no cars on that street; there had been no traffic for me to look out for. I was alone out there, so I thought.

I felt that spiritual pull was my sister. If not for that, I would not be here. My term of being a drug court judge would have been cut short. However, because that evening ended the way it did, I continued doing the job I was put on Earth to do. That evening reinforced for me that I am not alone, because I know my sister's spirit is always with me.

◆ My Last Two Contacts with Leona

In the late spring of 2012, I was attending a National Association of Drug Court Professionals (NADCP) conference in Washington, DC. As a member of the board of that organization, I participated in our board activities. Attending a luncheon with twenty-five board members, the CEO, and his administrative staff, who ran the day to-day operations of the organization, was one of the board functions. At the luncheon, the staff sat at tables alongside two or three board members. The luncheon was the only time, once a year, when the staff got to meet and sit face-to-face with the board members. Each seat had a name placard in front of it, so people knew where to sit.

I had attended the conference luncheon many times before as a board member. There was nothing new or different about that luncheon, except the people at the table were all different. After everybody said hello and introduced him- or herself, we all began buttering our rolls and eating the salads. I was talking to the judge sitting next to me, when a young lady of Native American descent said, "Excuse me, Judge Lloyd, but do you have a twin sister?"

I directed my attention at her and said, "Yes, I had a twin sister, but she passed ten years ago."

She responded, "I know."

I focused on her and thought it odd that her question had been in the present tense, as if my twin sister were still alive. Quickly, I wondered why she had even asked about my sister if she knew that Leona had passed. It bothered me slightly, but I managed to smile faintly and continued to butter my dinner roll, when she said, "Excuse me, Judge Lloyd. I hate to bother you again, but your sister won't leave me alone."

My eyes stayed on her. I did not understand what in the world the young lady was talking about.

"She told me to tell you *hello*."

I put my knife down, and tears flowed from my face like a waterfall. I was frozen. I could not speak. The judge next to me was concerned and asked if I was okay. I wanted to say yes, but I could not talk or move. Everyone at the table stopped eating. Their concerned faces all turned toward me. After about ten minutes, I finally found my voice.

The young lady continued. "I didn't mean to upset you, but she kept insisting and wouldn't leave me alone."

With tears still streaming down my face, I told her, "No, that's okay; you didn't upset me. You see, I have not had a direct message from my sister in ten years, which was shortly after her passing so, I was not prepared for this. Thank you for the message."

After convincing the judge next to me that I was all right, I slowly began to eat my food, but my mind was not on my food; it was on my sister and her reaching out to me with one simple word: *hello*.

That moment stayed on my mind when I returned to Detroit. I had been so unprepared for the delivery of that message that I had totally forgotten about the carjacking incident in 2006, when a message from my sister had been indirectly given to me in a protective spiritual way. That occurrence had happened in Detroit, six years before the luncheon incident, which occurred in Washington, DC, at a conference. As I said, her spirit is always with me.

After that experience, I wanted to reach out to the lady, but I did not know her name. I called the main headquarters of the NADCP and asked to speak to the person in charge of the joint luncheon at the conference, and they connected me with a young lady. I told her who I was and explained I was trying to connect with a young lady of Native American descent who had been seated at my table. After pulling up the assigned seating arrangements, she gave me the names of two ladies who had sat at the table. One was of Hispanic descent; that was not her. The other lady was a liaison between the drug courts and the tribal courts. That had to be her.

I emailed the young lady and asked if she had been the lady who sat at my table and carried a message from my deceased twin sister, and sure enough, it was her. I explained I wanted to reach out to her because that had never happened to me before. An email discussion went on for a few minutes. She recommended a book for me to read that I could order online. I thanked her and immediately went online and ordered the book. It was about a man who discovered later in his life that he had the power to connect and speak with people who had left the earth and crossed over. It proved to be an interesting book. I guess she wanted me to know more about the people who had those special abilities.

Three or four months later, I received an email from her asking if I had read the book she had suggested. I let her know that I had read it and enjoyed it. She said she knew I lived in Michigan but wanted to know if I was interested in going to the author's meditation class. The only problem was that it was taking place in Canada and she did not know how far the location was from me. I responded that I had a house in Canada, near Chatham, so if she gave me the location, I would figure it out.

She sent me the author's information. I went online and saw that he had an entire itinerary around the United States, but the province in Canada was a three-hour drive from my house in Canada. I contacted her later after I decided I would sign up for the meditation class. I indicated to her that it was on an Indian reservation; I had no clue where it was, but I intended to sign up for it.

"Great! I hope you enjoy it," she said. She added that many people found it to be relaxing. That was the last time I spoke to the Native American lady that had made the connection to Leona.

The meditation class in Canada was scheduled to take place about four months after I preregistered online. That gave me enough time to convince Gwen to agree to go.

On the date of the meditation class, we set out four hours prior to the start of the class. The Indian reservation, which was beautiful, looked like a regular city. The houses were as beautiful as some I had seen in upscale Los Angeles. We arrived at the address and worked our way to a one-story building. I had brought the things the website had indicated to bring: a mat to lie down on, a blanket, a pillow, and a bottle of water. As Gwen and I were in the parking lot, trying to pull the items we'd brought out of the back of my truck, a man who stood outside in front of the building, smoking a cigarette, saw us struggling with the mat and blankets and asked if we needed a hand.

"Yes, please." I was grateful for his assistance.

He came over and grabbed the cumbersome exercise mat and pillow. I was happy for the help because I often had pain in my left hip.

When we crossed the parking lot and approached the entrance, the man abruptly stopped and looking at me he said, "Excuse me, but I have to say something to you."

We stopped walking and I directed my attention toward him.

"You have some very persistent relatives, and they won't stop pestering me until I deliver this message to you from them. They said they wanted you to know they are very proud of you and all the work you're doing."

Stunned and keeping my eyes on him, I said slowly, "Okay, thank you."

"I'm sorry, but they wouldn't have left me alone if I hadn't delivered this message."

I thanked him again, thinking; *I have been down this road before.* Gwen and I exchanged glances. Who was this man? I had never seen him before. This time, I did not cry, but I was too shocked to follow up with any questions.

We went into the room, and the lady who greeted us assigned us tables to put our mats and pillows on. She went on to introduce the group to the man who would be leading the meditation. He walked in and began to speak. As I gazed at him, I suddenly realized he was the same man who had helped us carry in our items from the car. He was also the author of the book I had read several months earlier. He was the man who had the ability to connect with people who had passed and crossed over. Stunned for a moment, I realized he had carried a message from my family to me. Gwen and I talked about it all the way home. Many years after her death, Leona is still sending messages. She has never left me.

The meditation class was great, and I felt so relaxed that the pain I had been having in my side for months was gone, at least for that day. However, the thrill of that day was the message I received from my family, and I have no doubt my sister was the ring-leader. That was the last time I heard from my family or my sister, but I know she is around me. She will always find a way to get through. She is my guardian angel, and we will forever have a bond that death cannot break. Oh, God's amazing grace!

It was God's grace that helped my sister and me get through all the obstacles we got hit with while growing up, as well as throughout college and law school. It was his grace that made sure help came when I needed it to lift me back up and give me the spirit and fortitude to keep going after Leona passed. It was his grace that allowed me to be his instrument to help others find their rightful path in life, and it is his grace that prevents the bond between Leona and me from being broken.

Me with my Mercedes 500 G-Wagon that helped me escape danger

Part FIVE

2009– to Present

CHAPTER 21

Veterans' Court

◆ What's Marijuana Got to Do with It?

Imagine returning from a war zone, and society expects you to just pick up the pieces from when you left and become a normal, contributing member of society. Never mind that you suffer from post-traumatic stress disorder (PTSD) that will probably be with you for the rest of your life, and you might also be in excruciating pain from injuries.

My father did not have to imagine; that scenario was real for him. He came back from World War II with issues, such as PTSD, that he did not know he had, but he was left to deal with them on his own, like thousands of other veterans. In the twenty-first century, we now have labeled the condition PTSD, but still, many veterans came into my courtroom with horrible problems or severe pain from military duty and addiction to opioids due to their injuries. These men and women had unique problems and issues that had to be addressed.

In 2009, I decided to go to a seminar on the new topic of veterans' treatment court (VTC) at the NADCP conference in Washington, DC. Judge Robert Russell from Buffalo, New York, created the first veterans' court in the United States and developed that initial seminar. He started his veterans' court because the vets in his drug court did not fit in. Even though they were defendants with drug problems, the path that had gotten them there was different from the one of the typical, defendant in drug court. As Judge Russell explained, "The vets in my veterans' court are there because of the things that happened to them while they were in active service."

Those vets would say in his drug court, as they said in mine, "I am not like them," referring to the other defendants in drug court.

Because of the similarities I saw between his drug court and mine when it came to veterans, I left that seminar convinced our court had to create a veterans' court because our veterans had different issues that needed a different approach from the ones used in drug court.

My first request in 2009 for a veterans' court was denied. That was a frustrating response I was not prepared for. I refused to take that as my final answer. For the next year, my work with the veterans in drug court was about discovery and investigation. I began to learn the differences between the veterans and the nonveterans. Yes, they were using the same drugs, but for different reasons. The usage for the veterans were all service-related, unlike with the nonveterans.

In May of 2010, I went to the NADCP's special two-day training sessions headed by Judge Robert T. Russell, the founder of VTC. He placed troubled veterans who had served our country and returned to the United States with challenges in readjustment, as well as mental health issues, in VTC and formed an alliance with the veterans' health resource organization. By doing so, he created and developed a program that would give the vets a second chance to turn their lives around. My investigation into the vets in my drug court helped me identify with everything Judge Russell spoke of.

After the sessions, I went to speak to Judge Russell and expressed my chief judge's reluctance to add any more specialty courts, though I felt a veterans' court was desperately needed, not to mention that the vets in regular drug court would be the ones initially transferred to that specialty court. He knew me as a member of the board of directors for NADCP, and he was an emeritus board member. He said, "I know how committed you are to your drug court and helping your vets, so if you need me to fly into Detroit to speak with your chief judge, then I will do so. Your veterans' court would be a great asset to the vets in Detroit." I thanked him for his generous offer of assistance and said I would be in touch.

I came back from that conference determined to convince Chief Judge Atkins that we needed a veterans' court and all the benefits that came with it for the veterans. At my meeting with Judge Atkins I said, "Judge Russell, who has been honored by Congress for creating this innovative specialty court that is saving the lives of vets, indicated he would fly here to speak with you about the importance of letting me start a veterans' court."

I was just getting started, when the chief said, "It won't be necessary for him to fly in to speak with me. This is the second time you have requested this specialty court, so I know this is important to you. You have done an excellent job with drug court, and since you feel so strongly about the need for this court, you got it. We will meet to set up a date for when it will formally start and discuss how we will staff and create the program and identify our partners for the program."

I thanked her and left her office, and I danced my way down the hallway. The chief saw my determination, and she knew I was not going to let the matter go. Usually, when a chief judge says no, that is the final answer, but I was determined because with the new vet court, I would have access to many more resources for my vets and could cut through the red tape for them. Yes, I was going to fight for them, if necessary, but I was so glad she changed her mind and agreed to the creation of the new veteran's court.

In November of 2010, we started our veterans' court. It was the second established veterans' court in Michigan and the first in Wayne

County. Our veterans' court joined an alliance with Veteran Affairs (VA). By doing so, we expanded our availability to the resources the veterans needed for their recovery. I worked closely with their representatives, Ms. Nanette Collins and then Ms. Barbara Reyes, who attended all veteran court status hearings in the courtroom, assisted in cutting through all the red tape, and expedited all health appointments. They made sure all doctors understood the concerns of my court when it came to my vets in VTC.

In November 2012, on Veterans Day, the local newspaper, the *Detroit News*, featured our VTC on the front page. The *Detroit News* wanted to inform the public about what our court was doing to help the veteran population who were struggling with alcohol abuse, substance abuse, and PTSD. As the article pointed out, "One in four veterans living in southeastern Michigan had alcohol problems," and "81% of vets who had contact with the police or a court officer had a substance abuse problem before their incarceration." The article also stated, "As many as one third of veterans were identified as having alcohol dependency and self-medicated with alcohol or drugs due to their PTSD." The need was great for the development of a special program like veterans' treatment court for the men and women who had risked their lives for our country.

In VTC, I encountered many vets who had fought hard for this country and had their lives turned inside out. They were no longer the same women and men who had entered the service. Their lives had changed for the worse. They came home expecting our country to welcome them with open and nurturing arms, but that was not the reality. Many vets were not receiving help for PTSD because they feared being labeled as "crazy." When they were labeled in that manner, many found it impossible to obtain employment to help support themselves and their families, so many vets decided not to get the help they desperately needed. Instead, they turned to alcohol or narcotic substances. Sadly, the VA assisted the vets in obtaining narcotic meds for pain management so readily that the narcotics became a new addiction for them. They might not have felt any pain, but they were becoming addicts. *CBS World News* reported, "Veterans are twice as likely as non-veterans, in 2018, to die from an accidental overdose involving prescription opioids."

Interestingly, marijuana came to the forefront as a remedy for the new addiction veterans were falling victim to. Now, let us be clear: marijuana is an addictive, mind-altering drug. However, it has medicinal benefits. It has been found to be helpful to people who are in pain and who have glaucoma and other ailments. I had to open my eyes to the realization that it could be helpful for veterans.

In my VTC, I ordered the vets with PTSD into counseling. Not going to counseling could result in danger to themselves or to others. I insisted on talk therapy for my vets before any narcotics were recommended for them, because far too many times, I had heard that going to counseling only meant getting pills. No one wanted to spend quality time talking to them. However, I knew a pill was not going to fix everything; in fact, it might create more problems.

In 2016, I went to VTC seminars in Washington, DC, where I heard vet after vet explain his or her battle with prescription pills. They expressed that they were given many pills for PTSD, anxiety, pain, or sleeplessness. They revealed the enormous number of pills they were on and how easily they could obtain pills from the VA. I was shocked. However, the real problem was that none of those pills were helping the vets. They said they never slept, nor could they sit for more than five minutes in a classroom for courses they had enrolled in. Their home lives were a wreck; the pills they took turned them into strangers to their spouses and children. Many talked about contemplating suicide as an answer, a way out.

Listening to the vets at the conference, I was glad I insisted on no narcotics unless every possible remedy had been tried and had failed. Unlike the men I heard speak at that seminar, 99.5 percent of my graduates of vet court graduated drug and alcohol free. That did not include the vets who were already on methadone.

I saw vets enter veterans' court with feelings of despair, hopelessness, and distrust but graduate the program and leave as persons filled with hope for their futures. We worked hard to make sure those who needed job training received it and obtained jobs, regardless of past counseling for PTSD. The VA assisted and bent over backward to make it happen for our veterans. Several vets who graduated VTC decided to pass on to others the help they had received in VTC by starting their own organizations to assist vets. The programs targeted vets who might not be lucky enough to walk through the doors of a VTC.

Having graduates like that made me beam with pride. I knew the creation of the VTC program would end up benefitting other people indirectly.

◆ Southeastern Michigan Veterans Stand Down Inc.

In 2012, as a judge of the Thirty-Sixth District Court, I accepted an invitation from the board of Southeastern Michigan Veterans Stand Down Inc. (SMVSD) to participate in their program and hold court at the upcoming stand down to hear the misdemeanor cases of homeless veterans, including many who were in warrant status. The then president of the board, Gunnery Sergeant Norman Wilcox, and a spokesperson for the board met with me at the location of the stand down to plan out the design of the courtroom for the upcoming stand down.

Once a year, for the following four years, I presided over the court at the stand down to help homeless veterans handle their unadjudicated legal cases. My court team and I cleared up a lot of legal baggage for those vets. Many of the veterans at the stand down were in substance abuse recovery, getting their lives back in order. Many times, veterans used substances, whether alcohol or drugs, to buffer the problems created by their time in the service. Ironically, it was the substance abuse that resulted in veterans becoming homeless and therefore not handling their legal matters. By holding court at the stand down, my court and I helped to remove legal obstacles that prevented many vets from moving on with their lives and obtaining jobs. Jobs could lead to better housing, thus eliminating homelessness.

After I retired from the bench, I accepted the board's invitation to become a board member. Joining the board was a natural transition for me because it allowed me to continue to help remove the legal obstacles blocking the lives of homeless veterans. I made sure Thirty-Sixth District Court remained a viable resource to help vets by securing the help of Mr. Wright Wade, the director of probation as well as the help of their veterans' treatment court judge, Judge Shannon Holmes, to preside over the Southeastern Michigan Veterans Stand Down court. The Thirty-Sixth District Court has been a steadfast participant for the last seven years, and they continue to make a huge difference in the lives of the vets at the stand downs.

As a board member, I enlisted the help of Mrs. Yvonne Barnett-Greene, the manager of specialty courts at the Third Circuit Court. She helped formulate a vast amount of resources for the vets at the stand down who had legal issues and needed referrals for legal services. Additionally, she brought experts from the court to answer the vets' questions about child support issues, and she brought Mr. John Marr, the veterans' court coordinator, to help people who were interested in joining their veterans' court program to receive help with their circuit court cases. She got the Honorable Deborah Thomas, a Third Circuit Court judge, on board to speak and provide a blueprint for the vets and their family members to help them navigate their journey to obtaining felony expungements.

All in all, both courts have become an integral part of the Southeastern Michigan Veterans Stand Down. Hopefully, other courts around the country will become part of the military stand downs taking place in their states.

◆ Medical Marijuana versus Opioids for Veterans

The vets at the stand down suffered from the same problems as my VTC participants and vets all over the United States. I felt there had to be a better way to help veterans other than slipping pills down their throats. After I retired, I started researching the issue to see if there were alternatives that would not have the dangerous effects that pill popping had on many. There had to be a better way. Through my research, I discovered there is a better way to help vets.

As a drug court judge, I was initially a staunch objector to any defendant's use of marijuana, but just as the laws have shifted, I had to alter my stance. Numerous states have now legalized the medical and recreational use of marijuana (cannabis).

At the time of this writing, vets can now use medical marijuana and participate in state-regulated marijuana programs without losing their benefits. That was not the case before. They can now discuss their usage with their VA medical providers to make sure there are not any negative effects or interference with any other medicines they are receiving, without receiving any repercussions.

As a former drug court judge, I have seen the effects of marijuana usage by teenagers as well as adults. It would be safe to say that at least 95 percent of the young adults who appeared before me in drug court admitted they had dropped out of high school in the tenth or eleventh grade because of regular marijuana smoking. When I questioned them regarding why they had dropped out, they admitted that after they smoked weed, their comprehension of the materials studied in the classroom was poor. Smoking weed had everything to do with their dropping out of school, they said. I saw people in my drug court who had smoked marijuana regularly for five or ten years suddenly become full of energy and drive after they stopped smoking marijuana. In fact, they were unrecognizable and developed an unstoppable zest for life.

Despite, what I and many other judges have seen in drug courts, more than thirty-three states, including Michigan, have approved medical marijuana for people with chronic pain. In 2018, Michigan became the tenth state, in addition to Washington, DC, to legalize recreational marijuana to be used by people twenty-one years of age and older. As of 2020, a total of eleven states in the United States have legalized recreational marijuana. In October 2018, Canada legalized marijuana federally.

There is no question in my mind that medical marijuana is a better option than opioids for helping to alleviate pain. Opioid addiction has caused far too many deaths. However, whether in the case of medical marijuana or recreational marijuana; we have to realize, too many people are getting behind the wheel and driving while high.

Scientists at the University of Michigan Addiction Center conducted a study involving 790 medical marijuana patients in Michigan who were seeking recertification for chronic pain during 2014 and 2015. The researchers asked about respondents' driving habits over the past six months. More than half of the medical marijuana patients surveyed admitted to having driven while under the influence of cannabis. According to the findings, 56 percent reported driving within two hours of using marijuana, 51 percent said they drove while "a little high," and 21 percent reported driving while "very high."

My issue is this: How does one determine what is a little high versus very high? Can anyone really know how high he or she is? Shouldn't there be a standard for measuring this?

"To know that folks are driving and may be impaired from using their medical marijuana is concerning from a public health perspective," says Erin E. Bonar, PhD, the study's lead author, who is an assistant professor of psychiatry and a practicing clinical psychologist at U-M Addiction Treatment Services. Bonar says that when people drive under the influence of marijuana, their reaction time and coordination may be slower, and they might have a harder time reacting to the unexpected. In a risky situation, they may be more likely to be involved in a motor vehicle crash, because they will not be able to respond quickly. As of May 2018, hundreds of thousands of Americans have state approval to use medical marijuana, including nearly 270,000 in the state of Michigan, according to Statista.[3] Michigan has the second-highest number of medical marijuana patients next to California, according to the study.

There is uncertainty about how marijuana could affect driving for chronic daily users, who might have some even longer-lasting effects that linger in their system, Bonar says.

According to Bonar, "When it comes to driving, we haven't yet figured out the best way to know how impaired marijuana users are at any given time. We also don't have specific guidelines yet about when exactly it would be safe to operate a vehicle."

Bonar says the goal of her team's study is to help medical marijuana users be safer on the roads. "We also need clearer guidelines about marijuana dosing and side effects with an understanding of how individual differences in things like sex and body weight interact as well."

◆ The Change I Hope For

I would like to see the federal law that classifies marijuana as a schedule 1 controlled substance changed. That would result in declassification of marijuana and products made from the hemp plant, such as CBD products. That way, universities as well as the VA could research marijuana and hemp products to determine how effective or ineffective marijuana and CBD products are for treatment.

An American Legion poll released November 2018 found that more than 90 percent of veterans, support expanding research into

---

[3] https://www.statista.com/statistics/585154/us-legal-medical-marijuana-patients-state/.

medical marijuana, and more than 80 percent believe federal doctors should be allowed to prescribe it to veterans.

Any medical discoveries from VA cannabis testing could have wide-ranging effects on the broader national debate about the validity of cannabis as medication.

Veterans are suffering from chronic pain and PTSD. A CBS report claimed, "They are not your typical lobbyists. They're veterans whose lives were nearly ruined—first by their injury and then by their meds." A US Navy veteran stated that she took opioids for seventeen years after she suffered a service-related head injury. She was basically a walking zombie. Once she started using CBD oil, which did not give her the effects of feeling high, she found relief for her pain. She cannot get CBD oil from the VA because it is not legal. Her story is an example of why I am pushing for the legalization and separation of hemp products, such as CBD products.

As a drug court judge, I was once opposed to marijuana in any form, but during my last two years off the bench, because of my research, I have made some drastic changes in my beliefs.

I still do not believe anyone under the age of twenty-one should use marijuana. The rational part of a person's brain is not fully developed until the age of twenty-five. Researchers need to study whether early use of marijuana causes an impairment of growth of the brain and whether that impairment is permanent.

For those who want to use recreational marijuana, I look at marijuana as any other mind-altering drug, such as alcohol. People need to be educated about the long-term effects of marijuana. The pros and cons must be delineated so people don't look at it as just a party drug but realize that if it's used incorrectly, like alcohol, it can lead to addiction and many pitfalls in one's life, affecting career choices.

I strongly believe that if the marijuana laws are changed, the VA and leading universities will be able to do the research necessary to help veterans, athletes, and others suffering from traumatic injuries. If that research is done, other Americans who want to be free from pain would not be led down a path of self-destruction with opioids. America has a chance to get this right by changing the classification of marijuana in its entirety. If Congress decides not to change the classification of marijuana, there should at least be a modification to reflect a declassification of the hemp portion of the plant, from which CBD products are derived. This separation and declassification would pave the way for researchers to determine what the product can do and how it can benefit the health of Americans, which would eliminate the guessing games people play out of desperation for an alternative to opioids.

Me holding court at Southeastern Michigan Veterans Stand Down for homeless veterans, in 2016

CHAPTER 22

You Have Only One Life to Live

IT'S A FAMILY AFFAIR

Leona used to quote Mae West in saying, "You only have one life, but if you do it right, once is enough."

Every time she said that, I would laugh and agree. "You're right."

My sister thoroughly believed and lived by those words.

That powerful statement rubbed off on me. Sometimes, if I were cautiously trying to decide on something, she would roll in like a whirlwind and say, "What's there to think about? Just do it."

She did not mean I should throw caution to the wind. Instead, she meant "Don't sit on the fence when there's something in your heart that you really want to do." It was not unusual for her, after she had traveled on a trip, to come back and tell me how beautiful the location was and insist we go back to visit that place. Whether it was another country or an island, off we went.

Her "I can do it" spirit was contagious. She did not believe in sitting around; she believed in seeing the world, and she made sure her sister—lucky me—was never left out.

If it were snowing in Detroit, she would ease down to my house, and before I knew it, we were planning a winter getaway in February. Then—hocus-pocus—when we got off the plane, the white stuff beneath our feet and tickling our toes was sand, not snow.

We would relax and recharge our batteries in the island sun of Aruba, St. Martin; St. Thomas, US Virgin Islands; Mexico; or the Cayman Islands and be ready to take on the world when we came back.

I passed that joy for living on to friends and even defendants in court. I let defendants in drug court know that they had the capability to travel and go beyond the borders of Detroit. When you spread hope, it becomes infectious. It was something I wanted them to catch. Many of them did.

It filled my heart when one graduate of drug court went on to become a licensed practical nurse and then a registered nurse. She came back to visit me and let me know she was now living a great life. She brought a T-shirt for me from one of the islands she had visited on a cruise.

Leona and I both preached that can-do spirit to others because it was a rule we lived by. We would tell them, "Why not you?"

◆ Paradise Island

On one of our visits to the Bahamas, my sister was busy playing at a slot machine. Neither of us were gamblers; we did not like throwing money away, so we set a budget for gambling at the casinos. The amount was usually fifty dollars. Once the allotted money was gone, it was time to stop. Well, my sister had been sitting at one slot machine for so long that I teased her about growing roots.

"Every time I hit the button on this slot machine, I win! I haven't lost yet!" Leona exclaimed.

Well, my machine was not that lucky. Leona had buckets and buckets of quarters—so many that she gave me a bucket of quarters to go play a machine and leave her alone. Gail, our girlfriend, and I finally convinced her to leave the machine to go to a nightclub with a Vegas-style show. Leona was not thrilled to go, but she came with us.

After the show, she strolled by the machine she had been playing, and another woman was sitting there, winning like crazy.

My sister said, "See? That could have been me winning."

We all laughed because she had already won a lot of money that night. The point was just to play and have fun, and we did that.

Over the next few days, we ran up and down the Bahamian island, visiting the fancy lit-up clubs at night and shopping during the day. Those are fun-filled memories I will never forget.

There is one trip I wish with all my heart my sister could have taken with me. It was not to an exotic place like Thailand or Korea, even though I would have loved for her to have gone with me to those places, because I know we would have had a ball. I am speaking of our mother's birthplace: Rock Hill, South Carolina. By the time I went there, it was fourteen years after Leona had passed. However, the trip was not something I had planned. It was one of those things that happened in divine order.

◆ A Letter That Opened My World

My sister and I had been to my father's birthplace in Memphis, Tennessee, many times. However, when we asked our mother to go visit her birthplace with us, she always firmly said no. She said it brought back sad memories of the passing of her mother, so we reconciled ourselves to the reality that we would never see where our mother had grown up.

But that was not in the plan for me. In 2014, a cousin of mine named Pamela Chisolm contacted me. After reading her letter, I immediately called her to get acquainted with my new relative. We had a great conversation, and Pam, being the family historian, enlightened me on all my relatives past and present. Wow! The newfound knowledge was beyond my greatest expectations.

Pam and her two brothers had worked in the law enforcement field. One of her brothers, Linwood, was a retired Secret Service agent who had served under six presidents, from President Carter to President Obama. Pam lived in Washington, DC, so I asked her how in the world she had found me. Once I learned she was a retired DC police investigator, I figured she could have found me or anybody else easily. She said her late father had told her that his cousin, my mother, lived in Detroit and had a set of twins. From that point, she had searched the US Census and several obituaries.

After connecting with her, I accepted her invitation to the Chisolm family reunion, and a few months later, I was on my way to Rock Hill, South Carolina.

I met more than a hundred new relatives. Pam and my cousin Allen took me sightseeing so I could learn about the Chisolm family history. You could have knocked me over with a feather when I saw a street named Chisolm after our family. As I learned about my family, I could not stop wishing that my sister had been there to see all of it with me.

Before I left Rock Hill, I told my cousin Allen there was one place I had to see if we had time: the burial site of my grandmother. My uncle Napoleon had erected a statue to honor her at her burial site, and I had to see it because my mother had never seen it. I asked him if he could take me there. Without hesitation, he made a few quick maneuvers on the expressway, and we were there in no time. While driving, Allen said there was a beautiful statue at the grave site that looked like an angel.

As we approached her tombstone, I instinctively recognized it. "That's the statue of my grandmother. She looks just like her picture, from the wire-rimmed glasses to the little gold hoops in her ears. That picture of her has been in my mother's house on display since I was a little girl." The statue was dressed in a long, flowing gown, and just as Allen had said, she looked like an angel. I stood there and read the phrases inscribed on the two stone tablets that stood on each side of her, which described her character perfectly.

I stood there with tears cascading down my face yet overwhelmed by a sense of peace I had never experienced before. Wiping my flowing tears, I felt that Pam's outreach to me had been God's way of letting me know I was not alone. My connection to my mother's family tree, with all its branches lovingly surrounding me, made me feel at home.

Through his grace, God placed Pam in my life. However, God was not finished connecting me with my family; through Facebook I have met a ton of relatives from my father's side of the family. Through an invitation from my cousin, Earl Rayford, I intend to meet and connect with many of them next year in June at the Lloyd/Rodgers Family Reunion 2021. What a blessing; my family tree of life will blossom and bear fruit from both sides.

Enjoying winter in Canada at my beach house, named "Tranquility"

◆ Tranquility

I did something else I had not planned on, but as Leona said, "You only live once"; after her death, I bought a house in Canada, on Lake Erie. I named it Tranquility because of the serenity it brought to me. It became my retreat and a place where I could recover from and process the loss of my dear sister. The undulating waves and lake breezes brought me solace and peace. I moved some of her furniture into the house, and it was a constant reminder of her comforting voice and unwavering support. It was truly a home away from home. On many days, as I gazed at Lake Erie's sparkling blue water, I remembered Leona and myself dancing to the island music in the sunlight, while riding on a catamaran near an island on the Caribbean Sea.

Springtime...Me gazing out at beautiful Lake Erie at my beach house.

CHAPTER 23

From Where I Sat

REACH OUT AND TOUCH (SOMEBODY'S HAND)

I want to express a message to my fellow judges. Now that I have left the bench and taken off my robe, I can say what is really in my heart regarding the role of a judge and how a judge can be effective while on the bench.

No matter what type of court I presided over, I was determined that any litigant who walked into my courtroom, regardless of his or her problem, walked out an improved person. I wanted defendants to feel that the court cared about them as people and that they were more than case numbers. I wanted litigants to realize when they exited the courtroom that their situations had improved.

Focusing directly on defendants and quickly figuring out what type of mood they are in and what is really going on with them is the key. I knew that before placing a fine on an individual, my job was to communicate with him or her, one on one so, the defendant would let down his or her guard and talk to me. Even if defendants told defense counsel, they wanted to accept a plea deal and plead guilty, I questioned was that really what they wanted to do?

If the body language of the defendants indicated otherwise and instead screamed that they were angry, then as an observant judge, I looked beyond their words and asked if that was what they really wanted to do. If the response was yes but they wanted to explain something to me, then I gave them time to talk after the plea was given. In those cases, immediately, the whole temperament of the defendant changed. The heightened voice calmed down, and I would hear a response of "Okay."

Listening to the defendant and hearing his or her explanation is sometimes more important to the defendant than the assessed fine. The most important thing to the defendant is being heard. Any judge who wants to give the appearance of fairness should always afford the defendant the time to give an explanation. Defendants understand that the fine does not go away, but the above approach gives the judge another opportunity to explain how the law works and why the person's actions prompted the issuance of the ticket. Before I ended each case, I always took the opportunity to thank the defendant for his or her explanation to the court.

My golden rule was and still is: if judges treat each person who comes before them the way they would want to be treated, they will see a positive outcome for their court as well as for the defendant, regardless of a finding of innocence or guilt. There are no obstacles here in the United States blocking judges from doing so, except themselves. I have talked to representatives from other countries who were amazed at my demeanor in the courtroom. One visitor said that in his country, the defendants were afraid to look at the judge. He went on to say, that a judge shaking a defendant's hand for a job well done was unheard of because the judge, in their country was beyond reproach. My response was that I was glad I did not live in those countries, but God places you where you are supposed to be.

A good judge will always connect with the defendant. My first year on the bench, a defendant was amazed that I looked directly at him, as I spoke to him, as opposed to looking down at him.

"You actually looked me in the eye and talked to me, not at me. No other judge has done that for me," he said.

He waited in the courtroom to see how I treated other defendants and was surprised to find out that he was not an exception. "You talked to everybody like you talked to me, like we were real people."

Communication, consistency, fairness, compassion, individuality, thinking outside the box, and the ability to step out on faith are the components of the formula judges can use while still operating within the canons of judicial ethics and upholding the integrity and independence of the judiciary. They can turn their courtrooms into empowerment zones, making the world a better place.

A picture of me relaxing in my Judicial Chambers at the 36th District Court

◆ Life for Us Ain't Been No Crystal Stair

When Leona and I were little girls, my mother often read to us a poem by Langston Hughes titled "Mother to Son." Every time she read it to us, we would gather around her, fascinated by the animation in her voice and the twinkle in her eyes. However, when she read the poem, tears would stream down her face. She never told us why she was crying, but we still loved listening to her read it.

As we got older and took interpretive reading classes in college, both of us chose to read that poem out loud in class. Luckily, we were in separate classes; both of us loved that poem.

As a high school teacher, I introduced the world of Langston Hughes's literature to my students, including that poem. The message of the poem was one of hope and courage. Even though the mother in the poem had a life full of obstacles and hardships, she never let that stop her. She kept climbing, elevating herself higher to improve her condition. That was the message to her son. We believed it was also the message from our mother to us.

As Leona and I got older, the poem came to mean so much more to us. We had a mother who did not stop trying to be the best she could be after her physical and mental illnesses; she kept going. Maybe her tears reflected her awareness of the changes in her life that she had no control over, but she could not stop going forward. Perhaps reading the poem to us was her way of saying, "Life may get hard, but don't you dare quit. I expect you to tackle head-on what comes your way, because if it doesn't kill you, it will make you stronger."

From all the stories my mother told us, as well as all the things we saw her experience, we knew her life was anything but easy, but the challenges she faced did not stop her. She escaped the fear of burning crosses in the front yard of her home and the brutality of racism as a little girl living in the South. Later, she barely escaped death from a brain hemorrhage, which caused her life as she knew it to be erased. She lost a career she had trained for and worked in for ten years. She had to pick up the pieces of her life, reshape it, and go into the unknown, only to go through a series of nervous breakdowns. Through it all, she kept going; she did not stop.

Leona and I said in many speeches to young people that when they were traveling down the road of life, they were going to hit speed bumps, curves, potholes, and many other obstacles, but they couldn't let those obstacles stop them or make them turn around. That is called life.

Leona and I hit many obstacles, but we did not quit. When my sister died, I wanted to stop and turn back or at least sit down. I felt it was too difficult to go on, but I could hear my mother's voice reading the words of that poem, "Don't you set down on the steps / 'Cause you finds it's kinder hard." Her message to me was *"Baby, don't you stop what you and Leona started. You have to keep going."* I had to keep going, even if I was alone and even if it was hard and felt impossible. I could not turn back, not now. My mother never turned back. My father never turned back. They kept going and finished their missions. I could not turn back either; I had too much to do.

Me standing tall, wearing my sister's favorite color of power- RED. Photo Credit: by Victor A. Toliva

The path God set me on led me to drug court and veterans' court. I was not on that path alone; I had many more individuals with me: my defendants. I told them they could not stop because it was hard, and they could not turn around because life was not easy. Together, we kept moving forward, and I would not let them fall. Like them, I found that life had not been easy; it had been "no crystal stair." I went to law school when racism was rampant, I had to face racism in places where I worked, and I had an imperfect family life, but each of those things taught me how to hold what I truly wanted in the forefront as I became stronger and more focused on creating a positive outcome for those I served and those around me. For that, in the words of the song "Rise Up" by Andra Day, "I'll rise up a thousand times!"

Appendix

◆ List of Awards

The State Bar of Michigan honored Judge Lloyd with the 2009 Champion of Justice Award. This award is given to a practicing lawyer and judge "of integrity and adherence to the highest principles and traditions of the legal profession, superior professional competence and an extraordinary professional accomplishment that benefits the nation, the state or the local community."

Additional awards include the Sojourner Truth Award from the National Association of Negro Business and Professional Women's Clubs (2008); the Mark of Excellence Award from Alabama A&M University (2009); the Distinguished Service Award from the Detroit City Council (2009); and a Certificate of Tribute from Governor Jennifer Granholm (2009). Judge Lloyd and her drug court team received the Recognition Award from the National Association of Drug Court Professionals as the second-best drug court in the nation (2005–2006).

Judge Lloyd's team received the coveted Transformation Award from the National Association of Drug Court Professionals (2009). She was also a recipient of the Women of Wayne Headliner's Award, the Distinguished Board Service Award from the National Association of Drug Court Professionals (2015), and the Benjamin Hooks Visionary Award presented by the Greater Mount Moriah Missionary Baptist Church (2016).

For her work with veterans in Michigan, she received the following awards: the Emmanuel House for the Homeless Veteran's Program Award (2013); the Deepest Appreciation Certificate and Coin presented by the director of Veterans Services (2013); a Certificate of Appreciation from the City of Southfield Veterans' Commission (2015); the Southeastern Michigan Veterans Stand Down Appreciation Award (2015); a Michigan Veterans Foundation Certificate of Appreciation (2016); and the American Patriot Award, the Michigan Veterans Foundation's highest award presented to a civilian for supporting veterans (2016).

In 2017, Judge Lloyd received the Treasure of Detroit Award from Wayne State University Law School. This prestigious award is given to those who are innovative and have made changes in the legal profession.

Acknowledgments

I would like to Praise God, my Heavenly Father, from Whom all blessings flow.

I thank my mother and father for the love and support they gave my sister and me over the years. Thank you both for the many sacrifices you made to allow Leona and me to go forth into the world. Thank you for being there for us even during your hardships.

I would like to thank Daniel Brightwell for the loving and caring bond we have. Thank you for your constant support, guidance, patience, and encouragement with this project as well as many others. Thank you for making the time on many occasions to review draft after draft. Your input was invaluable, and it helped support my vision. Thank you for sharing this journey with me.

I would like to thank Reginald Turner, my attorney, manager, and friend. Thank you for your encouragement, guidance, and support in helping me publish this book, as well as the great career advice you have given me.

I would like to thank iUniverse for helping to bring my book to life.

I would like to thank Fred Russell for his patience in allowing me to interrupt his life with all my computer problems during this project. He helped me stay on track in a timely manner.

I would like to thank Wayne Law for preparing me for my legal career and allowing me to create the Judges Leona and Leonia Lloyd Twins for Justice Endowed Scholarship fund. It was created in memory of my twin sister, Honorable Leona L. Lloyd. The purpose of the fund is to recognize academic achievement and provide financial assistance to deserving law students who want to help rebuild and reshape the City of Detroit.

I wish to thank Judge Adam Shakoor, the late Mayor Chokwe Lumumba and Attorney Godfrey Dillard for being great mentors for Leona and I during our first year in law school. You gave us the guidance we needed.

To the late Attorney Carl B. Bolden, Jr., who mentored us as new lawyers and helped lay the legal foundation for us.

I wish Florence Dunklin were still here on this earth to allow me the opportunity to thank her for the invaluable assistance she provided as my court reporter, secretary and my friend. Florence was my right and left hand. Most of the judges envied me because I had Florence as my reporter. They would say, "I wish I had a Flo." She encouraged me constantly to write this book after my sister passed. I promised Flo I would write it. I was lucky to have read her several chapters of the book while she was hospitalized. It brought joy to her heart and laughter from her soul as she listened to me read. I will always miss her.

I would like to thank Judge Miriam Clark for allowing me to bug her to death about this book. Her advice to me was invaluable. She is one of my other sisters.

I would like to thank Gwendolyn Hill, Cheryl Mason Bush, Gail Shakoor and Bernadine Rodgers, for all the assistance they constantly gave me to keep things moving for me. They have been with me through the years, and I consider them my other sisters, just as Leona did.

I want to thank Wanda Weaver for her valuable input and the editorial skills she brought to this project in helping me tell my story.

I want to thank Laura Hill, Jasmine Brimage and Lola Holton, who not only worked with me at the court as a court reporter and case managers, respectively, but also are my friends. When I retired, they remained connected to me and constantly made me feel special. No matter what projects I worked on, I could count on them for their support. Their friendship is priceless.

To Kelvyn Ventour, I thank you for believing in Leona and me and becoming a valuable member of our team that made an indelible mark in music history. You helped the world get *Ready* for a new musical sound.

To Dan Henderson and Otto Williams, who had our backs and were always there when we needed you, thank you. You were an integral part of our entertainment team.

I want to say thank you to Bruce Tucker, who believed in us as lawyers and introduced us to his clients; the music icons David Ruffin and Eddie Kendricks, which resulted in them becoming our clients. They arranged for us to receive a gold record, which we proudly displayed on the walls of our law office and judicial chambers.

To the many artists we worked with as lawyers, I want to say thank you for investing your trust and faith in us.

There were artists that we worked for and formed unique relationships. I want to thank them for believing in us as we believed in them. God gave you extraordinary talent, and Leona and I wanted to be his instrument in helping to showcase your talents to the world: Mojo, Ready for the World, Kiara, Eddie Kendricks, David Ruffin, Robert Bell, and Davina.

I want to say thank the late Attorney Jerome Crawford Jr., Benjamin Holloway Jr. and the team of people who worked diligently on all the election campaigns for Leona and me. Without your hard work, we would have never made it to the bench.

I want to say thank you to Grover McCants, a former student of my sister's, Durand Walker, and David Zeien, for all the work you did on all the election campaigns Leona and I were involved in. Your input in our elections made us shine and stand out from the crowd.

I want to thank the late Dr. Margaret Bennett for always being my bridge over troubled waters.

I want to thank Lynne Williams and Ernest Black for supporting this book by letting me tell their stories in their own words. Our paths crossed through legal pathways, but now they are my friends, and I am so proud of them both and the positive impact they are making on the world today.

I want to thank my cousins from both sides of the family: Beverly Sims for taking the time to answer all my questions regarding the Lloyd family and Pamela Chisolm, Allen Chisolm and Lawen Becote, for answering a lot of questions for me about the Chisolm family and connecting me to that side of my family.

I want to thank all the nieces, nephews, and cousins I have connected with on Facebook, you reached out to me, and I love you all for adding more value to my life. To Earl Rayford, my cousin, who helped me connect to the relatives on the Lloyd side of the family by inviting me to the 2021 Lloyd/Rodgers Family Reunion. May we always stay connected.

To my beta readers—Sonya Lindsay, Darlene Tolbert, Barbara Reyes, Mildred Davis, Dawn Outland, Pamela Chisolm, Miriam Martin Clark, Dr. Cheryl Mason Bush, and Daniel Brightwell—I want to say thank you all, from the bottom of my heart for painstakingly reading through the early drafts of my book and providing invaluable insight for me to follow.

To John Winston, thank you for your invaluable advice and support on this project.

To my entire Thirty-Sixth District Drug and Veterans' Treatment Court team, the late Dr. Calvin Trent and all the treatment providers, including the VA representatives, I want to thank you for your hard work, kind spirit, and dedication. The care and personal attention you gave our clients made a monumental difference in their treatment and in their lives. For several years, you helped hundreds of people accomplish what they never thought they could attain. I could not have done my job without you.

I want to say thank you to the following members of the 36th District Court administration, past and present, for your complete and unwavering support for the Drug and Veteran's Treatment Court programs and your complete faith in me to head those programs: Judge Marilyn Atkins; Judge Patricia Jefferson(my fellow co-DTC judge partner) and Mr. Otis Davis.

To the Southeastern Michigan Veterans Stand Down Inc., thank you for allowing me the privilege of working with such a great organization. Working with homeless veterans has been one of the highlights of my life, both as a Judge and later as a Board member.

To Judge Deborah Thomas, Judge Shannon Holmes, Mr. Wright Wade, Mr. Adrian Greene, Mrs. Yvonne Barnett-Greene, and Mr. John Marr, thank you for helping bring compassion and dignity, year after year to the homeless veterans at the Stand Down by bringing the court system to them.

I would like to thank the following photographers and graphic artists for the work they provided for this book: the late Victor A. Toliva (Mrs. Lisa Toliva), Al Cooper, Dave Zeien, Stan Johnson, John Hill, and Attorney Butch Hollowell. Your pictures breathed visual life into my book.

I would like to thank Calvin Tucker, the CEO at Tee Shirts Galore & More, who always came through and had his company provide me with all types of promotional products to help Leona and me with our elections, our court programs, and now this book. Calvin is the type of person I could always count on, "To make it happen".

I would like to thank the following persons who did the research I needed, helped me find much-needed information, and cut through red tape to acquire the needed legal licenses for this book: Karen Love, Karen Dinkins, and Brenda Perryman.

I would like to thank my Canadian "family" who took me into their hearts and always looked out for me.

I would like to thank every client and every defendant who asked me for help when his or her hope was low. I will never forget what you have brought to my life by inviting me into yours.

I want to say thank you to all my friends on social media who support me and interact with me.

Lastly, I want to say thank you to any of my friends I inadvertently did not mention. Blame it on my head, not my heart!

Photo Album

Our Mother Mattie N. Lloyd

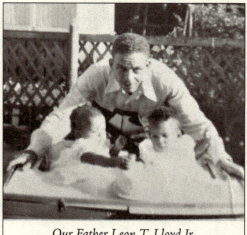
Our Father Leon T. Lloyd Jr.

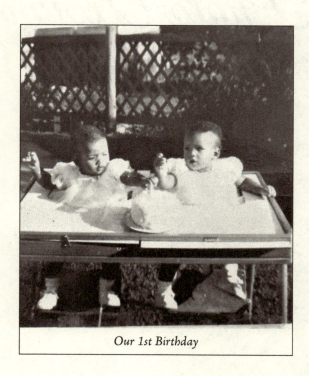
Our 1st Birthday

Six months old with our Grandmother Juliece Lloyd

Our First Christmas

Easter Day – 5 years old

12 years old

Janie Mason Chisolm
Our Great Grandmother

Fannie Chisolm
Our Grandmother

*Fannie's husband Anderson, our Grandfather,
their 11 children and their spouses*

Our Grandmother Fannie Louise Chisolm's Tombstone

Juliece Lloyd
Our Grandmother

Our Dad, Mom, Uncle Napoleon, Aunt Kathryn, Aunt Net and Uncle Zodis

Our Aunt Kathryn, Grandmother, Dad, mom, Aunt Carolyn

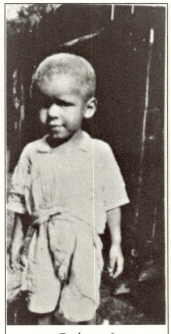
Dad - age 2

Leona and Leonia modeling at the Autorama

Leona and Leonia modeling at the Autorama

Leona's High School graduation picture

Leonia's High School graduation picture

Leona and I walking down the halls of Mumford High School on our way to the Honors Convocation ceremony

Modeling Photos By John Hill

Leonia's Law School Graduation Picture

Leona's Law School Graduation Picture

LLOYD AND LLOYD ATTORNEYS AT LAW. *Our law office in the Renaissance Center*

In the conference room of our law office

In the reception area of our law office

Leona in training under me at 36th District Court

Leona's third year on the bench

Speaking to high school students at their school

Campaign Billboard   Graphic design by David Zeien

At a speaking engagement

My Judicial Portrait Photo by Stan Johnson

Leonia and Leona Photo by Victor A. Toliva

Leonia and Leona in Hawaii

My cousins, Kenneth, Pam, Linwood

Leona- Deep sea fishing in Puerto Vallarta

Leonia in Florida

Leonia horseback riding in Puerto Vallarta, Mexico

Leona and I at Dunn River Falls in Ocho Rios, Jamaica

Leona, Cheryl and Joan at Niagara Falls in Ontario, Canada

Leonia in Seoul, Korea

Leona, Gwen and Leonia at the Half Moon Resort in Montego Bay, Jamaica

Leonia and Leona having dinner in Mexico (I am wearing the hat)

Leonia, Gail and Leona at the Atlantis Hotel in Paradise Island, Bahamas

Leona and I in the Cayman islands getting ready to sail off

Leona, Gwen and Leonia in MGM Grand Las Vegas

Leona in California

Leonia in Western outfit Photo by Victor A. Toliva

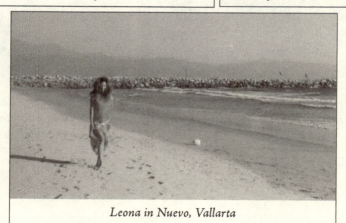
Leona in Nuevo, Vallarta

Leona in Jamaica about to board a Catamaran dinner cruise

Leona dancing in the evening on the Catamaran boat in Jamaica with a Jamaican citizen

Leonia relaxing at Belle Isle, Detroit, MI
Photo by Al Cooper

Leonia relaxing at Belle Isle, Detroit, MI
Photo by Al Cooper

Leonia writing at Belle Isle, Detroit, MI
Photo by Al Cooper

Sunset off my beach house in Canada

Leona speaking at the Hope Academy Graduation. Her last speech given on the evening she ascended to Heaven.

"ANGEL WINGS"
Photo by Melvin Butch Hollowell

This photo reminded me of my guardian angel Leona flying over me and the City of Detroit, keeping watch.

About the Author

Judge Leonia J. Lloyd's careers as a model, teacher, lawyer, and judge have spanned more than fifty years. She shared all her careers with her identical twin sister, Judge Leona L. Lloyd. She and her sister received their Bachelor of Science degrees in Education and Juris Doctorate law degrees from Wayne State University.

In compliance with her commitment to the community, in 2001, in memory of her sister, Judge Lloyd endowed a scholarship foundation at Wayne Law that assists students pursuing a law degree. Every year, the scholarship foundation presents scholarships to deserving law students.

She has been presented with numerous awards for her work in the field of substance abuse and recovery, as well as, her work with veterans.

She lives in Detroit, Michigan.